FATAL
ILLUSIONS

FATAL ILLUSIONS

Shredding a Dozen Unrealities That Can Keep Your Organization From Success

James R. Lucas

AMACOM
American Management Association
New York • Atlanta • Boston • Chicago • Kansas City • San Francisco • Washington, D.C.
Brussels • Mexico City • Tokyo • Toronto

This book is available at a special
discount when ordered in bulk quantities.
For information, contact Special Sales Department,
AMACOM, a division of American Management Association,
1601 Broadway, New York, NY 10019.

Library of Congress Cataloging-in-Publication Data

Lucas, J. R. (James Raymond), 1950–
    Fatal illusions : shredding a dozen unrealities that can keep your
organization from success / James R. Lucas.
       p.   cm.
    Includes bibliographical references and index.
    ISBN 0-8144-0359-X
    1. Psychology, Industrial.   2. Self-perception.   3. Industrial
management.   4. Organizational effectiveness.   I. Title.
HF5548.8.L683   1997
158.7—dc21   97-1324
                                         CIP

Printing number

10 9 8 7 6 5 4 3 2 1

To my father
James Earl (Lefty) Lucas
1924–1981
I miss you, Dad.

And to his grandchildren

Laura Christine

Peter Barrett

David Christopher

Bethany Gayle

Contents

Acknowledgments

My thanks to Janette Jasperson, my executive assistant, for all of her input, substantive and detailed editing, and typing. Janette, as usual, you've helped this book to come to pass, and made it a joyous adventure along the way. Your dedication and commitment to excellence are outstanding!

My thanks also to my daughter, Laura, who as always has provided excellent input and editing to this project, and encouragement to me.

I am very appreciative of the efforts of my colleague and friend Walt Lantzy, who took the time to read the entire manuscript in various forms and provided both good ideas and inspiration to the work. I am also grateful to Steve Bangert, John Hughes, Ed Oakley, Gerry Share, and Adrian Ulsh for their time and thoughts.

Although they're too numerous to list, I want to thank those for whom and with whom I've worked as either a consultant or manager over the past twenty-five years, for all of the input, advice, opportunity, growth, and both good and bad examples that have led into the thoughts and conclusions in this book.

My deep thanks to my family and friends who have been so supportive during the writing of this book and who have not only put up with me but have seemed somehow to enjoy the process as well.

My gratitude to Adrienne Hickey, my editor at AMACOM Books. She is at one and the same time gracious, encouraging, honest, and very professional in both her expectations and her advice. I feel fortunate to have ended up with the best. Hats off also to Barbara Horowitz and Kate Pferdner at AMACOM for shepherding this project through the production phase.

Finally, my thanks to C. P. for all of your inspiration and encouragement.

Introduction

Why, sometimes I've believed as many as six impossible things before breakfast.

—The Queen of Hearts in Lewis Carroll's
Alice's Adventures in Wonderland

You hear it all the time.

"The main thing we need is more [information/resources/training/education/experience/innovation/teamwork]."

Baloney.

The main thing we need is truth.

Truth—a proper and clear understanding of reality—is the key to success in organizations, teams, relationships, and careers. In fact, the departure point for all achievement is a relentless commitment to truth—truth about who we are, where we're headed, where the market is going, what our customers want, what our core competencies are (and whether anyone cares), what our core *limitations* are (and whether anyone can help us), and what our employees are thinking.

The enemy of truth is illusion. Illusion is "a false interpretation by the mind . . . a belief or hope that has no real substance." Illusion comes when we perceive something to be true that isn't true or is only partly true. Illusion comes because we want to believe the thing is true. Illusion is often—perhaps always—tied into false hope.

This false hope is usually driven by our desire to avoid facing problems—and the pain that comes from facing them and attempting to solve them. It's easier to search for ways to market a formerly successful product that is now falling in sales than to gaze unflinchingly into the reality that the product is on the verge of extinction. "When the horse is dead, get off," says the old proverb—but it's incredibly

easy to keep trying to ride an old horse even after the stench of death
has set in.

It's always easier to hope that a problem will go away or solve
itself than it is to shred bad ideas or to abandon good ideas that have
gone sour. And the more the reality of the situation diverges from our
desire to avoid pain and from our false hope, the more we need and
will use illusion to disguise the gap.

Illusions are living things. Like layer upon layer of paint added to
a rotting wall, illusions tend to produce more illusions. We may, for
example, deceive ourselves into thinking that the problem is marketing, rather than acknowledging that the product is a goner. This first
illusion leads to a second one—that the marketing department needs a
shake-up—and, when that fails, to a third illusion—that what we really
need is a new marketing concept (read: fad) and a guru to help us in
our ignorance of the "higher" ways.

This is the disastrous path that illusions put us on and then drive
us along. They cause us to "solve" a problem by adding another layer
of illusion and, when the rot breaks through, to paint it again. Illusions
cause us to head into the netherworld of organizational fantasy and to
"solve" problems that may not be *the* problem—or any problem at all.
Organizations spend an unbelievable amount of time and energy attempting to treat symptoms. Much of this effort merely shuffles illusions around.

Finding and facing truth is hard enough, given our human pro-
pensity to cling to and seek out illusions. The difficulty is compounded
by the fact that the situations we're in aren't static. Everything—
visions, directions, needs, customers, rosters—keeps changing. We
have the stress-filled assignment of finding reality in the eye of a hurricane. And we've got to find it before the 175-mile-per-hour winds hit
again.

Change is the norm, and it won't be managed. "The world doesn't
care about our opinions. Or feelings. [It] rewards only those of us who
catch on to what's happening, who invest our energy in finding and
seizing the opportunities brought about by change."[1]

It takes courage to "seize." But finding those opportunities requires even more than courage. It also requires that we shred our illusions.

This may be the hardest part. Our pride, our self-images, and our
dreams are all affected when we know we need to stop painting a
rotting wall. It can be very difficult to admit that we just wasted three
years on a lousy idea. The alternative to admitting it, however, may be
organizational death.

The value of shredding illusions is that we begin to face the real
problems, which are the only ones worthy of being solved, the only

ones that make a difference. We peel off the paint, layer by layer, so that we can determine the condition of the wall. Then, and only then, can we determine accurately whether to repair the wall or tear it down and build something better.

A word of caution: As we aggressively peel off the illusions, we can't allow ourselves to become discouraged on the one hand or ruthless on the other. Facing reality without humor and heart leads to either depression or cynicism, both of which ultimately produce—can *only* produce—a self-destructive organization. The goal is to shred illusions, but not so that we can conclude that people are worthless and life is a bad joke. We do it so that we can build something of great value, something that really satisfies us and all of our stakeholders.

To that end, also, should you think of additional illusions in need of shredding after you read the dozen I came up with, I would be pleased to have you share them with me. Please contact me at my consulting firm:

James R. Lucas
Luman Consultants
P.O. Box 2566
Shawnee Mission, KS 66201

Telephone: 913-248-1733
Fax: 913-671-7728
E-mail: JLucasLC@aol.com

I want to give you an explanation and a couple of warnings up front.

First, the explanation. When you come across the words *illude and illuding,* don't go scurrying for a dictionary. You won't find them there. Describing the omnipresence of illusions and their devastating effect on our organizations, I simply found no existing words that could so precisely and simply convey the meaning. I took the responsibility—so graciously provided by the fluidity of the incredible English language—of coining these words and their derivations. May they be of great use to you as you go about the critical business of shredding organizational illusions.

And now for the warnings. Warning 1: This book doesn't have all of the answers. *Nobody* has all of the answers. And most of the answers you need you probably already know. Our problem isn't lack of information—most of us are *drowning* in data. Instead, this book is about the built-in obstacles that keep us from *implementing* answers based on that information.

Warning 2: This book won't leave you alone. It's designed to make you and others in your organization uncomfortable. *Very* uncomfortable. It tries to do that by holding up the mirror of truth and inviting you to take an honest look.

An old saying reminds us that when we know the truth, we can be free—free from myths, free from misperceptions that lead us down unhelpful paths, free from bad ideas disguised as "traditions" or "culture," and free from opinions that just don't hold up under the relentless flood of marketplace reality.

You can know the truth. And you can be free—to succeed.

NOTE

1. Price Pritchett, *New Work Habits for a Radically Changing World* (Dallas, Tex.: Pritchett & Associates, Inc., 1994), p. iv.

Section I
Illusions

1

What Are Illusions?

It's not what we don't know that hurts us—it's what we know that just ain't so.

—American humorist Kin Hubbard

Robert had worked for the Wanderlust Corporation for eight years. He had brought an excellent academic background to the job, as well as four years of top-notch prior experience. He had devoted himself to his work and had inched up in responsibility, title, and pay.

Robert was sure that his performance was not only satisfactory but notable within his department. He felt that he was respected, and he was certain he'd be given the opportunity to take on new assignments as his career developed. He was confident that his relationships with his peers and management were very good. His most recent performance review was the best he had ever received.

On a beautiful spring morning, Robert was downsized.

IGNORING THE GROWING CANCER

What happened to Robert?

While I'm not suggesting that being downsized was Robert's fault (or at least it was not entirely his fault), it's quite apparent that Robert was operating under a serious and fatal illusion about his job security and his connection to his organization. The decision to let Robert go wasn't made one minute or five minutes or even a day before he was put on the street. This decision, and the economic and personal driving forces behind it, may have been in the works for weeks or months—or even years.

This is how it is so often in our careers. We go along and think we're living in reality. Suddenly—or so it seems—a problem explodes into our lives.

But the problem was there all along. We just didn't see it. It's the "not seeing it" that can cost us so dearly in the work that's so important to our personal satisfaction and to our livelihood. Organizationally, it can cost us our competitive edge, our profits, our group's morale, our best people, our very reason for existence.

Only clearly seeing and shredding illusions—especially the fatal variety—will allow us to achieve our life, career, and organizational goals. When Kin Hubbard said, "It's not what we don't know that hurts us—it's what we know that just ain't so," he was telling us that holding on to ideas that conflict with reality will damage us in many ways. It's the things we know "that just ain't so" that will trip us up hundreds or thousands of times in the course of a long career.

Holding on to illusions is a very easy thing for a human being to do. Getting the insight to break through an illusion—and then having the courage to do it—is very difficult; the easiest thing in the world is to sit complacently in the midst of a rose-colored bubble. But at their worst, illusions are the essence of folly—doing things on the basis of what we *want* to be true instead of what is actually true.

There once was a man who wanted to catch a mouse but had no cheese. He came up with what he thought was a clever solution to his problem. He cut a picture of cheese out of a magazine and used it to set the mousetrap. The next day, the man went expectantly to the trap. He was pleased to see that it had been sprung—until he saw that what he'd caught was a picture of a mouse.

PERCEPTION IS NOT REALITY

We're told over and over again that "perception is reality." As with all things that can be disastrous, this idea can be appealing, and there's a sense in which it's true. Our perceptions do color what we think, say, and do. We can carry a perception that our rude treatment of others has no effect on their relationship with us. So we might continue to be rude, deceiving ourselves that we're merely being "candid," "honest," or "straightforward" and that people will understand. And we can hold on to that perception—right up to the moment that one or more of those people move heaven and earth to bring us to our knees.

Perception is *not* reality. Perception is perception, and it can be either right or wrong, good or bad, helpful or not helpful, depending to a great extent on how well it aligns in the long run with reality. Our perceptions have intrinsic value only as they correspond ever more closely to the reality that surrounds us. Illusions lead to confusion, inconsistency, and sabotage of stated goals.

Taylor was sure of his "instincts" about people. He seldom looked at résumés, applications, or any other detailed information about potential employees. He felt that he could perceive the character of people just by interviewing them, and that on this basis he could make an accurate decision about their value to the organization and their ability to fit in.

But Taylor's perceptions were skewed by factors both internal and external. His illusion about his ability to evaluate people led to a pride that kept him from asking and seeking the answers to many critical questions. He often did most of the talking in interviews—always a fatal step. The most important part of recruitment—finding out what the prospective employee really thinks and feels—had no place in Taylor's scheme.

His arrogance led to a second internal illusion, which was the assumption that if he hired people who (he thought) were pretty much like himself, they would work well in all types of jobs and situations. He never considered involving others in the process in order to get a different perspective.

Compounding the problem were the illusions of the applicants. Often they didn't know what they were looking for, so they made their decisions about the organization on the basis of outward appearances. In interviews, they frequently projected an image that they thought Taylor wanted to see. When these external illusions were added to Taylor's internal ones, his actual ability to make a good, productive, and mutual "match" when hiring was greatly reduced. After starting work, many of the people Taylor hired pretended to like their jobs, confirming Taylor in his "I have good instincts" illusion. But the resultant frustration, conflict, turnover, and less-than-excellent results eventually made a sure—even if not fully perceived—mockery of Taylor's illusion.

ILLUSIONS ARE MORE THAN BLIND SPOTS

A blind spot is something we need to see but don't. It isn't generally blind because we *can't* see it; it's blind because we *won't* see it. "No one is as blind as he who will not see," we're reminded. Blind spots are usually unseen because we want it so. It's an act of the will.

Illusions are much more than blind spots—they are willful constructs. They are systems of deceptive thought about what life around us really is. At the extreme, they can become whole alternate worlds built to avoid the reality in which we are physically living. Our bodies can be on planet Earth while our minds are in a galaxy far, far away.

These constructs can take several forms. We can illude that something is true when it isn't. We can choose this path when we want to continue in a direction that is no longer viable (or that never was). This path resembles wishful thinking, but it can be much more than a mere daydream or passing fancy. It can be a complex web of self-deceit. In its most insidious form, it's based on situations that once were true.

At the end of World War II, Adolf Hitler was directing the movement of armies that didn't exist—but he had once had armies at his disposal. In the 1960s and 1970s, U.S. companies ignored the threat of Japanese products because they were seen as very poor in quality—which they once were. Hitler's illusion didn't keep him from losing World War II. The illusion of the U.S. companies didn't turn out much better.

We can also illude that something isn't true when it is. We can choose this path when we don't want to take a direction that is no longer ignorable. Change is pounding on the door—either the change that says it's always been this way and it's time for us to sign up or the change that says there's something new going on and it's not going to go away. Demand for continuous learning is an example of the first; demand that we become comfortable with communication technology illustrates the second.

In any case, illusions gain and maintain their power, not because we're ignorant of reality, but because we sense or know the reality and choose to avoid it. We might *tell* ourselves that we don't know anything different or have all the facts, while what we're really doing is entering more deeply into the process of illusion building. We don't like parts of reality, so we use the mammoth capability of our minds to put it in a dungeon.

This deception is compounded when we reinforce each other's illusions. I tell you your layoff plan sounds appropriate (suppressing doubts about the long-term effect on morale and innovation), and you tell me my reorganization should fix our poor customer service (suppressing questions about my lack of agreed-upon goals and training). We can all have ears that itch to hear what they want to hear. Reality is present and available.

And evaporates in a friendly conspiracy of illusion.

HOW EXTENSIVE ARE ILLUSIONS?

Illusions surround us. They are much more pervasive than most of us are willing to admit. Some examples from our culture at large:

➡ Over the past fifteen years, the United States has had many more tax "cuts" than tax increases. During the same time frame, the number of actual dollars taken in taxes has multiplied. Tax cuts are almost pure illusion. Usually, what the politicians are really talking about is cutting the *rate of increase* of tax growth, not actually taking in fewer tax dollars.

➡ Although in many ways we have an excellent health care system, we can operate under the serious illusion that what we have is medical "science." Most people, if asked, would assume that all surgical procedures are thoroughly and scientifically tested before launched into general use, but as many as 85 to 95 percent of all such procedures *may never be tested at all* before being put into wide practice.[1]

➡ Illusions in military encounters permeate history, from the unconquerable British who didn't beat the ragtag Americans to the unconquerable Americans who didn't beat the ragtag Vietnamese. Power and control—whether in politics or business—are often illusions.

➡ Political campaigns are about style, opinion polls, and putting the proper "spin" on statements and events. Candidates project an "image" that may have little or nothing to do with their actual character—that may, in fact, be the *opposite* of who they really are. Why does it work? Because most of us are willing to believe the "story" that campaign masters are so capable of telling. And then? We're "disappointed" when we begin to see a little of the truth about who the now-elected official really is.

➡ We assume that "best-seller" lists are an accurate measurement of the number of books actually sold. The reality? The *New York Times* submits to *selected* bookstores a *short* list of books it *thinks* will be best-selling titles for the coming week. The stores then fill in their weekly sales. The lists submitted to the stores are censored works of fiction. How does the *Times* select the books that go on the list to bookstores? It relies in large part on publisher-created illusions—things like advance publicity and the size of print runs and advertising budgets.

➡ Most of us "know" that membership in religious organizations has generally gone down over the last 200 years. But by how much? A lot? Or has it been a long, slow decline? And has the drop-off increased dramatically since the turbulent, tradition-busting 1960s? The reality? Membership in religious organizations has *increased* dramatically over this time frame, from a low 15–20 percent of the population at the end of the 1700s to a still tiny 30–35 percent at the end of the 1800s to 65 percent by the 1960s—and 75 percent today![2]

➡️ As parents, we can accept the oft-quoted and sweet-sounding illusion that our children are just going through a "phase." It's a cheap explanation that soothes but doesn't solve. These "phases" can turn out to be entrenched personality traits. Our children do change as they grow, but rotten behavior is still rotten behavior, and it's giving us a clue. Stalin went through phases as a child, and it was too bad for the world that his parents didn't stop him. The corporate equivalent is "We're just in a [business cycle/time of transition/period of growth pains]."

FACTORS THAT AID ILLUSIONS

There are a number of factors inherent in an open society and economy that help us believe illusions.

Credentials

We live in a credential-enamored society. In many ways, the actual knowledge or wisdom people have isn't even considered. If people have a degree or other credential from the right university or organization, surely they *must* know what they're talking about. Right? Wrong! A credential may guarantee much—or it may guarantee nothing. Credentials may be useful as a guide in making decisions, but it's certainly harmful, and can be fatal, to use them as the sole (or even main) criterion for making a judgment. Someone with multiple business degrees but no actual experience in the gritty world where you and I have to make decisions may still offer some real help—or may offer us an illusion-ridden theory that knocks us flat. Peter Drucker, the management guru, when asked if business school education was making entrepreneurs "smarter," said, "No. Education gives you neither experience nor wisdom."[3]

Hype

In a "go-go" economy, sales so often seem to be the way to riches, success, and fame. Sales as a profession can be honorable, satisfying, and rewarding. But the kinds of sales that come with exaggeration, "spins," and outright falsehood can create illusions that have little or nothing to do with the actual product or service being offered. Perhaps you, like me, are ready for vendors and service providers to begin underpromising and overdelivering. If the products and services are really good, the salespeople won't *have* to hype them.

Gullibility

Mark Twain reminded us that the main difference between a cat and a lie is that a cat has only nine lives. Amazingly, we can steadfastly refuse to believe the most obvious facts while at the same time accepting gigantic lies on the basis of gossip, slander, fads, or someone's off-the-cuff opinion. Gullibility is one of the most destructive attributes, and any of us can be all too easily susceptible to it. During the oil "crisis" of the early 1970s (itself an illusion), many people where I lived dutifully, as requested, turned off lights to conserve oil—even though the utility that served us, and others in our grid, didn't have a single oil-fired power plant.

Prejudice

Because of our upbringing, past history, laziness, or any number of other factors, we can make surface judgments all too readily. I have heard profound truths from cab drivers who looked like they'd just crawled out of a hole and have heard pure hogwash from people in custom-tailored suits. We all know the old maxim "You can't judge a book by its cover," but, if we're not careful, we may still do it a hundred times before lunch. Being patient, making sure we have enough data to draw conclusions, and taking time before we reach those conclusions take more work but are excellent destroyers of illusions.

Growth Rate and Size

Growth impresses us (unless it's our waistlines that are doing the growing!). But growth for growth's sake is the philosophy of the cancer cell. Many companies have grown in the last several decades through mergers and acquisitions, often involving unrelated businesses, only to be left with an unwieldy conglomerate that can't be managed, coordinated, or directed. Others have added thousands of people to their payroll in an orgy of growth, only to institute mass layoffs during the next downturn (some organizations don't ever figure it out and keep running through boom-and-bust, hire-and-fire cycles). Size is a false measure of impressiveness or security. Most new jobs, as well as many creative and new ideas, come not from the largest companies but from the wild and wooly start-up companies that have passionate and energetic workforces.

Mass Media

The media so very often tend to the reporting (and, occasionally, the real analyzing) of bad news. There seems to be a belief among many journalists that truth is found only in the broken, collapsing, and ugly things of life. One major company announced 40,000 layoffs (later reduced to 18,000) over several years. The layoffs were front-page news and gave the company much bad publicity. At the same time that the company was revising the number down to 18,000 (not *nearly* as widely reported), the U.S. economy created more than 700,000 *new* jobs in *one month* (which, incredibly, some "analysts" reported as bad news because it meant the economy was "heating up" too fast). We're drowning in bad news, which, rather than leading us to shred illusion, can lead us to shred hope. We sometimes forget that successful businesses were built during the Great Depression.

The mass media also influence our perceptions of reality through their advertising and other propaganda. "The people most vulnerable to indoctrination are those in media-managed, high-technology societies," according to one author.[4] Marketing and advertising experts have reduced the production of illusion to a science.

Polling

We all know what we believe—we've got the polls, don't we? "Polling looks scientific because of the way the results are expressed— percentage points, cross-tabulations, margins of error, statistical significance. But, claims one writer, much of polling—the asking and answering of questions—is a soft science built on the shifting sands of human language and psychology."[5]

Poll results can be altered dramatically simply by changing the wording of the question. One presidential adviser charged that the President made decisions based not on principles but on polls. That's scary in its own right—but when you add the reality that the poll results themselves are illusions, it becomes absolutely terrifying.

Celebrityitis

If Deming said it, it must be the best way—or so we may think. From Hollywood's dream factory, from sports stars, from business gurus, we draw conclusions and directions that may be half-truths or worse. "A leader must have the courage to act against an expert's advice," said the British Prime Minister James Callagon (1976–1979). People try to sell us things—from products to business fads—on the basis of what noteworthy people say. But there are product spokespeople who have never even used the product they're promoting, and there are management experts who have never followed the business philosophy they're expounding in the real world.

Ultimately, it's not *who* said it that's important but *what* was said—and whether or not it's true.

Familiarity

The old saying "Familiarity breeds contempt" applies to illusions. This contempt can keep us from taking the problem as a serious threat.

The data we see and our instincts tell us that a downturn is coming, and expert commentators say the same thing. But how many downturns have we all heard predicted in our careers that didn't happen? Even when the threat is obvious, it may be so routine that we refuse to take it seriously.

Myths

Many ideas that are generally accepted in a society simply aren't true. But they've been talked about for so long that they've taken on the mantle of fact.

Many people, for example, believe that Franklin Roosevelt's New Deal dramatically reduced the horrific unemployment rates of the early 1930s. The reality? The unemployment rate, about 25 percent, was essentially the same five years after the New Deal was implemented. As one writer said, "The Great Depression outlived the New Deal."[6] This illustrates how illusion can piggyback on illusion: The illusion of shrinking unemployment, once accepted, leads to giving credit where no credit is due. It was World War II that finally ended the unemployment crisis.

WHY ILLUSIONS WORK

Illusions are powerful attractions. They postpone the day of reckoning and offer us a false hope of better days. There are at least twelve reasons why illusions work:

1. It's less frightening to go on the way we are than it is to change—better a known and thorny problem than an unknown and risky solution: "Our workers don't seem to care about their work, but this empowerment stuff scares the daylights out of us."

2. It's very easy to base our lives on traditions and secondhand opinions—better to make decisions on hearsay, presumptions, and inferences than to think for ourselves: "Our punitive disciplinary system doesn't seem to solve the problems, but hasn't everyone been doing it this way for decades? Isn't this approach approved by the courts?"

3. Unraveling illusions can be a long and messy process—better to simplify life by accepting pretensions than to dig through a mountain of conflicting and confusing ideas: "Our market share is slipping, but didn't our benchmarking study show that we were better than our competitors on every critical measurement?"

4. Core change is extremely difficult—better to live with the unsatisfying aspects of our careers or organizations than to begin the labor of change from the inside out: "It seems like we've got a lot of internal warfare and political posturing going on, but do we really want to dig into all of these petty battles? What are we supposed to do—become psychologists? Besides, we're implementing procedures throughout the organization that should fix the problem."

5. It's difficult to diagnose and investigate—better just to draw quick conclusions and write out quick prescriptions: "Not very many of our people seem to be happy in their jobs, but that's just normal. We're not here to make people happy, are we? Maybe a bonus program would help."

6. For their own gain or safety, people are willing to tell us what we want to hear—better a pleasant lie than an ugly truth: "I'm a little uncomfortable with the plan I presented, but nobody at the meeting seemed to have any problems with it. That should mean full support during implementation."

7. Truth is often ugly—better to listen to the positive things people will say to our face (flattery) than to learn about the ugly things people will say behind our back (slander). "Why is he telling people he disagrees with our new strategic plan? He gave it strong support in our last staff meeting."

8. Gossip and slander about others are "juicy morsels"—better an interesting lie than unsensational truth: "I was glad to hear Bob's report about all of the people problems at Idea Corporation. Those guys have been killing us. But could you believe Renee's comments about the new products they have in the pipeline? Why would she defend a competitor like that?"

9. Facing reality can be very painful—better to pretend: "I'd be better off arguing that this technique is really working than admitting that we've just wasted two years on a bad plan."

10. Illusions are usually positive—better to believe a lie than to face an unpleasant truth: "We must be a close-knit organization. Look at the nice time we had at the Christmas party. It can't be true that there's no mutual respect or understanding."

11. The world is full of "bad guys" who are experts at looking like "good guys"—better to believe the theatrical outward appearance than the nasty inward reality: "With a résumé like that, how could she not help us? Did you see how she handled herself in that interview?"

12. Powerful opponents can spend much effort weaving complex webs—better to believe there are no schemes to damage our plans or careers than to understand that there are people who will hurt us and the organization if it seems in their own best interest: "People keep talking 'global, global, global.' What can a company in Sri Lanka possibly do to hurt us?"

I invite you to look at illusion-cleansing—dis-illusioning—not just as a good idea but as a leadership style and a management method. Reengineering and total quality management often treat symptoms or outcomes and, at their best, processes. Learning organizations attempt to treat the disabilities. Dis-illusioning goes deeper.

Dis-illusioning probes our core in order to treat the human sickness that cripples us all to one degree or another: our avoidance of problems, the pain that accompanies the problems, and the pain that accompanies the shredding of the illusions we use to cover up the problems and the pain. "It is through the pain of confronting and solving problems that we learn. . . . The less clearly we see the reality of the world—the more our minds are befuddled by falsehood, misperceptions, and illusions—the less able we will be to determine correct courses of action and make wise decisions."[7] The essence of wisdom is giving clear thought to our ways—our assumptions and our primary ideas—and avoiding self-deception at all costs.

What is an illusion? It is a false idea or conception, an unreal or misleading appearance or image. Illusions can finally lead us to the point where we no longer even want to hear the truth. It's up to us to keep this from happening.

NOTES

1. "That Operation You're Getting May Be Experimental," *USA Today*, September 13, 1995, 4-D.
2. J. Gordon Melton, ed., *The Encyclopedia of American Religions* (Tarrytown, N.Y.: Triumph Books, 1991), pp. xvii–xxvii.

3. Peter F. Drucker, "Flashes of Genius," *Inc.*, May 1996, 36.
4. Wilson Bryan Key, *The Age of Manipulation* (New York: Henry Holt, 1989), pp. 94–95.
5. Cynthia Crossen, *Tainted Truth: The Manipulation of Fact in America* (New York: Simon & Schuster, 1994), p. 104.
6. Robert S. McElvaine, *The Great Depression* (New York: Times Books, 1984), pp. 75, 297–299, 306–307.
7. M. Scott Peck, *The Road Less Traveled* (New York: Simon & Schuster, 1978), pp. 16, 44.

2
Why We "Buy In" to Illusions

Truth above all, even when it upsets and overwhelms us!
—Henri Frederic Amiel, *Journal*

Joan's strong personality had carried her far.

She had become president of her multimillion-dollar company in her early thirties. She had hired a talented, high-energy staff. Building her ideas on the autocratic methods of former ITT CEO Harold Geneen, a micromanager, she had turned the business into a tightly controlled, well-oiled machine. Sales had more than doubled since she had taken the reins.

But Joan was full of illusions about her leadership abilities. She had convinced herself that her employees liked and respected her, while they actually feared and loathed her. Her own micromanagement (she had a radio on her credenza to monitor all transmissions to and from company vehicles), her arrogance (no ideas were good except her own), and her demeaning treatment of her employees (she once turned a one-hour meeting into an all-day affair without breaks—even for food—as she methodically ripped apart each person present) had created a paranoid organization where the best energies and creativity were directed at not getting called on the carpet.

Joan gave bonuses, but they bought her nothing. She talked about cooperation, even "love," in her annual meetings, which only produced countless jokes about her hypocrisy. She encouraged innovation with her words but got none because she ridiculed and gutted all ideas. She spoke about building a stable organization, but good people left in direct proportion to how often they had to interact with her. She asked everyone to be as "committed" as she was, which brought snickers since no amount of overtime or effort would convince her of dedication. She spoke of having "worked her way up," which led to even more resentment, since she was the daughter of the owner and no one believed that competence had gotten her her position.

19

Was Joan, as she believed, a beloved and respected manager? Or was she an illusion-ridden tyrant? The only time freedom and joy prevailed in her company was when she was gone. Her absence was often the occasion for pot-luck parties in the office.

Joan believed that total control was the only way to success. She believed this, not because it was true but because she wanted to believe it. She had learned this approach to life from her domineering father (who had been well hated in his own day) and had had it confirmed in a search that led her past humane managers and onto Harold Geneen. (She called Managing, *Geneen's exercise in self-justification and machismo, her "MBA.") It was in a book, so it must be right. Right?*

Far From Reality

Illusions are ideas we've accumulated that cause us to look at ourselves and our organizations in ways that are far from reality. They originate in our upbringing, our education, our work experiences, our personal relationships, and the things we read and watch.

These ideas seem so right to us (the most effective illusions are *always* appealing), and they can peacefully lodge in our subconscious, but they have disastrous results. They skew our decision-making ability, causing us to choose unproductive paths and directions. They cause us to translate and reinterpret truth to fit our manufactured "grids." We can read a book with a hundred good ideas, even talk them up with our coworkers, and implement none of them because they don't match up with what we "know" to be true.

We "buy in" to illusions for many reasons. Some of the more important ones are as follows:

➡ Illusions permit us to avoid facing problems.
➡ Illusions produce a soothing or anesthetic effect on the pain that comes with the problems.
➡ Illusions keep us from having to do the hard and painful work of making changes.
➡ Illusions allow us to avoid responsibility.
➡ Illusions give us a sense of control and dull the sense of powerlessness.
➡ Illusions enable us to avoid conflict and retain an external aura of cooperation.
➡ Illusions allow us to disregard the fact that individuals and organizations are all dysfunctional to one degree or another.

Let's look at each of these in turn.

Avoiding Problems

Problems are really hard to solve.

We need every bit of wisdom we can muster to solve many of the problems that we face as we lead people and organizations. Truth is the way to solutions, but truth is often the first casualty when a major problem arises.

"Acknowledgment of truth provides an exit from seemingly unworkable situations."[1] Truth is the way out, but it can be negated by industry practice ("This is the way we've always done it"), prejudging ("Top management would never go for that"), false teaching ("———— said it, so it must be true"), and our own pride ("I've done all right so far"). It was the false teaching of Hal Geneen, combined with overweening pride, that spelled "fatal illusion" for Joan.

We're surrounded by bad news. One study of television news reporting found that there were 6,500 negative news stories to 300 positive in a selected time frame. Some experts believe that the average person has negative ideas stored in a seven-to-one ratio to positive ones. Nobody gossips about people working out their problems.

We can use illusions to shield ourselves. We certainly want to learn what we can from the negative and then move on with what we've learned. We want to focus on the positives that are real. But illusions allow us to avoid dealing with the negative by pretending a false positive. This is a refusal to face the fact that life is, to a great extent, a series of problems to be solved. Life is a test.

Illusions enable us to think we won't get a bad grade if we just avoid taking the exam.

Avoiding Pain

"Nobody dies nowadays of fatal truths," said Nietzsche. "There are too many antidotes to them."

Illusions are extremely unhelpful in the long term, but they are astonishingly appealing in the short term because they have a soothing, painkilling effect. They keep us from having to face ugly organizational realities. A dentist who injected anesthetic as a substitute for a root canal or tooth extraction would be offering the same kind of solution that we sometimes seek to relieve organizational pain. A lot of organizations, for example, inject short-term goals as a substitute for development of a compelling vision.

Fads are so marketable precisely because they have such an anesthetic effect. We don't have to root out the cancer; we'll just take some drugs so that it doesn't hurt! There are no easy answers to organizational illness. Reorganizing, reengineering, and refocusing always take hard work and lots of time, never get implemented without creating many problems (planned and unplanned) of their own, and often aren't even the right place to start.

Titan Technologies had some decent precision manufacturing capability but declining sales and profitability. The owners tried a series of anesthetics: management shake-up, technical staff shake-up, reorganization, quality-certification process, new production planning system, new cost-accounting system, and relationship building with key customers. They never faced the painful reality that their market had changed dramatically and had no long-term need for their core competencies—certainly not at a profitable level. Titan was finally sold to a company that needed its manufacturing capability but not its products, and Titan ceased to exist.

The anesthetic effect of illusion gets magnified because we're often looking for good news about our situation (or bad news about others'). We're in the market. We want to illude. And if the illusion ties into something that's worked for us before, that we've been even moderately successful with in the past, the "hook" can be complete.

Erroneous polling procedures led all of the major polling organizations to predict not only a victory but a landslide victory for Thomas E. Dewey over Harry S Truman in the 1948 presidential election. The main problem? The same procedures had "worked" in the previous two elections.

Past success, misapplied, can produce great illusions.

AVOIDING CHANGES

Are you doing today what you thought you'd be doing five or ten years ago?

Illusions do some of their greatest damage when they keep us from making necessary changes in our lives and organizations. We keep "hoping" something will change for the better—a new product will "show up," unexpected sales will allow us to hit budget, the nasty manager up the line will leave (or, if we're honest, die).

But hoping to win the lottery to solve our financial problems is a disastrous way to live. Change either is going to happen to us or is going to be initiated by us. As someone once said, there are only three kinds of managers: those who make things happen, those who watch things happen, and those who get hit over the head and ask "what happened?" We can wait for change to happen to us while illuding that it won't and end up spending our time feeling like victims of the fierce changes taking place in the marketplace. Or we can make the necessary changes that are under our control.

Deciding to make deep core changes puts us on a path of uncomfortable and inexact effort. It takes soul sweat to initiate and sustain the process of change. "Change is not made without inconvenience, even from worse to better," said Samuel Johnson, the famous British novelist. It's so much easier to reinterpret (or be selective about) advice and inputs so that we won't have to make any major adjustments. We want the minimum of work and the minimum of pain, the easy life rather than the successful life, smooth operations rather than stunning achievement.

The harmful effect of these understandable but unhelpful feelings is compounded by the fact that nothing in life is as simple as it seems. Rather than accepting this, we can illude that everything is a matter of black and white. We've spent years constructing our worldviews, our grids of how organizational life works, and we can choose as a path of least resistance to force all new data into our existing grids (rather than enlarging or discarding the grids). In our yearning to oversimplify reality, we can miss reality altogether.

It's astonishing how simplistic and unalterable our grids can be. "All Democrats are _____." "All Republicans are _____." "Conservatives are _____." "Liberals are _____." "Big companies are all _____." "Government workers are _____." Isn't it amazing how rapidly our grids help us fill in quick and simple answers? A book could be written about every one of these groups (in fact, may have been) and not even begin to touch their complexity.

In an illusion-based organization, we spend our time either fact testing or gut testing. Questions like "Can we get some more data?" or "What do your instincts tell us?" are often used as substitutes for the more important question "What's the truth here?" We may be more comfortable fact testing or gut testing than we are *reality* testing. More important than what we think about change or feel about change is recognizing the change and *doing* something with it.

Reality consistently demands that we embrace rather than avoid change.

AVOIDING RESPONSIBILITY

"Everything is your own damn fault," said Ernest Hemingway.

Well, maybe not everything—but an awful lot of it is. One of the signs of a healthy mind is the willingness to accept responsibility for one's own decisions, mistakes, and consequences. One of the signs of an illuding organization is a large investment in blame-delegating activity.

It's very easy to fall into a victim orientation. We can blame our individual failures on lack of information, lack of resources, lack of support, sabotage, and misunderstanding. We can blame our organizational failures on the market, "stupid" customers, "worthless" suppliers, incompetent employees, and "bad luck." The common ingredient in these excuses is that we locate the cause somewhere other than in ourselves.

Few points of view are less conducive to making progress than that of victim. It's a totally disempowering perspective. If the problem lies elsewhere, we can't do anything about it. But if the problem—or at least a substantial part of it—lies with us, we're in a position to make a difference.

If we're honest, we'll admit that we often don't want to face the reality of who we are, what our organization is, and what fears and desires are driving us. This includes the negative realities: the warts, pettiness, and inelegant areas. And it includes the positive realities: the challenges, opportunities, and dreams that scare the heck out of us. Only deep thought about these realities can empower us, but blame delegating can seem like an easier strategy.

Blame delegating becomes possible on a large scale only when we allow ourselves and others to do it. If we play the "blame game," we're in a poor position to insist that those who work for us don't. Florence Nightingale said that the secret of her success was that she never gave or took an excuse. Explanations, yes; excuses, never.

The avoidance of responsibility and delegation of blame become doable in part because the real damage often isn't obvious until the very end. Illusions are supported by the fact that disasters can be a long time in the making. The real answer to the question "How could we have known?" is that we probably could have, had we chosen to know.

The alternative to avoidance is to take responsibility for everything that is under our control or subject to our influence and to insist that others do the same. Rather than avoid them, we can choose to face problems, the pain the problems bring, and the pain that goes with solving them. We can accept what's ours to accept.

And plan the pain.

AVOIDING POWERLESSNESS

Avoiding powerlessness is the logical follow-up to the avoidance of responsibility. If we choose to avoid taking responsibility, then we have to find some way to avoid feeling powerless. That way is to take control. The more responsibility we avoid, the more powerless we feel and the more we try to take control.

In our desire to avoid powerlessness, we can illude about control that we really don't have. Since we don't like seeing our plans turned upside down, changed, or canceled, we can tenaciously cling to old ideas and methods even after it's been proven multiple times that they don't work. We can claw our way to tight control of our environment and the people with whom we interface.

Darryl, a classic control freak and the president of his own company, had always depended on his secretary to oversee the purchasing of office supplies. When she unexpectedly resigned, Darryl responded in fear that the office staff who remained would take advantage of the organization. He began acting as if people would either send the company into bankruptcy by buying too many office supplies or else would run out of something and force the company to grind to a screeching halt.

Rather than realizing that this fear was completely illusory (how many pens and paper clips would someone have to buy in order to bankrupt a multimillion-dollar company?), Darryl responded with total control. He had people count the office supplies (including the number of styrofoam cups) every Monday morning. He even made them count the number of internally typed and copied forms in the company's form room.

It never occurred to Darryl in his control illusion that it didn't matter if the company did run out of internally made forms (they could easily copy more). He never seemed concerned about how much he wasted in salaries for those meaningless exercises. He was never perturbed about the demeaning effect on the people who were required to count these items, nor was he aware of the fact that they just guessed the quantity and wrote a number down.

It wasn't control; it was the *illusion* of control. Darryl thought that he was taking control of the situation by instituting those procedures, but nothing really changed from the way it had been before his secretary left (when she had also guessed the quantity of on-hand supplies).

AVOIDING CONFLICT

An old Turkish proverb says, "Whoever tells the truth is chased out of nine villages." An East European proverb says the same thing with a warning: "Tell the truth and run."

One great illusion is that we can build our relationships on unreality. Another illusion is that truth always triumphs in relationships. It does always triumph in the long run (if you tell people that slow response is going to cost you customers, you'll eventually be vindicated). Truth usually finds its way to the surface eventually, but in the short run it may get us "killed" (e.g., ostracized for telling the truth).

Our employees or competitors can use our illusions against us. Employees can tell us what we want to hear, even if they know it to be wrong or unworkable, because they don't want the stress that piercing illusions always brings. They don't want to be chased out of nine villages, or out of our office.

Because many people won't tell us the truth about what they really think and feel, we can superficially conclude that they agree with us (or at least won't work against us). This illusion is made worse by the fact that people can go beyond nonresponse to an active illusory response: "I agree." "That's a great idea." "I see no problem with that." And all the while they wouldn't risk a dime of their own money on the proposal.

We buy into these illusions because we want to believe what people are "selling." Most of us are playing roles to some extent, at least in some situations. Many of us are projecting illusions of some kind—giving verbal agreement or superficial support or implying "honest input" where there is none and where none will be given. If people project illusions that match up with what we *want* to believe about them or their opinions, we "buy." Others, of course, are eager to buy our illusions, too. Projecting and believing these illusions are often encouraged under the banner of being a "team player." One leader said, "Peace if possible, but truth at any rate." We need to make sure we're buying the right thing.

Competitors can talk about cooperation at trade association meetings, for example, while they're working to steal our customers or employees. Sun-Tzu said (in a book studied avidly by many businesspeople around the world), "Warfare is the Way of deception. Thus although [you are] capable, display incapability to them. . . . When [your objective] is nearby, make it appear as if distant; when far away, create the illusion of being nearby. . . . Display profits to entice them."[2] Much of business life consists of unrealities and deliberate deceptions circulated among those willing to believe them.

People will say, do, and display misleading information and actions to beat us. Many people have become expert at professional illusion-projection (read: lying). They'll use euphemisms, slogans, changes in the meaning of words, and the manufacturing or altering of reports, studies, and statistics to get us to believe concepts that aren't real. Some of these deceptions can be very hard to see through.

Another way we use illusions to avoid conflict is by illuding that we make only rational decisions. We can agree rationally about something (such as empowerment), but our rational decision gets overwhelmed by nonrational feelings (such as anger) when empowered people make big mistakes. We'd rather illude that "things will work out" than do the hard and thorny work of training ourselves and our people to build a better organization on the principle of constructive dissent. It's easier to avoid learning how to direct, redirect, and control our intraorganizational passions, emotions, and prejudices.

AVOIDING FUNCTIONALITY

Illusions work so well for us as individuals because they play to our personal foibles and prejudices. Our father told us that everyone's lazy, which leads us to constantly monitor and prod people. We got burned early in our career, which leads us to be street-smart and do it to others before they do it to us. A relative was mugged by someone of a different color, which leads us to avoid hiring or promoting people of that color.

But not everyone is lazy, and treating all people as though they were will prove destructive as self-motivated people come to resent our heavy-handed management. "Doing it" to others will kill cooperation and give us a reputation of being no better than the ones who did it to us. And jerks aren't jerks because they're a different color—they're jerks because they're jerks. No group has a corner on that market.

We all have some inherent flaws—dysfunctions—that contribute to illusions. We take inappropriate paths in our thinking that let us feel we're being rational when we're not. "We often use a somewhat anomalous form of intuition, and adopt—often unknowingly—a number of little rules not just different from but also *incompatible* with the golden rules of rationality. . . . All of us employ, and pursue to their end, some genuine and easy (as well as fallacious) shortcuts in our minds [that] serve to render our thinking inaccessible to correction. . . . We reason in an intuitive, impromptu fashion, and are often convinced that we have really reasoned."[3] These "mental tunnels" can be discarded only with great effort and often with outside intervention.

We also have a penchant for latching on to and holding on to first impressions, a process psychologists call "anchoring." These first impressions can hold sway over all of our future thinking on the subject: "Early scripts, stereotypes, and scenarios prove surprisingly impervious to change."[4]

We can choose to ignore facts that would shatter our long-cherished beliefs. But because fear is so paralyzing, we can also choose to systematically ignore data because they *confirm* what we fear. Leaving out the information that makes us anxious is a sure sign of personal or organizational dysfunction.

This effect of illusion gets amplified when we hear the people around us expressing and living in illusions. I agree to support your plan as a good idea and you agree to support mine, but what if both plans are bad plans? This compounding of illusions magnifies their effect within the organization. Mutual reinforcement of illusions, propped up on the structure of compromise, can lead a Napoleon into a Russia or a Russia (Soviet Union) into an Afghanistan. Or you and me into a career-limiting or -ending move.

When our illusions encounter the illusions of others, we set in motion a circular process of deceiving and being deceived. The result? We build a system that seems to work (for a while) but that doesn't meet the needs of customers, doesn't respond to the challenges of competitors, and, in the end, doesn't meet the expectations we have of ourselves.

Finally, we can ignore illusion-shredding advice or input by rejecting the source. We can do this because we don't believe people like us, respect us, or care about us. We can do it because we don't like, respect, or care about them. But the real question isn't "How do they feel about me?" or "How do I feel about them?" The real question—the *only* question—is "Are they right?"

Part of maturity and wisdom is the ability to see the things in our established grids that are untrue and (because they're untrue) unworkable. Truth—facing reality—sets us free to make good decisions, while illusion—avoiding reality—leads us to one bad decision after another. Life sells illusions by the truckload.

But we don't have to buy.

Notes

1. Averil Marie Doyle, *Delusional Relationships: How They Are Formed, How They Falter and Fail* (Westport, Conn.: Praeger, 1995), p. 132.
2. Sun-Tzu, *The Art of War*, trans. Ralph D. Sawyer (New York: Barnes & Noble, 1994), p. 168.
3. Massimo Piattelli-Palmarini, *Inevitable Illusions: How Mistakes of Reason Rule Our Minds* (New York: Wiley, 1994), pp. 6–7.
4. Howard Gardner, *Leading Minds: An Anatomy of Leadership* (New York: Basic Books, 1995), p. 28.

3

Harmless, Hurtful, and Fatal Illusions

A primary survival capability of the future will be the ability to cast off what you have learned.

—Ken Matejka and Richard J. Dunsing,
A Manager's Guide to the Millennium

On December 7, 1941, one of the most grandiose illusions of the twentieth century came crashing to the ground.

The surprise bombing of the U.S. naval base at Pearl Harbor was the same tactic the Japanese had used in 1904 to open the Russo-Japanese War. The United States had plenty of warning that the Japanese, eager to protect their gains in Asia, might do it again. The Americans had broken the Japanese code, leaders in Washington had a constant flow of accurate intelligence, and radar warned of movements by Japanese ships. Why was the U.S. Navy caught off guard? "We had all the information and refused to interpret it correctly."[1]

The only reason this misinterpretation didn't turn out to be a fatal illusion for the United States (although it was for many individuals) was that Japan was operating under an even bigger illusion. The majority of Japanese leaders believed that they could attack the United States and consolidate their empire before their enemy could muster its vast industrial and military might and respond. But within three months, U.S. pilot Jimmy Doolittle was bombing Tokyo. Within six months, the Japanese navy was in shambles. Within a little more than three years, Japan was in shambles.

How can we pile illusions on top of illusions, until we bring our quicksand-based plans down on our heads? Our capacity to avoid reality should not be underestimated.

An important concept that is seldom taught by our schools and our on-the-job training programs is reality testing. Reality testing isn't something that comes naturally; in fact, quite the opposite is true. As we've already seen, we resist painful reality and spin our illusions to "deal with it." Those around us can operate in their own illusory worlds and spin their webs of illusion around us and others. This mutual illuding can be an ongoing process—nonstop, unless we stop it.

Reality testing is a self-reinforcing and cumulative process. It's self-reinforcing because the more times we face situations honestly, the easier it is to resist when the next temptation to illude comes along. It's cumulative because the net effect of a long series of purposeful reality testing is a savviness that won't be easily pushed aside.

Reality testing takes time and courage. The persistence and revivability of illusions is one of the great themes of history. Illusions aren't shredded quickly or without a war. Reality testing can begin by reading this book as a leadership team, slowly working your way through each of the concepts, and spending extensive and concentrated time on each of the twelve fatal illusions. If you take the necessary time and muster the necessary courage, your organization will be very different and much healthier than it is today—not because of the book, but because of your investment of yourself in the process.

Illuding, like reality testing, is self-reinforcing and cumulative. Illusion leads to more and stronger illusion, misperception invites misperception, and accepted or agreed-upon unreality confirms us in a deadly direction. This happens partly because reality keeps intruding into our illusory world. Reality demands—probably now with a higher level of pain—that we make serious changes to bring what we're doing into alignment with it. The same kind and degree of illusion will no longer do the job; if we won't stop illuding, we'll have to take the next step into a higher level of unreality.

Most of us are a mix of reality testing and illuding. The problem is that, without concerted effort to avoid it, illuding will win. "The great enemy of the truth is very often not the lie—deliberate, contrived, and dishonest—but the myth—persistent, persuasive, and unrealistic," said President John F. Kennedy.

Not all illusions are fatal. In this chapter, we look at illusions in three major categories: harmless illusions, which can lead to inconsistency; hurtful illusions, which can lead to limitations on our success; and fatal illusions, which can lead to organizational disaster.

HARMLESS ILLUSIONS

A harmless illusion is one that keeps us from facing reality in some small area of our life or organization.

I have a friend who says she's concerned about her weight. If a plate of brownies is nearby, she won't take a whole brownie, even under great pressure. But I've seen her polish off a whole batch—one small bite at a time, broken off as she walks by. Her behavior is definitely illusory, and—since her weight is not really a problem (it's another illusion that she's overweight)—relatively harmless.

Our careers can be loaded with harmless illusions: "I'd be happy if only I had *that* job." "I think I tell jokes pretty well." "These clothes will make people at the office respect me more." "I'll come in a little early so I can finish that project without interruption." This is the stuff of daydreams and fantasies. At a certain level, they help us feel less anxious about facing a very challenging world.

What are some relatively harmless illusions about our organizations?

"All this talk about 'casual Fridays' is nonsense—nobody really cares about that."

"Our people like the 'buzz' of our open-office arrangement, and privacy isn't much of an issue."

"Reserved parking spaces for management won't cause any resentment."

"Canceling the company party shouldn't have any effect on morale."

"Flextime is a fad."

We have to be especially careful about the sound bites—the little ideas, quotes, or slogans that sound so good but are really illusions. We need to be leery about their humor or catchiness, the very things that can lead us to "buy." For example:

Although relatively harmless in themselves (if the slogans just listed don't seem to be illusions, then you're illuding), these illusions can lead us to buy into other hurtful or fatal illusions later on. "To see things in the seed, that is genius," said Chinese philosopher Lao-Tzu. The small unrealities establish a pattern of illuding. It's the *pattern*—not necessarily the individual illusion—that will kill us down the road.

HURTFUL ILLUSIONS

The early 1990s brought what appeared to be a manufacturing boom to the United States. Domestic shipments of U.S. computer equipment

Slogan/Illusion	*Resulting Attitude*	*Reality*
"No good deed goes unpunished."	Why bother?	Great efforts often lead to great victories.
"——— happens."	Why plan long-term?	Sometimes it doesn't happen—and something caused it when it does.
"The one who dies with the most toys wins."	Possessions are top priority.	Organizations with lots of assets frequently go belly-up.
"Life is uncertain; eat dessert first."	Fads are better than fundamentals.	We can't live on fluff.
"TGIF"	Work is a hellhole.	Something that takes up thirty-five or more of our waking hours each week can and should be satisfying.

and peripherals rose from $55 billion in 1991 to $66 billion in 1994. Shipments of U.S. automotive parts and accessories rose almost 20 percent in the same time, to $112 billion. During those same years, computer-supply employment dropped from 250,000 to 190,000 and auto-supply employment declined by almost 50,000 jobs.

What happened? "U.S. multinationals are more and more meeting their distribution and service needs with goods designed and manufactured by . . . production networks from abroad."[2] In other words, sales of U.S. manufactured goods *look* as if they're going up because of sales by huge "nameplate" companies, even while the supporting domestic manufacturing base erodes. This illusion is permitting our domestic manufacturing base to gradually deteriorate and disappear. A hurtful illusion now—perhaps, later on, a fatal one.

A hurtful illusion keeps us from full effectiveness in achieving our goals but still may allow us some measure of success. In other words, the illusion has a "payoff" that can seem to offset some or all of the negative effects. In the example just given, the payoff for the nameplate companies was increased sales, even while the hurtful long-term erosion of the supporting manufacturing base was lost in the illusion of statistics.

We can be content to live with hurtful illusions because we're getting some things accomplished, even though we can find ourselves wondering why we're not getting over the hump and achieving all we'd like to.

Hurtful illusions can cloud our personal lives and careers: "I don't have time to read." "Exercise isn't that important." "They don't care if I'm late as long as I get the job done." "I've shared my complaints with a few people, but I think they're trustworthy." "My job is safe." It may be a long time before the pain is apparent.

In our organizations, if we're not careful, we can operate with a higher percentage of hurtful illusions than reality:

"If I can measure it, I can manage it."

"If it can't be measured, it can't be managed."

"Management is logical—if we use these means we'll get to that end."

"We can anticipate the major consequences of this decision."

"We can live up to the expectations of our employees and customers."

Prejudices and biases are almost always harmful (if not fatal). They are constructs that allow us to feel good about ourselves compared to our competitors and customers. They let us pigeonhole others rather than force us to do the hard work of learning and reality testing. We might continue to succeed at some level if our bias isn't too far removed from reality, but the problem is that biases (like bacteria) tend to grow over time.

FATAL ILLUSIONS

A fatal illusion leads to short- or long-term disaster. The disaster could be loss of customers, loss of market share, declines in sales or profits (or both), major personnel problems, legal assaults, or release from organizational problems (in the form of bankruptcy). Fatal illusions are killers, and they're hard to put behind bars.

Fatal illusions grow out of a number of crippling maladies: self-

centeredness, where we believe that whatever brings us the most pleasure and the least pain is best; pride, where we believe that we have all
the answers, or at least all the important ones; and hubris, where we
believe that we will win no matter what.

Along with these "we're terrific" diseases come some "we're unable" ones: self-contempt, where we believe that we're not smart, worthy, or valuable enough to win or even try; and other-centered
contempt, where we believe that our customers, suppliers, and fellow
workers are stupid and incapable of building a winning team.

Fatal illusions usually have a number of characteristics in
common:

➡ Their influence is pervasive throughout the department, division, or organization.
➡ No one talks about, or even hints at, their existence.
➡ Evidence that could expose the fatal illusions is systematically
and relentlessly suppressed by force and by agreement.
➡ Often, only a major shock or a strong outside influence can
break the power of the illusions.
➡ The illusions are implicitly defended in meetings, reports, and
decisions.
➡ Information that supports the illusions (books, articles, slogans, audiotapes, videotapes, seminars) is enthusiastically re-
ferred to and distributed.
➡ The illusions have one or more high-level and powerful pro-
ponents.

Illusions move toward fatality as errors of mind, heart, and will
coincide and reinforce one another. When erroneous ideas combine
with negative emotions and there is little determination to change, we
have a primordial brew out of which horrific illusions can grow.

In the next section of the book, we take a close look at twelve
illusions. In a world of accelerating change, fierce competition, always-
shrinking profit margins (or budgets), and a steady flow of innovative
ideas and products, any one of these twelve can be fatal to a business.
Two or more can ensure that our organization will die.

NOTES

1. Barbara W. Tuchman, *Practicing History* (New York: Ballantine Books, 1982),
p. 250.
2. David Friedman, "The Enemy Within," *Inc.*, October 1995, 48.

SECTION II
Twelve
Fatal
Illusions

In this section, we discuss twelve fatal illusions—one per chapter—that over time, can kill any organization that buys in to them.

There is a logical progression to these illusions and our coverage of them. The first illusion concerns our *vision*. If we illude about vision, we have no idea who we really are or where we ought to be going. *Priorities* show us how to put our feet under our vision; if we illude about them, we'll crawl about aimlessly. *Quality* (i.e., satisfying our customers through constant innovation) has to be our top priority; illuding here will destroy our bottom line, both now and down the road.

Our *expectations* for ourselves and for our organization affect not only how high we set our vision but also how we translate our priorities into actions; illusions in this area will make the achievement of our goals, including our quality goals, impossible. In order to reach our expectations, we have to be willing to *change;* if we illude here, we'll just end up transferring all of our yesterdays into tomorrows. By bringing real change to our organization, we can select the *consequences* we want and avoid the ones we don't want; illusions here will leave us feeling bewildered, angry, and helpless.

Proper use of *comparisons* can highlight where we need to change and help explain why we're getting the results that we are; on the other hand, if we're illuding, they can lead us into complacency and a false sense of security and dupe us into thinking that our organization is doing well right up to the moment that disaster strikes. Having the right *people* in the right place is absolutely vital to an organization's success; illuding about our staffing will result in wasted talent, inefficiency, employee dissatisfaction, and high turnover. No matter how good our people are, they won't achieve anything noteworthy unless we give them the information they need; illusions about *openness* will limit an organization to the capability of one person—the one hoarding the data.

Appropriate and adequate *incentives* are absolutely necessary for spurring our good people (the only kind we ought to have) to their highest level of achievement; illusions here can prevent us from opening the door to peak performance. Finding the right balance between individual and collaborative efforts will allow us to utilize all of our people's talents; illuding about *cooperation* will turn our organization into either a war zone or a cemetery. And *passion*. It all comes down to passion. Illuding about passion will leave our organization with no heart, no fire, and no future.

A word about the format of these chapters. We begin each one with an anecdote to illustrate the illusion in action. Next, we provide an overview of the illusion to give you the big picture. Then we dig in, taking a hard look at some of the causes of the illusion. Next we provide a twenty-point self-test to help you evaluate whether or not each illusion is lurking in your organization. Don't rush through these tests—doing so, and believing the answers, would lead to a major-league illusion that you're doing better than you are. A thorough and painstaking job here can reap rich rewards. After rating your organization (with input from others, including the curmudgeons and the revolutionaries) from 0 (lowest) to 5 (highest) on each statement, total your answers. A score of less than 90 in any chapter indicates that there is work to be done on that topic; less than 80 calls for some major illusion shredding; less than 70 says cancel all meetings, set up a cot, and concentrate on this item fast; less than 60 is a call for 911. A good way to start improving the situation is to take the lowest-scored items for each illusion and go to work correcting them.

Some of the statements on the self-test may leave you asking, "What does *that* have to do with this illusion?" You may need to spend a lot of time on these. The fact that the connection isn't apparent is likely a commentary on the deep-rootedness of the illusion.

In the last part of each chapter, we offer some ideas to help you shred the fatal illusion. We discuss these ideas under four major headings: "Organizational Viewpoints," in which we explore necessary changes in the overall orientation and structure of the organization;

"Leadership Attitudes," where we analyze our individual roles in the shredding process; "People Responses," in which we dissect the areas where our people's collaboration is essential; and "Learning and Asking," where we suggest some ways to keep ourselves open to the necessity of ongoing shredding.

If you consider each of these chapters as a place to stop for a while on your journey while you look at your organization with fresh, unflinching honesty, it can be a beginning point for a whole new era of personal and collective growth.

Let's start shredding.

4

Vision: "Having a Mission Statement Means We Know Who We Are"

Where there is no vision, the people run wild.

—Hebrew proverb

It was just a simple memo.

Doug, a young engineer, had been concerned about the direction of his company, CPT, for quite a while. He felt that the company was floundering, trying to beat the bushes to get some orders. He saw that any competitor with a focus would be able to defeat CPT in the long run.

It was then that Doug saw a magazine article, "A Call for Vision in Managing Technology." It said everything that Doug had been feeling for months. He sat down and wrote a memo to his boss with ideas about how strengthening the company's vision could make CPT more successful in the industry. He attached a copy of the article and dropped it in his boss's "in" box.

It nearly killed Doug's career.

Doug was young and enthusiastic. He needed a vision to inspire him, but none was forthcoming. His boss, obviously offended, told him that "vision" wasn't Doug's concern—doing his job was. Doug's boss didn't understand that working toward a vision is what gives employees a sense of pride, a feeling of being special, a confidence that nobody else does it quite as well. And he didn't care. He didn't want Doug to be a visionary. He wanted him to be a human resource.

Doug's boss carried an illusion that vision was unimportant to—more, a distraction from—the real business of getting orders and making money. Doug's illusion was his belief that his boss wanted input; he didn't, because he already knew everything.

Vision is the quality that elevates the mundane into higher realms of achievement. Vision excites passion, bestows meaning on otherwise routine or dreary days, gives direction to goals, and provides guidance for daily decisions. Without vision, organizations wither, and people lose interest. Yet most organizations don't have it.

THE VISION ILLUSION

Scott Adams, in his book *The Dilbert Principle*, defines a mission statement as "a long, awkward sentence that demonstrates management's inability to think clearly."[1]

My guess is that most of us would agree with Adams's assessment. The vision illusion says that "mission statements mean we know who we are," while the reality is that most of the vision and mission statements currently in use aren't in use at all. The vast majority of these statements are leading their organizations in the same sense that a hood ornament is leading a car.

The first vision illusion is to confuse vision with vision statements. We can easily confuse the output with the idea. Vision is a dream or picture of the future that draws us—no, *pulls* us—into the future. A vision statement is an attempt to capture that vision in words.

We don't know who we are because we've developed a vision statement—we know who we are because we know who we are. Because we've taken the time to work through the baloney to get to the core of what's important—to *all* of our stakeholders. Because we've spent the effort to get beyond warm maple syrup—and down to some "drivers" that both the new recruit and the hardened veteran can buy into and apply on the job. Because we've selected some things that are actually worth people's precious time. As a result, people throughout the organization can quote the statement because they're *living* it, not because they've memorized it.

An example of a visionless vision is "growth." In a survey of 150 executives at Fortune 1000 companies, 62 percent said that growth was one of their most important goals, and 20 percent said that it was their *most* important goal. What's wrong with that? Growth is a miserable measure of success, quality, or value. Why? Because cancer grows. Warts grow. The empires of Napoleon, Bismarck, Hitler, and Stalin grew. Organizations can grow—right out of their ability to be understood, much less led or managed.

Growth is a *by-product,* not a vision. Growth as a driving force (e.g., "Our vision is to be the biggest in our industry") is more likely to be a symptom of megalomania rather than a statement of value.

We also illude when we try to make vision statements either too short or too long.

The "too short" vision tries to condense all of what we want to be and do into one compound sentence. While the desire to think and write concisely can be commendable, it's illusory to believe that a single sentence, drafted by top management and "experts," can capture the essence of an organization and have an impact on the people in it on a *daily basis.*

On the other side, the "too long" vision can actually become a strategic planning document in which the vision gets lost. Once something gets too detailed, it loses its ability to guide and inspire, which are the only reasons to have an articulated vision in the first place.

Perhaps the most frightening illusions about vision are the belief that our statement has meaning for people who actually never give it a second thought and the conviction that we've produced a "masterpiece," when what it evokes in the trenches is ridicule. Laughter is a wonderful reaction at times, but not in response to our proposed guide to the future. If we think that the ridicule reveals a flaw in the laugher rather than a deficiency in the managers who wrote inadvertent comedy, fatal illusion is on the throne.

The opposite approach to the illusion of the visionless vision is the illusion that we don't need to have any vision at all. Without a vision, effort is scattered, and people run wild. Empowering people when there's no unifying vision only provides resources for empire building and intracorporate mutiny and revolution. Having no vision also allows too much room for inertia—continuing to do what we've been doing because we don't know what else to do. It was to fight this inertia that Doug sent his memo.

Causes of the Illusion

How can good ideas like vision and vision statements end up feeding our illusions and *becoming* illusions? Here are some of the reasons:

➡ Because we haven't really bought in to the idea that vision is important, either we don't want to spend the time to define it or we try to get the "vision" thing over with as quickly as possible.

➡ Because we're afraid that a detailed vision will rigidify our organization and leave no room for the flexing of our creative muscles, we make the vision statement hopelessly generic or merely avoid it altogether.

➡ Since we can easily confuse "vision" with "lofty," the final product can be so pie-in-the-sky (so "heavenly minded that it's no earthly good") that nobody can relate to it.

➡ When we really don't believe our people can contribute to the vision, we draft the statement "on high," leaving those who are actually doing the work (and thus reality) out of the process.

➡ Since we want to "sound good," we can formulate what we think we *ought* to be rather than what we truly want to be or can become, acting much like survey respondents who give the answers they think will impress the questioner.

➡ If we're lazy, it's easier to imitate or borrow a vision from a consultant or competitor and to look outside, rather than inside, for our ideas and our definition of who we are.

➡ If we simply want our vision to sound like the "best of class" of our competitors, we can forget the simple power of charting a unique course in inspiring people.

➡ Since it's so difficult to articulate a concise, detailed vision, we can begin to confuse strategies, plans, and goals with vision.

If we don't really have a vision (or at least not one worth articulating), simply avoiding the pain of that truth and opting not to develop a vision statement at all can seem much more desirable than wrestling with who we are.

How to Recognize the Illusion

Rate your organization from 0 (lowest) to 5 (highest) on the following statements:

_____ Our vision includes elements that will endure beyond the tenure of anyone currently working here.

_____ We are very careful not to confuse our vision with our vision statement.

_____ We developed our vision completely before attempting to write a vision statement.

_____ We don't try to substitute strategies, plans, and goals for vision.

_____ All employees gave input to the development of the vision (1 if 20 percent, 2 if 40 percent, etc.).

_____ Our vision incorporates (and is) an organizational story, with each point calling specific, vivid, and realistic pictures to the reader's mind.

_____ After thirty days, all employees could passionately articulate the vision in their own words.

_____ Our vision statement has at least five major, clear, focused subpoints that commit us to specific paths (1 if one, 2 if two, etc.).

_____ Our employees think our vision is worthy (ask *them* to do this rating).

_____ The vision statement relates to and affects daily decisions by our employees (again, ask *them*).

_____ Our vision is achievable in total as well as in all its parts.

_____ Our customers and suppliers know, understand, and agree with our vision (it's scary, but guess who we have to ask!).

_____ Our vision statement clearly differentiates us from our competitors in significant ways.

_____ We refuse to borrow any part of our vision from anyone else or to buy it from a consultant.

_____ Our vision statement is a declaration of what we want to become, not what we think others might want us to become.

_____ Our vision statement incorporates multiple tactics that neither we nor our competitors are now doing but that we know we'll have to do.

_____ Our vision has the passion to inspire and make our people run (ask your stakeholders).

_____ Our vision has aspects about which our employees can—and do—brag to their friends (we'll need to ask).

_____ Everyone gives us feedback on our vision and our vision statement, and the feedback is built into revisions as needed.

_____ We really believe that we couldn't operate successfully without a vision and a vision statement.

_____ TOTAL

Shredding the Illusion

Do we have a vision that passes the "reality" test? Does it "smell" real?

Organizational Viewpoints

To survive today, we must have a vision that can be captured in a vision/mission statement. (Some people recommend two different documents—pu-*leez!* We'll call it a vision statement the rest of the way.) We're illuding if we think that we can go somewhere when we don't know where that is, or that our vision is "unspoken" (read: absent). Good intentions won't buy the farm—or even help us find it.

From an organizational perspective, a vision has to have these five components:

1. *A sense of worthiness.* "The greatest use of life is to spend it for something that will outlast it," suggested the American psychologist and philosopher William James.

2. *An ability to inspire.* "I simply dream dreams and see visions, and then I paint around those dreams and visions," said the Italian Renaissance painter Raphael.

3. *An invitation to share.* "We all need to believe in what we are doing," said Allan D. Gilmour, executive vice president of Ford.

4. *Clear and understandable detail.* "Write the vision, and make it plain upon your tables, that he may run who reads it," recommended the ancient Hebrew prophet Habakkuk.

5. *Achievability.* "I never gave an order that couldn't be obeyed," American General Douglas MacArthur answered when asked about his key to success.

Brief vision statements are invariably hokey and nondirective. A one-sentence vision statement gives the illusion of saying something when it has all the substance of cotton candy. It needs to have enough detail to give guidance to the process. It has to flow from our understanding of the daily life of our employees, customers, distributors, and suppliers. *All* of our most important values ought to be reflected and given life in our vision statement.

On the other hand, a detailed vision statement doesn't try to "fix" an unchanging vision. A well-done statement instead "flexifies" our organization. It is dynamic, not static; a movie, not a photograph; a process, not a position. It gives subpoint detail that expands, rather than rigidifies, our scope. It broadens our understanding of the possibilities before us.

A vision statement is bigger than and different from strategies, which are bigger than and different from plans and goals. "Goals and plans are elements of creating a strategy, but in most cases neither (or even both) are sufficient for doing so. . . . [They give] the *illusion* of strategy. . . . The process of setting goals subtly leads to the feeling that a strategy is in place."[2] In the same way, having strategies can give the *illusion* of vision.

A vision tells us where we're going. "In many ways, the vision or mission statement is a test of whether there really is a message."[3] Strategies tell us how to get there—how to win in our competitive environment, how to give our customers what they need at the right price and with the right costs. Plans and goals tell us how to implement and measure our strategies.

Vision can and should guide a reengineering effort. Reengineering sometimes fails when it's a supereffort to erase an old structure and replace it with a new one. Reengineering often works best when we engineer *process*, not structure. It can also work well when we replace one structure with another *if* we have a clear vision to lead that replacement.

Vision shouldn't focus on the organization's "name" or "reputation." These things are by-products of an effective, energizing vision, just as a person's reputation is a cumulative picture of what he says and does over a long period of time. Reputation, like happiness, can't be achieved directly. Efforts to create a reputation lead to the spewing out of illusion-filled press releases and management speeches, and in the end we can buy in to the illusions ("we're the best in the business"; "nobody does it like we do") ourselves. Advertising slogans are all right, as long as we remember that they're not vision.

Vision statements, to be worth anything, have to *differentiate* our company from the competition. Anyone who interfaces with our organization should be able to identify the statement with us, even if our organization's name isn't at the top.

Perhaps the most important aspect of an inspiring vision is its affinity for "story telling." Does our vision tell a story about who we are, what we believe, and what we value? Is it translatable into "stories"? Do we have multiple organizational stories to illustrate each point of the vision statement?

The reason great vision involves great stories is this: Stories move the heart. They can interest, involve, inspire, and change even the most sophisticated and complex personalities. The simpler the story, the wider the appeal and, often, the deeper the impact. Many people simply won't "get it"—at least not at the level of their visceral, emotional drives and desires—unless the message is in story form.

To be effective, a vision has to embody a story, be illustrated and emphasized with stories, and be supported by an ongoing stream of stories. Rationally written vision statements have little power to stir an organization. When they're written to tell a story, nothing can stand in their way.

Leadership Attitudes

Vision can be one of the greatest illusion-shredding devices in our managerial repertoire. The process of developing a coherent and detailed vision can enlarge our worldview, help make our assumptions and biases readily apparent, and assist us in abandoning microcosmic (limited) views that don't align with macrocosmic (big-picture) reality.

As leaders and managers, one of our most important roles is to communicate the vision through our words and actions. Having uncommunicated vision is only slightly better than having no vision at all. A vision won't be absorbed into the organic response of our people and teams unless it's communicated to them consistently, in many ways, on many occasions. Stories are the best way.

It's important to remember that we can't do everything at once. My company's vision statement has three major categories with four major subpoints under each category (and all on one page). We select one of those subpoints and focus on it for a month (less than that is not long enough). During that month, we talk about the point in meetings, set objectives for improving our ability to achieve that point, institute change initiatives to support enhancement, get people's feedback. We notify everyone often about whatever point is coming up in the next month. Focus of this magnitude makes the vision run.

People Responses

If we're leading an effective vision-development process, we don't assume that we know what our employees and customers want from us; we assume that we *don't* know (we probably don't). We involve everybody because we know how easily our biases and preconceived ideas can cause us to illude.

Employees are not usually involved in this process, nor is their input welcome. The results of this exclusion become obvious over time.

Two stonecutters were working near a busy street. A passerby noticed that the two were working with very different levels of intensity.

He went up to the one who was working at a more leisurely pace, taking many breaks, and asked him what he was doing.

"I'm cutting stone," the man answered matter-of-factly as he sipped his drink.

The passerby then approached the second man, who was working industriously and with great concentration at exactly the same job as the first man. He waited until the man finally looked up and smiled. "What are you doing?" the passerby asked.

The man wiped his glistening forehead with his sleeve. "I'm building a cathedral," he answered proudly before taking up his tools again.

The passerby nodded in understanding and walked on.

What was the difference between cutting stone and building a cathedral?

Vision. Our vision *must* connect with the hearts and dreams of our people. Otherwise, they're just cutting stone.

When our people are responding because their hearts and dreams are in tune with our vision, we are ahead of 80 percent or more of the organizations that surround us.

Learning and Asking

If we want vision to mean something, we shouldn't "issue" a vision statement. We should ask for people's input to the process to get both their ideas and their "buy-in." And then we have to sweat through it together. "Vision does not come by inspiration," said Robert A. Weaver, a former secretary of housing and urban development. "It comes from knowledge, intelligently cultivated."

If a vision doesn't inspire us and our people to do or be something greater than we're already doing or being, then it isn't a vision, and we need to stop pretending. We need to ask our people to rate our vision statement—point by point—on a 1–5 scale of inspiration and passion.

5 = I'd do anything possible to help this come to pass.

4 = This is very important and worthy of some sacrifice.

3 = I'm glad we want to do those things, but they don't hit me where I live.

2 = I'm a little embarrassed about our vision, but I need the pay-check.

1 = This ship is in trouble, and I've got my eye on the lifeboat.

The best vision statements look to where we haven't been and are afraid to go. They understand that our current skill sets may not be "core competencies" but rather "core constrictions," since nothing fails like success. A strong, viable vision statement includes a section on "areas and things we're not doing now that we'd better stay up on or we'll be killed."

One of the most neglected components of rooting a vision deeply in our organization is feedback. How do people feel about it? Do they care? Do they think it closely relates to our customers and their values and needs? Is their visceral reaction to say "Wow!" or to laugh and make cynical comments? A vision is meaningless without communication, and feedback is an indispensable, loop-closing part of communication. Just talking about it begins the rooting-in process.

In a survey of top managers from more than 10,000 companies, only 30 percent of those polled said that their organizations regularly asked for feedback to ensure that what they were trying to communicate was actually understood.[4] This means that 70 percent *assumed* that the message was received and grasped (or didn't care one way or the other). It's no wonder that these same managers thought that fewer than 40 percent of their own employees understood the company's vision. Here it is: There's an uncomfortable feeling that people don't "get it," but we don't ask.

This is life in illusion-land.

Vision is a picture of a process, not a structure. It's something that can live, breathe, grow, adapt, and learn. At its best it is an ongoing, participative, flexible, ever-evolving part of every organization's life.

NOTES

1. Scott Adams, *The Dilbert Principle* (New York: HarperBusiness, 1996), p. 36.
2. Eileen C. Shapiro, *How Corporate Truths Become Competitive Traps* (New York: Wiley, 1991), p. 98.
3. Karl Albrecht, *The Northbound Train* (New York: AMACOM, 1994), p. 148.
4. Peter Lowy and Byron Reimus, "Ready, Aim, Communicate," *Management Review*, July 1996, 40–43.

5

Priorities: "Of Course Our People Understand What's Important"

Doing more things faster is no substitute for doing the right things.
—Stephen R. Covey, *First Things First*

Doris closed the door and sank into bed. She thought about pulling the sheet over her head.

The day had been as stressful as any she could remember. After her appointment as the new principal of Forest Trail Middle School, she had felt a flush of excitement as a stream of goals she wanted to accomplish ran through her mind. The night she'd accepted the job, she'd filled up eleven pages of notes.

All of that now seemed like another lifetime. Over the last six days, she had met with five disgruntled teachers, one of whom hinted at a lawsuit because she was unhappy with her assignment. Then one of the vice principals—the disciplinarian, of all people—had unexpectedly handed in her resignation. Replacing her was going to take up a lot of time that Doris didn't have. Doris had also met with about fifty parents, half of whom had complaints or special requests related to their children. As Doris was leaving the school that day, her head throbbing, the district administrator had handed her a list of twelve program deficiencies and asked for a plan to correct them—to be turned in within two weeks.

Doris stared up at the ceiling. She was furious. All she could think about was how much she hated everything.

Then she saw her again.

In her mind, she could picture her.

What's her name? Joanne? No. Starts with a "J," though. Julia!

That's it. She's . . . an eighth-grader, I think. Brown hair pulled back. Big smile with braces. She was coming for practice. Choir, maybe? Yes, choir. That's it.

She could see Julia handing her the note and then quickly disappearing down the hall. She had taken it, assuming it was from her parents. She had been stunned as she opened it and realized it was a note from Julia. "Welcome to our school. I hope you'll like it here. I know it's hard being new. I was new last year and was so scared until another girl said hello. The scared just flew away." She had glanced down the hallway, to where she had last seen the girl. Then she had looked down at the note. "I thought you might be scared, even though you are a principal. I thought if I said hello maybe your scared would fly away, too."

Then Doris remembered why she'd taken the job.

THE PRIORITY ILLUSION

Priorities can keep us focused and give us perspective when life is demanding and chaotic around us. For Doris, remembering that the children were her top priority made the challenges she faced seem less oppressive. Because our priorities are the path we take to realize our vision, the careful selection of priorities is one of the most important things our organization can do to succeed. They're also one of the easiest things about which we can illude.

The priority illusion often begins with the idea that others will set our priorities for us.

At the organizational level, we can illude that the market will define all of our priorities. But the market may not even *know* all of its priorities—particularly when we're looking at undiscovered directions and uninvented products or services. The reality is that we'll have to define and articulate our own priorities, in part because only we know who we are, and in part because those who have the needs often can't or won't tell us what they are.

At the individual level, we can wait for our organization to define our priorities for us. But organizations are in many ways incapable of doing this. They tell us they want one thing and then measure us on something else. They tell us to focus on something and then structure an environment that distracts and interrupts and is driven by the urgent, by meetings, and (at times) by pure nonsense. Organizations often don't even know what *their* priorities are; how can they direct us on ours?

Often worse than not setting priorities for us, people sometimes *do* attempt to tell us what our priorities should be. These priorities are frequently driven not by results but by someone's personal agenda, perception, or illusion about what's needed. "The time spent on any matter is usually inversely proportional to its importance," said C. Northcote Parkinson in his 1957 book *Parkinson's Law and Other Studies in Administration.* In today's world, waiting for someone else to set our priorities for us is a ticket to being downsized.

Another illusion occurs when we discuss and agree on our priorities, post them on our bulletin boards, then never think of them when we're making day-to-day decisions. This happens when we are driven by the urgent. For example, in one company, no matter what people said their top priorities were, all employee decisions were really made by considering what the president would think about the issue.

Our top priority as organizations or as leaders has to be giving our customers the (and only the) benefits they need and desire at a price they perceive to be a good deal and at a cost that allows us to operate both competitively and profitably. But we can illude that this is our top priority when we're really spending our energies on something else entirely. We can easily spend all of our best efforts on processes, methods, rules, and activities rather than on outcomes, objectives, values, and results—illuding all the while that "the customer is number one."

The way we achieve true customer satisfaction on an ongoing basis is through the second most important priority: constant innovation. But here we can illude that we're innovating because we've rewritten the policy manual (you still *have* one?), changed a procedure (are you sure it's the best way?), added some "customer-service" people (isn't everybody supposed to be in "customer service"?), or even added a new product or service (is this what the customers *really* need?). Making priorities out of peripherals is both a crippling distraction and a fatal illusion.

We can illude on both sides of the question of what leads to constant innovation. On the one hand, we can illude that substantial planning and analysis—getting all the facts in place—is the answer. But in today's world, we have to be able to get to the "prototype" level fast; we have to have a continual orientation toward speed, testing, remaking, and reintroducing.

On the other hand, we can carry the "ready, fire, aim" approach too far and illude that if we just try enough ideas in a short period of time, *something* is bound to click. But if our ideas are poor ones—or if they haven't had the necessary pruning to make them into good ideas—then trying to be successful by doing more wrong things per month than our competitors is a formula for organizational demise. "Any plant growing in the wrong place is a 'weed,' " noted the *Old*

Farmer's Almanac. And at times the best response to a crisis is to (for a while) do nothing.

Assessing the impact on our operations of globalization, internationally linked supply chains, and a shrinking world market is a third important priority; to think otherwise is to try to insulate ourselves from reality. Today, however, no organization can insulate itself from this reality forever. We don't know when a twenty-five-person company providing our service in Singapore may obliterate our competitive advantage in Columbia, South Carolina, or when a company in a totally unrelated industry in Amsterdam might innovate in an entirely new direction and leave us without a customer in Tucson, Arizona. The Industrial Revolution is over. Size, location, financial assets, years in business, even technology—all mean nothing. New knowledge, supported by speed, is king. We've all got to be on the cutting edge. The only alternative is to be cut to pieces.

If we're not careful, we can allow an illusion to become a priority. We can delude ourselves into thinking that using this illusion as a guiding star will lead our organization to success. Let's take a look at some of the worst offenders.

The "bigger is better" illusion still enjoys wide currency. But bigger isn't better; *better* is better. As stated earlier, if our priority is to get bigger, we've adopted the philosophy of the cancer cell. If our priority is to get better—which often means getting smaller so that we can provide better quality and service with *speed*—we've adopted the philosophy of the white blood cell and have a shot at creating a healthy body. The question isn't how we grow a 150-person department or organization into a 300-person one but how we make two 150s out of a 300.

Along with this illusion comes the "more information is better" illusion. Once again, better—not more—is the answer. In a world of information overload, where so often we're processing garbage at the speed of light, *selection* of the best and most relevant information is the way to better decisions. Having limits on a good thing (e.g., information) will serve to keep it "good."

We can illude that we don't have to train people in how to access, read, understand, use, and leverage new information and knowledge. We can illude that people will train themselves and know how to tie what they're learning into our organizational objectives. But they won't be able to do these things alone. Few, if any, periods of history have produced so much information and so little knowledge. Wisdom, not information, is the priority.

The last "bigger is better" illusion is the quest for the "break-through." It's crippling to wait for a breakthrough without taking the necessary small steps along the way. In fact, often the breakthroughs come at the end of a long series of small steps. Small things often add up—or lead up—to a breakthrough. This "breakthrough" illusion keeps us focused on the wrong end and eliminates the power that being responsible in creating the many small things can bring.

We also have to be ready to exploit a breakthrough when it comes.

> Lofty academic concepts of product cycles and technology life cycles and the theory of comparative advantage lend intellectual support to the view that we can stay on top by tackling new technological frontiers. A comforting image indeed: the U.S. makes breakthroughs and forges ahead, leaving older 'hand me down' industries to other countries.
>
> But reality is far more complex than these comforting images. Even though many important breakthrough innovations have been made here, the high-technology end products, along with the jobs and wealth they create, are being produced elsewhere.[1]

We can illude that a breakthrough will automatically lead to success. Not necessarily. Maybe not even likely. As with so many things in life, it's illusion to believe that long-term goals or improvements can come easily, fast, or without the dedication to the small but critical priorities along the way.

We also can illude that people will somehow be able to get everything done, with "everything" constituting a gigantic, growing, ever-changing, and devouring mass. We shouldn't sacrifice the "small" that has a big payoff for the apparently "big," or sacrifice the truly "big" for the urgent but worthless "small." We have to clear the debris from in front of our people and expect some things not to get done if we want them to help lead us to victory.

The truth is that we never really know where or when the payoff will be, but we need to focus on the activities—big or small—that will give us the best opportunity.

Causes of the Illusion

These are some of the factors that can lead to illusions about our priorities:

➡ If we haven't taken the steps to set our own priorities, put in place the structures to support them, and started the cheering, we can go into "default" mode and wait for someone else to start the applause.

➡ Since it's easier to measure what we can see (processes, methods) than what we can't see (outcomes, results), without wise and extra effort we can be overcome by daily details.

➡ Because constant innovation is incredibly difficult and taxing, it can be very easy to rest on our laurels and hope for the best.

➡ It's easier to be fascinated either by planning (the excellent scout motto "be prepared") or by intuition (best-selling author Tom Peters's insightful "bias for action") than it is to struggle to balance the two on a case-by-case basis.

➡ If we lack the security and the self-confidence necessary to go against the grain, we can opt for the false assurance that size ("all the kids are doing it"; "everybody else disagrees, so we can't be right") can give us.

➡ Since few of us have been trained or have trained ourselves to analyze, dissect, interpret, and discard information, we can become enamored of the quantity of information and confuse it with knowledge (which it is not).

➡ Since it's much harder to do the small but critical things that lead to success than it is to dream about "breakthroughs," we can be enticed by laziness and our resistance to facing pain into waiting for a solution to magically appear and save us.

How to Recognize the Illusion

Rate your organization from 0 (lowest) to 5 (highest) on the following statements:

_____ We set our own organizational priorities and don't let the market set them for us.

_____ We specifically determine, as part of setting priorities, what we *won't* become and *won't* do.

_____ We expect our people (in the context of mutually agreed-upon responsibilities) to set and maintain their own priorities, and we don't permit them to passively wait for us to do it for them.

_____ If we asked our people, they could explain how their priorities are leading to the realization of the organization's vision—that is, why their priorities *are* priorities (ask five of them and write down the number of people who can do this).

_____ If we asked our people, they could explain how everything that they do relates to one or more of their individual priorities (again, ask five of them and write down the number who can).

_____ We refuse to let people unilaterally set priorities for other divisions, departments, or people.

_____ We make outcomes, objectives, values, and results our top priorities and deemphasize processes, methods, rules, and "activity."

_____ We agree that customer satisfaction, supported by constant innovation, is our top priority, and we use it to guide all our decisions.

_____ In our quest for constant innovation, we strive to find the balance between planning and analysis on the one hand, and intuition and taking action (e.g., doing everything with an eye toward speed and fast response) on the other.

_____ We view the creation of stakeholder value as a by-product of customer satisfaction and constant innovation but also as a priority in its own right, and we determine how every major decision will affect it.

_____ Regardless of the size or location of our organization, we have adopted a global, expansive, diverse perspective that colors our daily decisions.

_____ In times of crisis we slow down our decision making and take time both to think and to plan before we respond.

_____ In times of crisis we look intensely for ways to squeeze opportunity out of the problem.

_____ Throughout our organization, we focus more on getting better than we do on getting bigger.

_____ We are fanatical about being on the cutting edge of new services, products, design, technology, processes, marketing approaches, distribution channels, and logistics.

_____ We have critical components (i.e., people, systems) in place to receive, analyze, select, and disseminate key information to our people.

_____ We teach our people how to use and leverage the information we give them and get feedback to ensure that our techniques are working.

_____ We focus our attention on creating training that is tied
into helping us achieve our organizational objectives.
_____ We believe that big breakthroughs generally come not
as a "flash," but rather from a long series of small,
faithful, responsible risks and actions.
_____ We expect our people to delegate, ignore, and otherwise refuse to perform low-priority, low-value activities.

_____ TOTAL

SHREDDING THE ILLUSION

Since we can be touting one set of priorities while we're actually living
by another, it's crucial that we shred illusions in this area before we
realize that the ladder we've climbed was leaning up against the wrong
wall.

Organizational Viewpoints

We have to find ways to convey to our organization that our top priority is giving customers what they need at a price they perceive as a
value and at a cost that allows us to continue to thrive and have resources to pour into the next innovation.

We also have to make sure that our people have gotten the message and bought in to it. If someone's top priority is to get promoted,
get a raise, or make it to Friday, either we haven't successfully con-
veyed the message or we've got the wrong person.

In our quest to live this priority, we've got to force ourselves to
take the initiative in defining what that priority means *for us*. We can't
wait to follow or copy someone else in the marketplace; sometimes
others are moving too fast for us to catch up, and often—through their
clever deception or simply through our failure to see the whole picture—we can wind up imitating illusion rather than reality.

In all of our discussions about priorities, we'll have to work hard
to impress others with the concept that values (what we believe is important) always take precedence over rules and that performance (results) is always more critical than activity. Doris remembered that her
most important value was to connect with an eighth-grader, not to captain a ship with a mutinous crew and surly passengers. A powerful
vision (as described in Chapter 4), if emphasized clearly enough over

a long enough period of time, can cause these values and a bias toward results to stand out in people's minds.

One of the most important priorities is to establish clearly who we *aren't* and what we *won't* do. It can be devastating to believe that because we're good at one thing, we can do well at other things that aren't directly related to it. Even if we are capable of doing something better than average (or even better than most others), it doesn't mean that we should do it.

Part of our focus has to revolve around the topic of *speed*. In our hypercompetitive world, response time has to be a major priority. We still have to do the planning and analysis, but we have to do them faster, and we have to be content with 80 percent of the answers and data (which we can often get with 20 percent of the effort and time). We've got to make getting to the testing, prototype, and market-response levels fast a top priority. Then we need to learn from our experience, hone our plans, and try again—fast.

If we think of our organization as a high-performance car designed to go very fast, we have to keep the pedal to the metal most of the time. But when things go haywire in front of us, we've also got to know where the brakes are. Our normal orientation needs to be to drive fast, but we have to know when to stop.

The more intense a crisis, the greater the need to stop and assess our options. It's illusion to believe that the best thing to do in a crisis is to respond fast, to keep moving ahead. Terrible decisions, with long-lasting results, can easily be made in a confused, chaotic, pressure-cooker time of crisis. The times when we're feeling the most pressure to make something happen are the times when we should force ourselves to go the slowest.

Since organizations with good products or services, plenty of talent, substantial facilities, plant, and equipment, and significant levels of inventory can still go out of business, we need to focus our entire organization to think like *money managers*. We need to focus on flow— cash flow, order flow, design flow, production flow, inventory flow (turns), information flow—anything where we can improve service, streamline operations, and reduce costs *all at the same time.*

Finally, we have to have an organizational humility—to know and believe that we don't know what all of the priorities should be, that big results can come from things that today don't look very important, that somebody in a satellite office 800 miles away might be working in anonymity on the idea that will one day save our organizational hides.

Leadership Attitudes

If we think about it, we'll admit that people seldom if ever get their priorities from official organizational messages that aren't lived out before them. Our example—what we talk about and do with our time—speaks much more eloquently than any pronouncement.

The factors that make our priorities clear are the issues we constantly discuss and measure, the actions we ourselves take, the achievements for which we reward and recognize people, and the way people are treated when they do (or don't do) certain things. Often, the best way to emphasize what's important is through the use of "stories"—talking about good results and the heroic (or ordinary-with-persistence) efforts that achieved them.

This is one way Doris could make a difference in her school. If the development of children is her highest priority, she should begin to take note of, catalogue, and share every story she can get her hands on where a teacher had a special impact or one child showed a special kindness to another—or where a little brown-haired girl with a pony-tail made the difference for a new but overwhelmed principal. Stories can do what rhetorical skills can't touch.

Effectiveness demands that we focus on results. It's illusion to spend our leadership energies on establishing orderly methods and making "discipline" a priority. We have to fight to avoid the error of focusing on methods as priorities rather than on objectives. The best approach we can take is to coestablish the mission with our people and let the methods evolve under the caring efforts of free and empowered employees.

We also have to help people balance the time they spend reviewing the past and the time they spend acting and "getting on with it." If we're prudent, we'll give thought to the past and learn all we can from it. But if we want to prosper, we'll spend as much time applying what we've learned as we did learning it.

Finally, as leaders and managers we need to understand the importance that people place on living balanced lives. Many people don't see their careers as the center of the universe, and over the long haul those who do often make pretty one-dimensional and overbearing colleagues. People want to know that we relate to them as whole people and that we honor who they are and what they do in nonwork areas of their lives.

People don't believe that work should always come before pleasure, that others' work (including ours) should come before theirs, that they shouldn't take breaks or lunch or walks, that reading industry-related magazines or chatting is a waste of time, or that workers' commitment should be measured by a willingness to sacrifice personal plans—or lives. They don't want to feel that if they don't get everything done, they're failures.

Leaders and managers who deal with people as whole, multidimensional beings often get a far better response than those who see people as production units.

People Responses

We can't assume that those who work for us always have our organization and its interests as their number one priority. To believe this, to be deceived by people's surface excitement, is truly a fatal illusion.

The priorities and interests of the people who work for us and around us are as varied as their personalities, needs, and desires. The need to read through their false fronts and to see the reality of what they really need and want is crucial. Only when we know what their priorities really are can we align those priorities with ours.

The first response we need from our people is a willingness to participate in the priority-setting process. We need to know that they understand and accept the organization's priorities, know their own priorities, and have taken steps to bring the two into close connection.

After realizing that young people were her first priority, Doris began setting aside three hours a day to focus on issues important to her students, including talking with them over lunch in the cafeteria. She still carried out her administrative duties and met with parents and teachers. But she never forgot her mission and tried hard never to let her three hours be infringed on.

After people have identified and begun following their true priorities, the next most important response is for them to do the very best job they can on whatever is before them. They can never just "mail in" an effort. If something is a priority, it deserves full attention and their best creativity and energy, because we never know where that attention can bring a big payoff.

This means that something isn't a priority because it's "big" or the boss is interested in it. It's a priority because it's important, no matter how small it may seem. We need to convince workers that great outcomes result from responsible dedication to what—at the moment—can seem like tiny assignments.

We also should expect employees to ignore assignments and details that aren't high-value. We'll surely fail with an "everything must be done" mentality. We should expect people to do daily triage and to save themselves for the big payoff. "It is better to lose the saddle than the horse," an old Italian proverb reminds us.

At least two to four times a year, we need to ask people what they think their top priorities are, why they think so, and where they picked them up. We need them to have a priority mind-set—one that hasn't been borrowed or forced on them by someone else.

Learning and Asking

To accomplish what we want to do and need to do in order to survive and thrive, our focus has to be on constant innovation. There is no status quo anymore.

Constant innovation means that we as an organization will have to move on to the new product or service before the old one is dead, or even used up. "[Leading organizations are] quite prepared to bring out new products at price and performance levels that savage their existing lines. Their reasoning? Far better to render your own products obsolete than have someone else do it for you,"[2] one writer has suggested.

We need to understand that we can't spend our time trying to squeeze the last ounce of profit out of a product at the end of its life cycle or continue to service customers the same way until our market share begins to slip. We can't wait for the need to innovate to be forced on us by others. By then it may be too late.

A key question to ask is how *what* we're doing can interfere with *how* we're doing. Organizational consultant Price Pritchett tells us that "our work processes are always cleanest when we design them to be solely in service to outcomes." We need results analysts more than systems analysts.

It's difficult to believe that in a world on information overload, where 90 percent of what we can learn is worthless or worse, we can survive organizationally (or individually) without an information-screening process. We can use an "information screening team" to accumulate, absorb, and pass along what's valuable. Even if they miss something, it probably won't be half as bad as allowing the organization to drown in data. Unmanaged information processing can use up time that would better be spent on our top priorities.

Finally, we need to continually pursue the answer to some key questions: "Where is the cutting edge? Are we on it? How can we stay on it? Do we know what to do with it?" There are only two places to be today: on the cutting edge—or on the cutting room floor.

NOTES

1. Richard Florida and Martin Kenney, *The Breakthrough Illusion* (New York: Basic Books, 1990).
2. Matthew J. Kiernan, *The Eleven Commandments of 21st Century Management* (Englewood Cliffs, N.J.: Prentice-Hall, 1996), p. 78.

6

Quality: "Everybody Knows What Quality Is"

From a dog you don't make salami.
—Hungarian proverb

Michael had finished an exhausting week.

He had finally collapsed into his window seat on the huge plane being readied for departure from Honolulu to Dallas. It was early evening. The mood was positive as people stashed their belongings in the overhead bins and pushed other items under their seats. The weather was good. After a week away from home on business, Michael was ready to eat, read, and sleep.

He stashed the three books he wanted to finish reading in the seat pocket. The plane began moving, and the safety announcements were made. The plane began its takeoff and then suddenly aborted it halfway down the runway. The pilot announced that an air pressure light had come on. As he headed back to the terminal, the light went off, and he tried to take off again. The light came on once more, and this time the plane was returned for inspection by mechanics.

After almost two hours of sitting in a now very hot and uncomfortable cabin, the passengers were told that they would have to get off the plane so that the mechanics could take it out onto the runway and "try some things" (not a tremendously encouraging thought). Michael got off, expecting to get on again soon. He left his books in the pocket.

The plane never took off. Michael was fortunate in finding another flight out late that evening. He asked the flight attendant to report that he had left his books on the canceled flight and gave her the flight and the seat number. She talked to the pilot, who called the information into the airline people on the ground.

The books were never returned. Michael made countless calls but got nowhere. His wife and daughter made more calls, still without success. They were transferred to Oklahoma, found out about a huge and mysterious ware-

*house of "lost" material in Utah, and waded through innumerable depart-
ments. Michael finally got the name and number of the head of the airline's
consumer affairs department and talked on different occasions with two secre-
taries who could actually see the executive in his office. No call was ever
returned.*

*The head of consumer affairs was too busy doing something else to take
care of a consumer.*

THE QUALITY ILLUSION

Few topics get more press than quality, and few topics get as little real
advancement as quality. Organizations like the airline Michael flew on
make claims about quality, and may even have some pieces of quality,
but then can't follow through or deliver on the simplest of customer
needs. But quality must be our top priority if we want our organizations to flourish.

The quality illusion begins with the often erroneous idea that we
know what the customer wants, when sometimes the *customer* doesn't
even know what he or she wants. Or we may talk with one or two
customers and, in our natural laziness, extrapolate from those conversations and generalize about "our customers."

This error is often compounded by another illusion: that everyone
in our organization knows what quality is. The reality is that after decades of talk about quality and countless books on the subject, the most
basic definition of quality still eludes many (if not most) people at the
supervisory and working levels.

The two basic quality illusions are fed by other illusions. We illude
that on any given problem, we have to get all possible information
before deciding (we can't), or, conversely, that we don't need all possible information before deciding (we must try).

We illude that mistakes are bad and convey that idea to people
around us by conducting witch-hunts, crucifying those who make mistakes, fixing the blame rather than the problem, and even shooting the
messengers. Except for those made with malice or repetitive hardheadedness, mistakes aren't bad; they're opportunities to grow and
improve and hone. One measure of organizational quality is how little
(or how much) time and energy are spent generating defenses, creating
"cover ourselves" paper trails, and reinterpreting reality to point organizational fingers in a different direction.

We can illude that complexity and sophistication are symbolic of
world-class operations, while the reality is that these are often the
things that drive up costs, extend lead times, compound and disguise

problems, and color everything with a gray haze of confusion. Few things can mislead us as effectively as the illusion of quality and success that impressive and costly systems can project.

The whole area of measurements provides fertile ground for illusions. In one sense, the management dictum "If I don't measure it, I can't manage it" is true. But we can illude at the extremes. We can believe that if we can measure something it must be important, giving us a feeling of control, when the reality is that we can measure hundreds of things that are easy to measure and worthless to report. On the other end, we can illude that if we can't measure something (at least easily), it must not be important, leading to a sense of smugness, when what we're not attempting to measure can be necessary for the organization's survival.

Even if we get past the smugness, we can still end up illuding that we can measure the more difficult or nonrational factors in the same way as the easily measured or rational ones. The reality is that all of these success criteria must be measured and managed, but in different ways. Rational factors are measured by numbers and charts and graphs. Nonrational factors are measured by dialogue and intuition and instinct. All important things can be measured—and must be.

Even if we pick the right things to measure, we can measure them from the wrong end or with the wrong perspective. Many measurements are of *inputs* (what we're doing) rather than of *outputs* (the results that our customers want). Illuding organizations usually focus on inputs, methods, and processes rather than on outputs, possibilities, and results.

Perhaps one of the biggest illusions in the quality movement is that we can and should measure quality from a *negative* perspective: number of defects, number of errors, number of customer complaints. But the *essence* of quality is that it is a *positive outcome*. Only massive illusion can cause us to believe that we can measure a positive criterion in a negative way and at the same time inspire a passion for positive outcomes in our organizations.

CAUSES OF THE ILLUSION

How can we kid ourselves about such an important topic as quality? There are a number of reasons, including these:

➡ Laziness—not the kind that won't work, but the kind that won't dig—can lead us to draw major conclusions from small samples and superficial impressions.

➡ Since it can be so difficult and destabilizing to current structure to scrap a service or product and start over, we can be tempted to illude that some tinkering with the current offering will be sufficient.

➡ Because we're saturated with information, we can conclude that the answer to the question is either more information (when we're already drowning) or calling a halt to our information seeking (when we have a lot of data but not what we need).

➡ From grade school on, we're taught that mistakes are bad, that they'll hurt our grades and limit our careers, and that the wisest course is to "protect" ourselves from pain by hiding mistakes or deflecting the blame elsewhere.

➡ If we want to be thought of in a positive way by others, we can try to project an image of ourselves that makes us look better than we really are.

➡ Because people tend to judge even extremely complex issues in simple black-and-white terms, we can illude that success and failure are opposites, instead of two points on a continuum.

➡ We can be fascinated with numbers and statistics, which can lead us to put too much emphasis on them ("*now* we know what our customer wants") or to give scant attention to topics that can't be easily reduced to numbers ("we can't run a business with 'soft' data").

➡ Because it's usually much easier to manage daily activities (inputs) than far-down-the-road results (outputs), we can choose to spend our time on the things we can more directly control.

➡ Since we can easily believe that people would rather avoid pain than seek pleasure, we can focus on the stick (negative measurements and penalties) rather than the carrot (growth and achievement).

Kidding ourselves about quality is a truly fatal illusion. If we think we know what our customers want but we really don't, we're only a step away from the cliff. In fact, the only way to build a quality organization is to have no illusions about quality, to believe that the organization will only grow and improve under the relentless scrutiny of reality.

How to Recognize the Illusion

Rate your organization from 0 (lowest) to 5 (highest) on the following statements:

_____ We give our customers everything they need, at a price they can afford, at a cost that leaves us with a profit.

_____ We don't give our customers anything they don't need.

_____ Our customers would rate us high on our quality (ask them in a one-question survey with a five-point scale and put the average here).

_____ If we asked five employees at random to define quality, they could do it confidently, accurately, and consistently (do it, then give yourself 5 points for five strong definitions, 4 for four, etc.).

_____ Throughout the organization, we understand the marketplace and know how our product or service is being used.

_____ We're close enough to our customers to be able to see and recommend other ways they could use our product or service, and we do so regularly.

_____ We have become an integral part of our primary customers' planning, design, production, quality, or service processes (5 if 85–100 percent, 4 if 65–84 percent, 3 if 50–64 percent, 2 if 25–49 percent, 1 if 10–24 percent, 0 if less than 10 percent).

_____ We have a strong commitment to, and ownership of, quality throughout the organization and from all of our key partners (e.g., customers, suppliers, distributors).

_____ We understand that quality starts with "first things" (e.g., planning and design) rather than with measuring and correcting end points.

_____ We design quality in rather than build or inspect it in.

_____ We understand that the essence of quality is simplicity, and we relentlessly work to simplify processes, products, and services to achieve faster, cheaper, better results for our customers.

_____ We steadfastly refuse to spend our best energies on revamping and retooling rather than on determining how best to deliver our chosen customer value to our selected customers.

_____ Our quality assurance system serves as a catalyst for, rather than as an inspector of, quality.

_____ We expect our suppliers to provide quality products or services to us and don't accept poor quality.

_____ We have systems (e.g., continuous sourcing, certification and recertification, mutual visits, real-time com-

munication, delivery logs) in place to keep supplier
quality at peak levels.

_____ We regularly and consistently train people to know
what good quality is and how to achieve it.

_____ We have developed and implemented a strong, results-
producing approach to problem solving when quality
challenges are uncovered.

_____ We have flexified our organization to allow employees
the freedom to change and make mistakes in a nonpu-
nitive environment.

_____ We baseline and measure quality in a positive way.

_____ We take an annual quality survey (internal and external) and set goals to address any detected shortcom-
ings.

_____ TOTAL

SHREDDING THE ILLUSION

Organizational Viewpoints

Quality is an attitude, not a system.

Every year, organizations that have implemented the principles
of quality experts Deming, Juran, and Crosby, instituted total quality
management, gotten ISO 9000 or other certifications, and won one of
the many quality awards develop very serious problems or go out of
existence altogether. "Executives are sometimes attracted to TQM for
the wrong reasons . . . [and] they often do not know how to support
the effort."[1]

Quality isn't a system; quality is a way of life. We can't tack a
quality program onto an organization that wouldn't recognize quality
if it walked up and introduced itself and hope to get good results.
"Quality is never an accident," said English critic John Ruskin. "It is
always the result of intelligent effort."

Shredding illusions organizationally begins with assuming that
we don't know what our customers want. In fact, it begins even earlier,
with the assumption that our *customers* don't know what they
want—at least not completely. Even if we could sit down and ask them
what they want, we *still* would be only part of the way (to be sure, an
important part of the way) to quality.

At times, we can get a better perspective on our customers' future
needs than they can. This is so for a number of reasons. First, we are
often working with a number of customers who are doing the same

thing (which gives us a broader perspective), while they are reluctant to share ideas with each other. Second, the longer we've worked in a situation and the more familiar we are with the details, the *less* likely we often are to be creative or come up with any breakthroughs (hence Honda's practice of putting interested people from unrelated departments on project teams). Third, since we're an "outsider," we can ask the "dumb" questions, which are not infrequently a gold mine of new ideas.

What we're really saying is that opportunity isn't something that drops from the sky. It comes from aligning our core competencies, skill sets, and latent, untapped potentialities with new, emerging, and even unknown market and customer needs.

We have to avoid the siren song of revamping, which calls us toward the destructive rocks of noncompetitiveness. We can't tack quality onto a bland service or product and expect big successes. "Where expectations of value are rising fast and today's leaders can be left by the wayside tomorrow, bolt-ons not only don't work, they actually make the situation worse. . . . They drug the management team into a world of illusion, a world where they feel that they are solving the problems."[2]

To be effective, we must force ourselves to overcome entropy. We've got to stop measuring things that are easy to measure and that we've been measuring for years if the measurements aren't about core issues. We can do this by asking our people to list the worthless or low-payoff measurements. After we've ferreted out the real time wasters, we can take what's left and ask our employees to prioritize them on the basis of their "usefulness in achieving results." The bottom items on those lists should be chopped off, also.

We've got to learn how to measure the unmeasurable, the things that are so critical but that take real insight to discover and track. This won't come so easy. We'll have to do some serious brainstorming, first to detect what these items are and then to find some reasonable and effective way to measure them (e.g., number of new and useful ideas generated for customers in the last year; number of customer mistakes saved by our intervention; number of existing product or service enhancements created for customers; number of unnecessary customer features or specifications reduced or eliminated through our input; dollar estimates for all of these; regularity of customers' decision to repurchase; reasons why customers go elsewhere; number of customer needs that we meet as well or better than anyone else; number of customers who would rate us "strongly agree" on the question "Do you consider us to be a vital and intimate part of your organization?").

Our organizational illusion shredding needs to include our suppliers. We should expect no less from them than we're willing to give our customers (and, if we're being honest and fair, no more). In today's ferocious market, we put up with poor suppliers at our own peril. Excuses ("they're going through a reorganization"; "at least they're cheap") should lower the suppliers even *further* in our evaluation.

In addition, we need to incorporate the best suppliers we can find into an effective network or supply chain. We need their help in taking the pulse of the market, in design, pricing, and production strategies, in repetitive cost-reduction projects, and in general quality improvement. No organization can stand alone today. The conviction that one can is hubris and a fatal illusion.

Finally, quality at the organizational level includes conscious caring about the enhancement of resources at all levels—human (e.g., safety, nurturing), community (e.g., avoidance of mass layoffs or dislocations), and the world at large (e.g., environment, future generations).

Leadership Attitudes

After top-drawer selection of people and effective matching of these people to positions and assignments (which we discuss in Chapter 11), the most important thing we can do as managers and leaders is to show people what good quality is and how to achieve it.

This means, first, that we've got to adjust the way we look at quality. Quality is a *positive* attribute, yet it is so often discussed and analyzed from a negative perspective. The question is: "Given our customer's needs—including features, service, pricing, and speed—what are the best things we can do to align ourselves with those needs?"

It means, second, that we understand that quality has both a general and a specific component. There are some things we do that allow us to meet some of the needs of most or all of our customers. But, like the sharp job seeker who tailors a general résumé on an organization-by-organization basis, we must do other things specifically, thoroughly, and continually for each and every one of our customers.

Mass customization—economies of scale combined with the flexibility to add or subtract features and related costs—is critical in our approach to quality. Even in mass-market retailing, we need to find a way to make every one of our customers feel as if she's our only customer—at that moment. Mass customization applies to service businesses as well. It's simplistic and illusory to believe that all customers are exactly alike and expect the same level of service. For example, some customers may appreciate the follow-up call to check on their satisfaction level, while others may consider such calls pushy or a nuisance. A world-class system, over time, knows the difference.

Third, the measurements by which we manage have to be both different and fewer. What difference do production efficiencies make if we're building the wrong things or creating excess inventory, with all of its associated costs? What good does it do us to respond quickly to customer calls if our price is perceived as a poor value? We've got to brainstorm to find out what the criteria for success really are, regardless of how "soft" they seem or how difficult they are to measure. The "invisible" criteria are often the most important. We can't risk measuring the size of an iceberg only by what we see.

Fourth, we've got to focus more on outputs than inputs. In the final analysis, who *cares* if people work four, six, eight, or ten hours a day, if they get the job done well? Outputs—results, achieving objectives—need to be the drivers. To focus on quality, we've got to focus on outputs, measure outputs, pay for outputs, reward and recognize for outputs—and leave inputs (means, methods, processes) in the backseat.

People Responses

People thoroughly understand only what they've participated in and helped to form. We understand by putting our hands into a project, getting messy, wrestling with the issues. Full understanding comes from *application,* not from theory. Believing that a quality program written "on high" and handed to the troops will be accepted and followed is pure illusion.

We can't let our people make unacceptable trade-offs with quality: cost versus quality, schedule versus quality, service versus quality. Which of these do we want? The answer is Yes. These trade-offs are illusions offered as marketplace facts. We want *all* of these attributes at the same time. In fact, to improve quality, we're going to have to make services, products, and processes simpler, which inherently reduces cost.

In addition to involving everyone in developing and implementing a quality *environment* (not "program"), we've got to get the right kind and level of information to the people who make decisions on a daily basis. This means that we've got to make sure they've got all critical inputs and—because it's so hard to wade through mounds of data—*no* uncritical inputs. And we've got to pay a lot of attention to the amount of data they get even on critical items, and the frequency with which they get it.

And, remembering that quality is a positive attribute, we need to talk about it, measure it, and report it in positive terms. Agents being taught to detect counterfeit money aren't shown counterfeit money

(the negative) during their training, but rather spend their time studying the real thing (the positive). They spend so much time on the positive that the negative stands out instantly. Let's measure successes
rather than failures, hits rather than misses, undamaged goods rather
than damaged, satisfactory production rather than scrap, victories
rather than defeats.

It's the difference between being encouraged to score a touch-
down and being told not to fumble. Do we want our people focusing
on touchdowns or fumbles? What we focus on is usually what we get.
So what will we get with fumble thinking?

Yup.

Learning and Asking

Vast amounts of organizational energies are spent on a horribly erroneous view of mistakes.

If we believe that mistakes are bad, we'll set up monitoring systems to make sure they don't occur (they will, anyway). We'll spend a
big piece of our time tracking down mistakes and spreading the blame
around. We'll constantly reinforce the idea that mistakes could be fatal
to a worker's career. Fear will reign supreme.

Our people won't miss this philosophy. They'll cooperate with the
monitoring system as much as possible, and co-opt it where they must.
They'll respond to our tracking by covering up their tracks, leaving
false clues, and pointing us in other directions. They'll learn to sell out
their associates when the blame is being delegated. I've seen organizations where half or more of people's best creativity was spent on self-
protective activity.

But the idea that mistakes are bad is a fatal illusion. Mistakes, in
an imperfect world, are normal. Mistakes can be frustrating. Mistakes
can even be fatal. But mistakes are not bad.

In fact, mistakes, properly viewed, are a mislabeled opportunity.

The Chinese symbol for "crisis" is made up of two symbols, one
of which stands for "danger." But the other one stands for "opportunity." In every crisis—in every mistake—the danger is often obvious,
at least in great part. But the danger can create an illusion: that there
is no opportunity.

What we're saying is that danger and opportunity aren't opposites—they're two sides of the same coin. Danger, rightly handled, can
create great opportunity. Failure, properly dealt with, can lead to fabu-
lous growth and success. "Success and failure are not polar opposites
. . . one can lead to the other with great ease. Neither is likely to be
permanent; the irony is that we believe both will last forever."[3]

The airline in the story at the beginning of this chapter had an opportunity to learn from Michael's three lost books. A commitment to excellence would have led the consumer affairs executive to answer his phone. Someone *inside* the airline could have called around and tried to find the books, experience the netherworld, and fix every non-customer-oriented attitude and glitch along the way. Opportunity or nuisance? Yes. Nuisance is just opportunity wrapped in a soggy news-paper.

We need to perform calm "postmortems" on mistakes. Why did this happen? What illusions were affecting the outcome? How can we avoid this mistake in the future? How can we profit from it? We can even have a eulogy over the "death"—a true eulogy, where we tell people we're sorry for their loss rather than accuse them of murder. Making an unintentional but serious mistake is a personal tragedy, not a crime against the organization.

With people collectively, we can discuss mistakes in a nonthreat-ening way. We can change the way we talk about mistakes to empha-size that we accept their normalcy and will spend *no* time blaming anyone. I call a mistake a phoenix—the mythical bird that rose anew from its own ashes. "We've got a phoenix here. We all see the ashes. Where's the bird?" If we could really see what mistakes could do for us, we'd welcome them with open arms.

With individuals, we can bring mistakes to the surface and make it normal to discuss them. We can have a section on our performance review that asks people to list the five biggest mistakes they've made in the last year, what they've learned from them, and how they've turned them into successes or profits. Let people know that not making mistakes is the biggest mistake of all, because it means they're playing it safe and hiding behind the status quo.

We have to drive self-protective thinking out of our organizations. Defensive attitudes, files kept for protection, the search for someone to blame—all of these things have to be squelched. Beyond that, we have to give glitches the most positive of spins. We can't just accept mis-takes. We've got to celebrate them.

Finally, we've got to go beyond dissecting collective and individ-ual mistakes and take the quality pulse of the entire organization at least once a year. We need to conduct an in-depth, organization-wide (internal) and customer-wide (external) survey to uncover the en-trenched systemic and relational flaws. The surveys need to be up-front, blunt, detailed, and probably anonymous. Once the results are compiled, we need to develop specific plans and objectives to address the problems highlighted. We can form teams to deal with the short-comings and set time frames for resolution.

• • • • •

Quality, in the long run, is the only thing that survives. It doesn't come with slogans, posters, programs, or measurements of statistical deviation. It doesn't come with fear or negative numbers. And it doesn't come easily or cheaply. Quality comes with total involvement, positive pursuit, opportunistic attitudes.

And a lot of sweat.

NOTES

1. Mark Graham Brown, Darcy E. Hitchcock, and Marsha L. Willard, *Why TQM Fails and What to Do About It* (Burr Ridge, Ill.: Irwin), p. 2.
2. Michael Treacy and Fred Wiersema, *The Discipline of Market Leaders* (Reading, Mass.: Addison-Wesley, 1995), p. 12.
3. Carol Hyatt and Linda Gottlieb, *When Smart People Fail* (New York: Simon & Schuster, 1987), p. 37.

7

Expectations: "We Don't Know *What* to Expect of Those People"

You cannot seek for the ideal outside the realm of reality.

—Leon Blum, *New Conversations*

Roberta was given an assignment somewhere between "Mission Impossible" and "The Impossible Dream."

She had been brought in to turn around a sagging manufacturing operation. In the first forty weeks of the fiscal year, the division had shipped $1.8 million of its $4 million plan. "Do the best you can," she was told. "Do whatever it takes, including firing everybody if necessary. We think everyone out there may be dead from the neck up."

The division was running about 10 percent on time. Due to sloppy order filling, about half of what was shipped required back orders. Quality was miserable. Morale was even worse. The targets with bulls' eyes drawn around the "fragile" stickers said it all.

There were no formal planning systems or written bills-of-material. Roberta wasn't able to offer any raises or bonuses until after the end of the fiscal year. She requested that a full-time quality assurance manager be hired, but again was put off until after the end of the year. "They told me to do whatever it took to turn things around," she told her husband with frustration, "and I think I can spend anything up to $500 to do it."

Roberta decided not to fire anybody. She met with her supervisors and laid out a recovery plan that produced shaking heads and near-laughter. But she was serious, which they soon found out. She then met with the workforce of seventy-five disgruntled and very unhappy campers.

"I know you think this place is a joke," she began, resorting to the sel-

*dom-used management tools of honesty and empathy. "I do, too. I know you
don't think your voice is heard or that you're making enough money. I agree.
But no more. I don't want to work for a bad joke, and I don't think you do
either. If you work with me, we'll make this place something to feel good about.
If we do well, we can avoid layoffs. And though I can't promise you how much
or how fast, if you work together to hit our budgets and production goals, I'll
fight tooth and nail for more money."*

*Then she hit them with the clincher: "To tell you the truth, I don't think
anyone in this organization thinks you can do it. But I'm new. I think you
can do it. Maybe I'm not smart enough to know that you can't. Maybe I think
you're better than you really are. But I think you can prove everybody wrong.
I think you can make them eat their words. In my gut, I think you can still
hit your budget for the year."*

Roberta turned and walked out.

*The division shipped $2.3 million in the last twelve weeks and beat its
plan for the year. At the same time, quality went way up (even without a
quality assurance manager), on-time performance went to 98.1 percent, and
back orders dropped to less than 3 percent.*

The difference?

Expectations.

THE EXPECTATION ILLUSION

On the one hand, we can want more out of the people around us than
they ever seem willing or able to give. On the other hand, we can end
up with a low view of what people are really capable of achieving. We
can expect too much, bringing discouragement, or we can expect too
little, bringing poor performance.

When we expect more than what people are able to do, we illude
that they will pull it off—*somehow.* We substitute wishful thinking for
realistic goals that stretch people.

Cliff had allowed Rachel, a valued employee who had served as
his personnel manager, to go to half-time after the birth of her child,
although he reduced her responsibilities by only a small amount. Rachel worked quite a bit at home (without pay) to keep up with her
duties, but she was still very happy about the arrangement and her
work. Everyone else was pleased with her performance as well.

Then Cliff decided that he could get a little more out of her; he
assumed that some additional accounting-related responsibilities
would be no problem for Rachel, even in a half-time position. Cliff was
illuding about how much work she was already doing, in part because
Rachel didn't talk about what she was doing at home, in part because

he had never familiarized himself with what it took to do her job. Rachel eventually quit in frustration. Cliff lost a long-term, knowledgeable, dedicated employee because of his unreasonable expectations. He had to hire and train a full-time person to replace Rachel. The new person never achieved what Rachel had accomplished half-time.

This side of the expectation illusion brings great frustration to the organization. When people can never hit their goals, no matter how hard or cleverly they try, they give up. Or, if the unreachable goals are in only certain areas, they may sacrifice other areas to try to hit the expected targets. An unreasonable sales goal, for example, might lead to unnecessary discounts, schedule pressure that leads to shoddy work, or excessive production overtime, all of which can flatten or destroy profit. "When we pursue the unattainable we make impossible the realizable," said Robert Ardrey in his 1970 book *The Social Contract.*

When we expect people to accomplish too little—often the more common illusion—we believe that people aren't interested in, or capable of, high levels of performance. We suspect that most people just want to put in their time and go home. But most people want more. Some don't, because they've been trained to believe that they don't matter, but most people can be persuaded to increase their goals. The few that never rise to the occasion will have to carry their illusion—that they can just get by—to another organization that isn't interested in high performance.

The problem with low expectations is that we tend to get what we expect. If what we expect is little and small, the response we get will be little and small as well. Having low expectations is no favor to our people. We can think we're just "taking it easy" on them, just being "reasonable," but what we're really doing is killing their minds and hearts. Small expectations have no power to move people, to make them care, to help them feel good about who they are and what they're doing with a huge percentage of their time and energy.

If we expect people to be machines, taking orders and performing daily routines (horrible word), they will be. If we expect them to be dynamic, intelligent, creative, flexible organisms, they will be. The few who want to be machines can do it—elsewhere. High-expectation managers know that these few can cripple a high-performance organization.

Don't expect too much. But expect a lot.

CAUSES OF THE ILLUSION

How, when we resent pressures to do more than we are able and willing to do, can we apply those same pressures to others? And how, in a world that demands so much of us, can we end up expecting so little of those around us? Here are some possibilities:

➡ Because we're all expected to do more with less (and faster), we can believe, in an effort at self-preservation, that the only way to get it all done is to squeeze more out of everyone else.

➡ Since we're usually not the ones initiating the pressure (someone else is driving us), we can justify our demands as "just trying to get the job done" or "just following orders" (or the really pathetic "what can I do?").

➡ If we were raised or trained in a performance-based manner (i.e., "you have value if you perform"), we can subconsciously adopt a performance-based, what-have-you-done-for-me-lately approach to others.

➡ If we forget that we're dealing with people rather than with "human resources" or even "personnel," we can operate as if we have machines that can be "upgraded" rather than living beings with minds, desires, and resistance points of their own.

➡ Because we've been let down by so many people in our personal lives and careers, we can—understandably but fatally—adopt a pessimistic or cynical attitude about people in general.

➡ If we don't want to face the possibility that we or the system are the problem, we can illude that the problem is "out there," find fault with our "unmotivated" people, and avoid our responsibility to lead.

➡ If we don't take the time to find out what we can expect from individual people and teams, to learn who they are and what they are capable of achieving, we can imagine capacities that exist only in our own heads or completely bypass capacities that lie dormant and untapped.

➡ When we have hidden agendas or privately held but unarticulated expectations ("If you don't know what I want, I'm certainly not going to tell you"), leading to constant rework on the one hand and mixed signals on the other, we can conclude that people just aren't smart enough to get it (or give up and conclude that people will simply never catch our vision).

➡ If our mental models of what we can expect are incorrect because we haven't read enough, studied enough, or talked enough with high-expectation managers, we can remain stuck in a stagnant status quo.

➡ When we're not willing to spend the energy, time, and resources on the kind of training and development that will help people to exceed their past levels of performance, we can inadvertently assign them to a career and organizational sinkhole.

➡ If we're uncomfortable exceeding the low expectations of our subordinates, thereby upsetting them or causing conflict, we can resign ourselves and our organization to a "most comfortable" (read: "least successful") level of performance.

HOW TO RECOGNIZE THE ILLUSION

Rate your organization from 0 (lowest) to 5 (highest) on the following statements:

_____ We make the selection, agreement, and clarification of expectations a high priority for managers as they relate to their people and for everyone as they relate to their own goals.

_____ We provide training for all of our managers in how to set and agree on stretching but doable expectations.

_____ We actively pursue learning about efforts and projects where people feel an imminent sense of helplessness and disaster.

_____ We consistently and without damaging people's careers or sense of self-worth remove people from assignments that they have little chance of completing successfully through no fault of their own.

_____ We monitor the stress levels of our people and make adjustments when either overall or individual pressure passes from a healthy to a crippling level.

_____ We have people who can alert each person in our organization when that person's own stress is reaching levels that are causing them to bear down too hard on others.

_____ We understand that performance has its ebbs and flows, and accept the small breaks (e.g., eating lunch, taking walks, reading magazines, staring out the window) that people need in order to regroup and recharge.

_____ When giving out major assignments, we give people the time to (and insist that they) evaluate, ask questions, and express fears before they take the assignment or (by mutual agreement) pass.

_____ *Loyalty* is defined as vigorous dissent and stretching the system rather than buying into plans without question and avoiding disagreement or conflict.

_____ We spend at least 6 to 10 percent of our payroll costs (1 if 6 percent, 2 if 7 percent, etc.—including people's pay while being trained) on training that builds both knowledge and confidence.

_____ At least half of our training budget is for things our people are not currently doing (5 if 50 percent or more, 4 if 40–49 percent, 3 if 30–39 percent, 2 if 20–29 percent, 1 if 10–19 percent, 0 if less than 10 percent).

_____ We provide opportunity for our people to advise their supervisors of the expectations they have for *them*.

_____ Performance reviews are used to establish high expectations for the coming one to three years (5 if five or more "stretch" goals are typically set, 4 if four, etc.).

_____ We regularly challenge people to tell us honestly where they think our expectations are too high or too low.

_____ We recognize and reward people who are constantly suggesting ways to achieve at higher levels in the future.

_____ We expect all of our employees to treat everyone else with respect at all times.

_____ We expect people to accept substantial responsibility for their success, failure, decisions, or indecision.

_____ We reward people for taking legitimate risks, whether the result is positive or negative.

_____ We expect people to admit all mistakes, share all bad news, and offer ways to profit from these problems.

_____ We evaluate our supervisors on the setting of appropriate levels of expectations for their areas and people.

_____ TOTAL

SHREDDING THE ILLUSION

When we take responsibility for setting high but achievable expectations, we've taken the first step toward shattering the expectation illusion.

Organizational Viewpoints

The first thing we have to do is find out what our organization is capable of achieving, given the proper environment. This is not a small or inexpensive thing to accomplish. One of the hardest things for leaders to do is to learn the true nature of both the incredibly multifaceted beings who work for us and the organic complexity that exists in even very small organizations.

Our expectations have to be high enough to stretch but low enough not to stress. Goals that don't require people to move in new directions, try new approaches, and feel a little uncomfortable aren't worthy of the name *goal*. If at least some people aren't a little uncertain about the doability of the goals, the goals probably aren't high enough.

One of the best tests of a nonilluding organization is its willingness to live with and even embrace the uncomfortable. Too much emphasis can be put on getting along and having a peaceful environment. The only place on earth where there are no arguments and where peacefulness reigns supreme is a cemetery.

At the same time, if goals are too high, the organization can crack under the pressure. One of the most destructive causes of tension is the collision of targets and reality, when the gap between expectations and the possibility of achieving them is wide and unclosable. Morale will surely suffer, but so will creativity, accuracy, and the ability to focus on the important priorities. All of these things and more shrivel under the heat of unachievable expectations.

Just as deadly are goals that are too low. It's a more subtle reality that boredom can produce just as much stress as unachievable objectives. When daily efforts become too easy for too long, something valuable dies in an organization.

The environment in an organization that has set expectations without illusions is fast-paced, high-energy, and moderately chaotic without yielding to fire fighting, frenzy, and crippling stress.

We learn how to achieve this organizational "calm fury" only through some testing, analysis, and lots of dialogue.

Leadership Attitudes

We as managers have to empower people by helping them to see and set high but achievable goals for themselves. Empowerment begins with *establishing* the expectations, not just achieving them.

Empowerment encompasses giving people the training, education, and mentoring that allow them to achieve goals in a way and at a rate that satisfies both us and them. To say people are empowered when they have little or no confidence in what they're doing is meaningless.

We also need to give the people the resources, including information, to allow them to achieve what we agree is both worthwhile and achievable.

For too many people given huge goals, little training, and inadequate resources, empowerment is an illusion. It sounds lofty, but in reality it means "more work," "you're a dumping ground," and "management doesn't know what it's doing, so you'll have to figure it out for yourself."

At the same time, we have to give up the illusion that we're responsible for people's actions. We've got to tell our people that we are *not* responsible for their success or failure—they are. To make this work, we must hire only the very best people we can find (with *best* defined as "willing to take personal responsibility for setting and achieving high goals and to grow beyond current skill sets").

We have to give up the "easy" solution of hierarchical micromanagement, where everyone eyes everyone else up and down the ladder. We also have to give up the ideas that knowledge can come quickly or easily, problems have easy solutions, and people don't need much training to be able to do well. Expectations aren't met in a vacuum. People need the support, resources, information, and practice to prevent *all* expectations from becoming unachievable.

Finally, we as leaders need to avoid being captured by the expectations of our followers. This is especially true if their expectations aren't about things that we can do or in line with corporate goals. "Followers easily project their fantasies onto their leaders, interpret everything leaders do in light of their self-created image of them, and fatally seduce leaders into believing that they are in fact the illusory creatures the followers have made them."[1] This means in part that we've got to be willing to let our people know what we don't know, hear about our mistakes, and see our warts.

People who work for us can expect us as leaders to do and be more than we are able to do or should be doing, or they can expect us to expect little of them. In either case, we've got to work hard to avoid trying to live up to their too-high or down to their too-low expectations.

People Responses

Together with our employees, we need to set some "stretch" goals and then go to work on them. People don't achieve great things by *talking* about them; they achieve great things by *doing* them, even if they're unsure, even if they make some false starts, even if they're scared to death.

Using performance reviews as a time to develop high expectations can put an otherwise tense and boring meeting to good use. We can use 25 percent of the review to cover the past and the other 75 percent to discuss expectations about the coming quarter or year. Having the employee think about expectations in advance will make the review much more profitable. "Goal setting has traditionally been based on past performance," Juran reminded us. "This practice has tended to perpetuate the sins of the past."

All of our expectations need to be related to results and outcomes rather than to effort or methods. It's too easy for people to expect to get paid or rewarded for how hard they work (whether or not they've achieved their goals) or for their longevity with the organization. We need to advance people—with pay, bonuses, promotions, comp time (give them the afternoon off if they achieve an outstanding goal in the morning)—on the basis of what they contribute.

We must insist that people be responsible for their own attitudes and responses, their own careers, their own lives. The highest form of empowerment in training involves two steps: first, to reach agreement with the employee about her developmental needs in a given time frame, and second, to allow her to design her own training program to meet those needs by selecting from a broad range of available resources and programs.

This can be very challenging for people who are or who have become comfortable *not* being empowered. Some people don't want to take or have responsibility, and they're uncomfortable with expectations in any form. They resist taking responsibility, leadership, or risk. They'd rather be told what to do. We have to find ways to overcome this resistance and move these people along. It's impossible to try to compete and achieve in today's world with people who have no expectations.

Learning and Asking

It is illusion to conclude either that people won't share with us how we can set and achieve higher expectations or that they don't have anything to share.

People will share if we can learn what's causing them to hold back—for that's surely what people do. They see a problem and discern some effective solutions, but they say nothing. They sense some new opportunity in the market or with a customer, and they remain silent about it. There is tremendous wisdom in an array of counselors and consultants, and *we have them working for us.* The future is out there, in our organization, waiting to be tapped—but we have to tap it. We have to ask.

If they won't share because they think they won't be listened to, we've got to create mechanisms for listening and convince people we mean it. These mechanisms can be anonymous surveys, off-the-record

critical discussions (one on one or in groups, with or without management present), or requested written responses that address a specific
challenge or possibility. We'll convince people that we're listening if
we respond in some way to *every* idea presented. Asking for input but
not guaranteeing follow-up is probably even less effective than sending out a mailer and taking no further action. At times it's tedious to
respond, but we've got to do it.

If people won't share because they think we have a faulty reward
system, we've got to fix or expand the program. One of the most com-
monly used and disastrous "rewards" is giving the person who makes
the suggestion the "opportunity" to implement it. We're illuding at
subterranean levels if we think people will continue to enlighten us if
their only reward is more work. If someone is the best person to do the
job and *wants* to do it, we'll have to make sure that person has the
resources and the time to do it, and we may have to lighten the rest of
her load. Few people will deliberately bury themselves on an ongoing
basis. Often, people want to be given the credit—but not the added
assignment.

The reward structure for new ideas has to be two-tier: one reward
for the ideas themselves and one for their successful implementation.
If we don't or can't apply a good suggestion, the person who made it
shouldn't be penalized—at least not if we want the flow of ideas to
continue. Who is greater—the one who invents something or the one
who figures out how to commercialize it? The answer is yes.

If employees won't share because they don't have enough confidence or background, we've got to give them the training and information they need to cross the threshold. Everyone has something to share,
but people have to believe that it's worthwhile to articulate their ideas
and that they won't be ridiculed for doing so. It's our job to give them
data or education so that the "something" they have to share has sufficient depth and perspective to make the idea more valuable and to
make them more willing to broadcast it. We've got to get our people
in "flow," where they have enough grid, new input, and time to piece
together previously unrelated ideas producing useful enhancements.
And it's our job to encourage their confidence by respectfully listening
to all suggestions for improvement, and insisting that others do the
same.

We can learn a massive amount about where to advance from our
own people. We've just got to ask the right way.

NOTE

1. Manfred F. R. Kets De Vries, *Leaders, Fools, and Imposters* (San Francisco:
Jossey-Bass, 1993), p. 13.

8

Change: "We'll Get to That Later"

The art of progress is to preserve order amid change and to preserve change amid order.

—Alfred North Whitehead

Karen knew it wasn't working.

She had just taken over as general manager of a small, high-tech firm in the medical products industry. The technology was leading edge, and the capability of the organization was good, but lack of leadership had produced staff wars and financial disaster. The company was choking itself to death.

Karen had seen immediately that the production manager, a brilliant but arrogant engineer, was a focal point of controversy and turmoil. She had let him and several others go. But underperforming managers in two key areas—marketing/sales and procurement—were long-term employees with ties to the owner. With great misgivings, Karen decided that the organization had had enough change and kept these two people on.

Karen was wrong.

At first, her energy, vision, and skill brought the company back from the grave and allowed it to turn its first profit in more than three years. But in the long term, her abilities couldn't counteract the ineptitude of the two managers. Over a two-year period, the company missed several excellent market opportunities, lost one major customer, didn't exploit several new customers, and developed no successful strategic alliances with key suppliers. With a shrinking future for the company, Karen ended up presiding over its sale to a large company, which cannibalized her operation and let her go.

Karen was concerned about the effects of change. She worried that there had already been too much change. She didn't want to affect the "stability" of the organization.

But the company hadn't had "too much" change.
It hadn't had enough.

THE CHANGE ILLUSION

"Yesterday I was a dog. Today I am a dog. Tomorrow I'll probably still be a dog," said Snoopy. While Snoopy can get away with this complacent attitude, for people it spells organizational death. In order to reach our expectations, we have to be willing to change.

Karen failed to revitalize the company because of illusions about change—that change is "bad," that people can't deal with change, that change brings problems, and (worst of all) that she could run a company without embracing change. She avoided making the necessary changes internally, which not only crippled her organization but also left it unprepared to deal with, react to, and get ahead of the changes that were occurring with incredible velocity in the external environment.

One aspect of the change illusion is that change is "bad." But change isn't "good" or "bad"—change is *reality*. The only thing constant in this world is change. By the time we get to where we're going, where we're going may not be there anymore. All change is "bad" if we ignore it and are crushed by it. And all change can be "good" if we're ready to prepare for it and exploit it.

Sometimes these changes can come in rapid-fire succession and seem incredibly negative. David Lloyd George, prime minister of Britain from 1916 to 1922, was once asked, in the middle of dealing with World War I, the Irish Liberation Movement, and severe economic challenges, how he maintained such a positive attitude. His response? "Well, I find that a change of nuisances is as good as a vacation." Humor can help us stay on our feet. Resistance to change is an invitation to be run over.

Another aspect of the change illusion is that change—internal or external—will slow down or stop. "If only things would settle down for a bit, then. . . . " In this post–Industrial Revolution age, things may never settle down again. The only "settling" that we're likely to see in the future is the dust settling on top of corporate coffins. The tombstone will read HERE LIES RESISTANCE TO CHANGE.

Another illusion is that we can "manage" change. If the totalitarian monolith of the Soviet Union's Communist party—with complete control of the government, military, and economy—couldn't control the change that swept it out of existence, neither can we. Can we look for change and try to figure out what to do with it? Yes. Can we initiate it when we see an opportunity? Of course. But manage it? No way.

We can fool ourselves by making a lot of small changes or completing a percentage of a big change. We can painstakingly revise the procedure manual, when the manual itself needs to go. We can tell ourselves, "We're half done implementing this change; we've accomplished a lot," when the whole change needed to be completed last month. William Gladstone, the legendary prime minister of Great Britain, reminded us that "nothing is so fatal to character as half finished tasks."

We can illude that we can "hold off" change. But resistance to change is pointless. It will come. We can stay in our little cottage by the sea, illuding that the hurricane won't destroy us—but when the monster waves come, they'll sweep us away without even noticing that we were there or leaving a mark to remember us by. Resistance to oppression is stirring. Resistance to change is futile.

Perhaps one of the biggest illusions about change is that we can anticipate it. Occasionally we can clearly see a change coming and ready ourselves for it, and perhaps a few times in a lifetime we can even be the *cause* of the change. But that isn't the norm. Most changes are seen only dimly, as a vague outline in the distant mist, or felt as an uneasy sense of pending upheaval or warning that causes us to shiver and look around.

We *can* position ourselves to respond to most changes—if we're really good, to react fast when the first tiny cracks appear—but nobody really knows what's going to happen in five years or what the world of five years into the future will look like. There are just too many variables—innovations, customer demands and tastes, political and social upheavals, economic surges and dislocations. It's reasonable to read about and try to get a feel for the future. It's reasonable to be as prepared as we can be. But it's illusion to believe we can know it. No one on this planet knows what it will be.

CAUSES OF THE ILLUSION

How can we illude about something—change—that is such an obvious and dominating aspect of life? Here are some reasons:

➡ Because knowledge can seem so real, we can substitute learning about change for actually absorbing or implementing it.

➡ Since change is scary and brings so much stress (sometimes massive pressure)—whether we're told the person we've been dealing with is "no longer here," our key customer no longer needs our product, or our favorite restaurant has closed down—we can try to function by avoiding the feelings the change engenders and illude that it's not a problem.

➡ The rate of change is so great that we can feel that facing it and dealing with it are more than we can do, want to do, or can even adjust to.

➡ Since the familiar is comfortable, and since as human beings we have some need for the stable and secure, we can cling to things long after their usefulness has passed.

➡ Even with all the writing and talk about risk taking, many of us have been trained to be risk averse, and since all change looks like risk, it can look like a career-enhancing move to avoid or try to minimize it.

➡ When a situation has gone on for a long time, we can falsely believe that it can't be changed or improved, when the reality is that *everything* can be improved by thoughtful and focused action.

➡ Since, psychologically, the longer we've invested in a certain course of action, the harder it can be to stop (and lose our investment), we can continue to plow ahead long after wisdom (or even horse sense) has told us to stop.

➡ When many of the people who work around us and for us don't like change, resist it, and grumble about it (even while they want us as their leader to like it, plan for it, and articulate it), we can tire of the double fight (overcoming resistance and fully preparing ourselves).

➡ When people have at times seen change used as an excuse to do them harm (e.g., they've been given the reason—the illusion—that "we have to lay off because of the changing market" when the reality is that the downsizing is needed because of lousy management decisions), they're naturally going to be skeptical about change-directed decisions.

HOW TO RECOGNIZE THE ILLUSION

Rate your organization from 0 (lowest) to 5 (highest) on the following statements:

_____ We are willing, even eager, to abandon the past rather than defend its value or pretend it was better than it was.

_____ We pay great attention to, and are very sensitive about, the timing of major changes in direction.

_____ We expend great energy preparing people for change, beginning long before the change is apparent to the majority of them.

_____ We in management are willing to change our leadership style and methods continuously to meet needs (not fads).

_____ Announcements about marketplace or directional changes are made in positive, opportunistic terms.

_____ We refuse to allow past successes to entrench us in directions, goals, or processes that can strangle us in the future.

_____ We're prepared to change our organizational culture, style, goals, and directions as often as necessary to meet changing conditions.

_____ We are willing to change structures, systems, procedures, and resources to support needed changes.

_____ We prove we're open to change by rewarding rather than punishing "rock the boat" behavior, actions, and challenges to existing ways of doing business.

_____ We advise all new employees, as well as regularly alert the rest of our staff, that change is the norm and that embracing it will be the key component in their success.

_____ We deliberately find ways to stir up discontent with the way we're doing things today.

_____ We spend substantial time exploring, exposing, modifying, and discarding our mental models.

_____ We regularly give our employees the opportunity to participate in the initiation and direction of internal change and in the preparation of our response to external change.

_____ We develop specific plans to deal with the fears about the future and about their security that grip people during times of upheaval.

_____ We are committed to the re-education and introduction of new skill sets that are required to absorb major changes and successfully exploit them.

_____ We continually have individuals and teams looking at the "scare-me-to-death" market and technology changes coming over the horizon.

_____ We are active in implementing changes without having to have all of the facts.

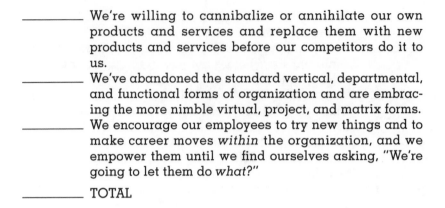

_____ We're willing to cannibalize or annihilate our own products and services and replace them with new products and services before our competitors do it to us.

_____ We've abandoned the standard vertical, departmental, and functional forms of organization and are embracing the more nimble virtual, project, and matrix forms.

_____ We encourage our employees to try new things and to make career moves *within* the organization, and we empower them until we find ourselves asking, "We're going to let them do *what?*"

_____ TOTAL

Shredding the Illusion

Organizational Viewpoints

The most critical step is to develop an organization-wide positive orientation to change—whether it's coming from outside and seems either positive or negative or whether it's coming from inside and seems either positive or negative. *All* external change—no matter how terrifying—represents some opportunity, and *all* internal change—no matter how stumbling—represents a chance to survive and grow.

External change can bring pressure to bear on our organization. Whether it's acknowledged or not is another matter (at least until the change overwhelms the organization). In the best (and most likely-to-survive) organizations, a culture of change exists, meaning that ways are found to immerse people in the coming change rather than let them insulate themselves from it. The pressure of external change is converted into the pressure of internal change. Few major changes in life are made without the appropriate application of pressure.

This is why effective organizations are able to look at crises not as the end of the old world but as the beginning of a new one. Crises often force a desperately needed change in an organization that is in the process of illuding itself out of existence. Crises can do what obvious, rational arguments can't.

A critical step toward developing a positive orientation toward change is developing a willingness throughout the organization to modify or abandon the past—even the most successful parts—rather than continue it because "we've always done it that way" or "we've done it that way and it works." In our opening example, Karen needed to terminate the two organization-disabling managers and restructure their functions. It would have been hard; the past argued against it.

But the past needs no defense; it is what it is. And it needs no pretense; it isn't what it wasn't. Learn from it—and lose it. "Never let yesterday use up too much of today," said designer Kobi Yamada.

We have to accept the fact that there is no permanence. In fact, the illusion of permanence is deadly. It causes us to rely on our market position, size, competitive advantages, or core competencies for future success, when those might be the very things that slow us down and blind us to needed change. We need to banish talk of "stable markets," "ongoing demand," and "permanent workforce."

We especially must make sure our mental models—our pictures of what life, markets, customers, and our own organization are like—are open to change. We can always get a picture of reality that's closer to the mark than the one we have today. Make the frank exposure and dissection of mental models a key agenda item at *every* management meeting. Don't skip any—erroneous ways of thinking and perceiving can sprout and grow to deadly size in an incredibly short time. Changing mental models or grids is the hardest and most time-consuming thing we can do. And today it's the most critical.

If Karen had reviewed the corporate mental models with her other managers and other advisers, she might have been able to see that the right amount of change is the amount that gets the job done. She could have embraced change and fixed the two dying departments.

Our organizational structures need to be flexified to enable us to respond immediately to change. Years ago, Hallmark Cards took two years to get a new greeting card to market. Although the company went through reengineering, it still takes a year to get a card into the stores.[1] It took less time than that for the Allies in World War II to move from the invasion at Normandy to winning the surrender of Germany.

In photography, exposure (which determines how light or dark the film turns out) equals intensity (of light) times the length of time the shutter is open. Our exposure in the marketplace is equal to the intensity of change times the length of time the shutter (the window of opportunity to exploit the change) is open. The intensity today is blinding. And the shutter isn't open very long.

We have to look for more than just the continuous improvement that we get from a long series of small changes that we can (and must) make to existing products, services, and processes. We must ready ourselves for the discontinuous change, the geometric or even exponential increases in the kind or degree of change, the blow-away shift that creates the opportunity for huge competitive advantage. The dialogue needs to look something like this:

"Wow! Can you believe that?!"

"No [*pause*]. Yes. How do we take advantage of it?"

The length of the pause?
About ten seconds.

Leadership Attitudes

We can't force change on an organization when we ourselves aren't willing to change. We have to be willing to change ourselves—what we believe, how we think about opportunities and problems, how we manage. And we have to be willing to flexify our organization, to change anything that blocks improvement and add anything that expands our capabilities and opportunities.

A great deal of effort should be expended preparing people for change, whether it's positive or negative. Change will always be traumatic, but the goals of an accomplished manager are to turn the stress of change into a positive energy, the confusion of the change into an opportunity to learn, and the insecurity of the change into a challenge to grow. It's giving ample and repeated information, assurance, and time to allow the change to "fit."

In times of crises or turnaround, we need to be extremely careful that we initiate the right amount of change. Too much too fast can destabilize the organization and send it into a tailspin. We can easily make cuts in staff that are too deep, kill morale, and prevent the organization from serving its customers. Businesses that slash their staffs to cut costs can end up hiring back people as employees or consultants, training whole new staffs, limping along, and being fit only for acquisition, merger, or cannibalization.

Too little change, on the other hand, can—as Karen found out—leave an organization improperly staffed, unable to get the job done, and status-quoing its way to the graveyard. We must make a significant adjustment to our course.

We need to really prepare people for change and not illude that they'll get onboard by themselves. The more preparation, the more likely that change will be accepted, even embraced. Timing is also important (and is seldom given its due importance) when announcing or initiating change. The tone in which the change is announced is an unbelievably important factor. Some managers could describe heaven and make it sound like hell.

Finally, we have to give up the illusion that we can keep managing the same way we did in years past.

Who cares if we're good at it, if it doesn't work?

People Responses

There are a number of things we can do to help our employees adjust to change. First, we can talk about change—a *lot*. They need to hear us talk about it in a natural, nonscary, "we-can-handle-it" kind of way. If we can recast the changes, especially the potentially terrifying ones, as part of our vision for the future, so much the better. People generally hate change, but they generally like dreams. We want them to respond to change with creativity and zeal, not fear and insecurity.

We can let our people know that 50 to 75 percent of what they know today won't be needed or cared about in two to five years. They're going to have to fill that gap with aggressive learning—at work, at home, on the beach, everywhere. They can't wait for us—they've got to be proactive. We shouldn't have people working for us who aren't. We can underscore this orientation by making *learning, response to change,* and *initiation of change* three *very* important criteria on performance appraisals.

We can't let ourselves illude that change can come without stress. When people's tolerance for anxiety is being pressed or exceeded, it can lead to desires to escape, to yield to spontaneous impulses, and to regress to unexpected and destructive (even primitive) behavior. We have to monitor and control the level of organizational stress.

One way to do this is to involve employees in the change process and let them help mold the direction of an internal change or the response to an external change. Another way is to rotate employees onto a "change response" team. In an age of teams, few if any are as important as an ongoing, multiviewpoint team in fostering innovation, responding effectively to change, and challenging the illusion of permanence. This team should meet weekly and be encouraged to challenge corporate illusions about the future and report its thoughts to the rest of the organization, preferably in open forums where questions can be answered, stress can be lowered, and the team can have *its* illusions challenged.

For centuries, except for a few periods of rapid transition, the lifetimes of most people were shorter than the time it took for sweeping changes to begin and become established. Not so anymore. Massive changes in the culture, government, and economy can occur many times in a human life span. The pace can leave us gasping for air.

In an era when so much of what people learned in school or on the job is now obsolete, and when their current useful knowledge can be obliterated almost overnight, people can at core be disoriented and terrified. "People today," says the futurist Alvin Toffler, "are scared silly."[2]

We have to find ways to help people respond to their fears by growing and running into the future. And we have to show them that we believe in them. "Enlightened leaders know . . . that people must feel okay with themselves *as they are* before they will be strong enough to look inside themselves for the possibility of change."[3]

We need a substantial group of mavericks who are willing to rock the boat, shake things up, challenge policies and procedures, and laugh at archaic rules. We should want, in fact, to stir up this kind of thinking and acting, with questions like:

➡ "Are you really saying that there's *no way* to do this [better/faster/cheaper]?"
➡ "What would happen if we stopped doing that?"
➡ "Would you do it this way if it were your company and your money?"
➡ "If we'd go out of business tomorrow unless you found a way to reduce costs by _____%, what would you change *today?*"

Learning and Asking

An important part of responding to change or creating effective change is looking at a change from multiple viewpoints, from multiple realities. "When [many] don't know what to do, they simply do more of what they do know. . . . Expanded choice enables managers to generate creative responses. . . . It may be comforting to think that failure was unavoidable and that we did all we could. But it can be enormously liberating for managers to realize that there is *always* more than one way to respond to *any* organizational problem or dilemma."[4] Assigning individuals or teams to create different perspectives—a customer point of view, an employee point of view, a process point of view—can open up whole new avenues for exploration.

Questions such as "What *is* our business?" and "How do we reengineer our process or structure to achieve our goals?" can be useful, but they may be the wrong place to start. Transformation may or may not be enhanced by focusing on core competencies (which are themselves often an illusion and even if not may not match up well with the marketplace). And by the time we go through a major reengineering (which so often fails to simplify the process, the number one—and two and three—goals), we can be beaten. Or we can be out of business.

The key questions to ask are "What *is* this change?" and "How do we exploit it?" Innovation comes when we "systematically identify changes that have already occurred in a business . . . and then to look at them as opportunities. . . . [It] means changing your products and services to keep up with markets that are changing faster than anybody has ever seen."[5]

This means that we need to carefully analyze where the change is going and to methodically ask how we can take advantage of the wrinkles. "What separates truly great corporate innovators from the competitors they leave in the dust is their ability to create conscious mechanisms to innovate consistently."[6] This approach doesn't eliminate intuition and hunches (although we have to be careful in areas where gut instinct has worked before and may have given us the illusion of wisdom). It means rather that we systemize our handling of 80 percent of change and then use enlightened hunches for the last 20 percent.

An important part of learning is losing unhelpful ideas, perspectives, and unschooled ways of looking at the world and how it's changing. We need to inquire deeply into the minds of our employees—in performance reviews, one-on-one discussions, and team meetings—to find out what pressing changes have made it into their conscious awareness and which ones they're blocking out.

And we need to learn what distant echoes of change they're hearing, so that they can help us unlearn what we "know" too be true.

"Only the wisest and stupidest of men never change," said Confucius. Today, it's only the stupidest.

The grand illusion that change is occurring too fast is crippling—and meaningless. External factors and changes that are forcing internal changes are *reality*, and it doesn't matter whether we like it or not. It isn't too fast, it just *is*.

Our reality is to create a change orientation and process that can keep pace with environmental changes. We need to embrace change, look for ways to exploit it, and—if we're really at the top of our form—find ways to make it occur faster. If we can't figure out how to make it work for us at the present moment, we can at least try to figure out how to keep it from killing us.

Change is exciting, scary, breathtaking, terrifying, full of opportunities, and fraught with dangers. And change is here to stay.

NOTES

1. Michael Hammer and James Champy, *Reengineering the Corporation: A Manifesto for Business Revolution* (New York: HarperBusiness, 1993), pp. 159–170.
2. "Cashing in on Tomorrow," *Time*, July 15, 1996, 52.
3. Ed Oakley and Doug Krug, *Enlightened Leadership: Getting to the Heart of Change* (New York: Fireside, 1994), p. 247.

4. Lee G. Bolman and Terrence E. Deal, *Reframing Organizations: Artistry, Choice, and Leadership* (San Francisco: Jossey-Bass, 1991), p. 4.
5. Peter F. Drucker, "Flashes of Genius," *Inc.,* May 1996.
6. Matthew J. Kiernan, *The Eleven Commandments of 21st Century Management* (Englewood Cliffs, N.J.: Prentice-Hall, 1996), p. 51.

9

Consequences:
"I Think We Can Get
Away With That"

Logical consequences are the scarecrows of fools and the beacons of
wise men.

—Thomas H. Huxley, *Animal Automatism*

It was just a small downsizing.

Just 3 percent of the workforce. Just a handful of people out of several hundred employees. No big deal. It wasn't even called a downsizing. Management was very careful to explain that this was simply a reorganization to streamline and improve operations and that it had nothing to do with business conditions or with the performance of the people who were downsized. Management was sure that the explanation was reasonable and that there would be no lasting negative repercussions.

Nobody bought it.

In a mixture of anger and fear, a key and long-term employee who had not been let go told me, "I've been through this kind of thing a couple of times before. I can't deal with it. I'm taking off a couple of days to get away from this place. I don't know where this is going to lead me." Another sharp and previously committed midlevel manager told me, "I don't know what this means. I guess I'll just do my best, try to get some good additional experience, and keep my eyes open for new opportunities."

These feelings permeated the organization. What went wrong? The cuts were so small, and management had been so very careful to explain what they didn't mean. They were sure that no one would interpret them "incorrectly," that the changes would not impact morale, that everyone would understand and agree. How could management have been so off the mark?

A grand illusion.

THE CONSEQUENCE ILLUSION

No one had really thought the decision through to all of its possible consequences. These consequences—damaged morale and reduced commitment to the company—weren't difficult to anticipate. Yet no one anticipated them or took precautions against them, not even in a world where job security is often employees' number one concern and fear. No one ever asked the simple but powerful question, "What are all of the possible consequences of this decision?"

The illusion was that actions don't have consequences, that the company wouldn't reap what it had sown. It grew out of a wild and unfounded optimism that allowed management to ignore anything that might have contradicted its wishful thinking.

There is a basic human illusion that we can get away with things, that actions will not elicit equal and opposite reactions, that we won't reap what we sow in our personal and organizational decision making. Consequences can be unwanted, ugly, and embarrassing, so we try to drop a screen between what we're deciding and the consequences we can almost sense in the offing.

The law of consequences—we always *do* reap what we sow—was compounded in our opening example by its corollary, the law of *unintended* consequences. In this case, the unintended consequences arose from employees' refusal to believe management's justification for the layoffs. After the downsizing, all of management's announcements and decisions were suspected of harboring hidden agendas. The statement that there was nothing personal or performance-based in the layoffs wasn't believed by anyone. People stopped taking the more dangerous—but also the potentially more valuable—risks. And virtually everyone began protecting his or her position and seeking cover for all decisions, one of the truly enormous wastes of energy and resources in organizational life.

Every decision has unintended consequences. A decision is a creative act; it either reinforces a current direction (good or bad) or takes our organization in a new direction (good or bad). People, whether we like it or not, respond creatively (and often unpredictably) to our decisions. Future decisions and circumstances will interact with our new direction differently from the way they would have with the old.

Ken seemed like the most expendable person in the department. He had the fewest credentials and the least seniority. His duties could be spread among the remaining employees after he was let go. The intended consequence, reduced payroll, was achieved. The unintended consequence? Management didn't understand that Ken, with his humor and wit, had become the primary source of the department's morale. His firing left the department without its emotional core.

The law of unintended consequences is fueled by the illusion of wisdom and thoroughness. This illusion says, "We've covered the bases, and we know what results we'll get." Amazingly, we can believe this even when we've never asked the corollary question, "What are all of the possible *un*intended consequences of this decision?" If we pursue the answer to this question, we can convert many otherwise unintended consequences into clear issues that can be dealt with.

The Hyatt Regency Hotel in Kansas City is a beautiful facility. In what was almost a warning, final construction work on the interior of the hotel was accelerated to accommodate a high-society celebration, leading to the unintended consequences of rushed and shoddy work. Unintended consequences should have been on every agenda after that, but they weren't.

The hotel was originally built with suspended skywalks in the lobby. Incredibly, no one asked these critical questions: Has this design been thought through? What if a lot of people are on the skywalks at the same time? Shouldn't we load-test these things before we let actual human beings in here? One of the biggest unintended consequences in the history of hotels exploded onto the front pages of newspapers in the early 1980s when the collapse of the skywalks killed more than 200 people.

Though we may not always know the full range of possible consequences, we can always try to anticipate it. We *must* try. There will still be unintended consequences, but let's not be caught unprepared by things that were foreseeable and then excuse our willful ignorance by decrying "unintended consequences."

Ironically, thinking about consequences at length but unrealistically can lead to another destructive version of the consequence illusion: imagining disastrous negative consequences if a decision is made or a current direction is changed. This illusion is especially destructive if the imagined (but unlikely, even ridiculous) consequences inhibit our actions or lead to an ongoing path of inaction and fear.

CAUSES OF THE ILLUSION

Most of us know in principle that our decisions will have both intended and unintended consequences. What keeps us from seeing these consequences and doing something about them in individual cases?

➡ Since it takes a lot of work to ask about and anticipate consequences (especially regarding "small" decisions—and there are no small decisions), we can choose the more comfortable path of just plowing ahead.

➡ Because it's more tempting to make the easiest decision (the one that takes the least trouble to implement or seems to get to the desired result most quickly) than to search for and implement the best decision (the one that achieves the desired result with the least negative intended and unintended consequences), we can take the path of least resistance.

➡ If our desire to do something is dominating, we can choose not to think about its negative consequences, since the action itself seems so right or satisfying.

➡ Because it's soothing, we can cling to the wishful belief that problems will go away or take care of themselves, even when our experience tells us that this will not happen. "It does not do to leave a live dragon out of your calculations, if you live near him," said fantasy writer J.R.R. Tolkien.

➡ Since we often grant a liberty to ourselves that we wouldn't accept in others, we may believe that the rules apply to everyone but us (e.g., that it's okay to harm others but it's not okay for them to harm us in return).

➡ Because it's much more comforting to our self-image and pride to blame others for consequences than it is to blame our own decisions and actions (especially if the consequences are very far removed from our decisions in time or distance), we can create an entire world of conspiracy and unreliability around us (e.g., low morale may be blamed on "lousy employees" rather than on a cutthroat decision made by management).

➡ If we accept less than full responsibility for a decision, it's easy to go into denial mode: "No one could have anticipated that"; "It's not my fault they reacted that way"; "There's no reason for customers to want something different than what we're offering."

➡ Since the world is, in some ways, a very frightening place and the media are constantly reinforcing that perception, we can easily imagine a host of disasters waiting to overwhelm us no matter what direction we take, which can cause us to freeze.

➡ If we've been trained to be negative about ourselves and others, conceptualizing positive outcomes can be almost an insurmountable task.

HOW TO RECOGNIZE THE ILLUSION

Rate your organization from 0 (lowest) to 5 (highest) on the following statements:

_____ We discuss consequences (intended and unintended) thoroughly before making any decision or changes.

_____ We understand that almost all decisions have positive unintended consequences, and we try to prepare in advance to exploit them.

_____ We understand that almost all decisions have negative unintended consequences, and we try to prepare in advance to minimize their damage.

_____ We don't believe that we can get away with anything as an organization or as individuals.

_____ We find ways to let our employees be trained and matured by the consequences of their words and actions.

_____ We don't assume that any problem will go away or take care of itself.

_____ We understand that morale (high or low, good or bad) is a consequence of a very long series of attitudes, interactions, and decisions.

_____ All employees understand the impact and consequences of missed deadlines (for internal and external customers) and work furiously to meet them.

_____ All employees (down to the janitor) have access to, are trained how to use, and pay close attention to budgets and numbers.

_____ Our practice throughout the organization is to under-promise and overdeliver.

_____ We constantly work on developing and *maintaining* key relationships and alliances with customers, suppliers, and others.

_____ We are more curious about the future (positive and negative) than we are satisfied with the present or the past.

_____ Everyone in the organization is aware of and keeps up with changes in our industry, customers' needs, technology, and society.

_____ Everyone is committed to learning about the aftermath of decisions.

_____ Everyone is free to question everything.

_____ We make the timing of decisions an important part of every decision-making discussion.

_____ We understand that untrustworthy people and organizations will kill us, so we constantly reevaluate relationships and terminate the unproductive ones.

_____ We are careful not to make any decisions that chip away at others' trust or our integrity.

_____ We don't assume that our problems are anyone's fault but our own.

_____ We try to avoid spending organizational resources on unlikely, disastrous negative consequences.

_____ TOTAL

SHREDDING THE ILLUSION

Organizational Viewpoints

We have to ensure that denial is never allowed to live and breathe in our organization. Whenever we hear comments like "There's no reason for customers to want that" and "Competitors are stupid for doing that," we know we're in the midst of avoiding the reap/sow principle. If customers want it, there's a reason. If competitors are doing it, there's a reason. We either need to find out the reasons or prepare to be demolished.

Lou Ann, the marketing manager for Polyweb Industries, had written half a dozen memos suggesting strongly that the company look into and implement bar coding. She could foresee that several of her key customers were going to insist on supplier-coded material deliveries and that lack of preparation could cost her some key accounts. She got either no response at all or the "you're right" response (i.e., "You're right, Lou Ann, we need to look into that"). When two major customers did take their business elsewhere, management was shocked. Rather than being thanked for her warnings, Lou Ann was blamed for the loss.

As is clear from this debacle, *inaction*, like action, has consequences. Psychologically, it's often easier to bear the consequences of inaction ("at least we didn't do it to ourselves"), but the results can be just as problematic.

There are four key questions that need to be asked whenever we're making or avoiding a decision:

1. What are the best possible outcomes of this decision?
2. What are the worst possible outcomes of this decision?

3. What are the best possible results that can occur if we do (or continue doing) nothing?
4. What are the worst possible results that can occur if we do (or continue doing) nothing?

Consequences are usually the result of a long series of small decisions (or nondecisions). If we're walking somewhere, we don't get there all at once; we do it a step at a time. *Any single step* in a different direction will lead to a different destination—perhaps even a radically different destination.

If we don't like the consequences, we shouldn't look at the most recent event that triggered them and vow not to repeat it. We should look at the whole process that got us there and vow never again to allow that process to begin.

Leadership Attitudes

Whenever we're about to make a decision (especially one about a major step or small first steps in a new direction), it's imperative that we involve everyone who might have an input about the possible consequences, good and bad, intended and unintended. The time spent will almost always be less than the time it will take to deal with the many strands of those consequences.

If we're concerned that people might not speak up, we need to use tools, such as anonymous questionnaires or surveys, to get at the heart of the matter. It is astounding how a disastrous decision can sometimes be stopped by someone in an unrelated area, way down the organizational ladder, or by a very new recruit. We've all said at times, "Gee, I never thought of that." The important thing is to say this *before* we make the decision, not after.

If it's a major decision, we can go the next step and do follow-up surveys (anonymous surveys are probably the best) to test what's come out of the decision. Four important questions are:

1. What are the specific results you see as an outcome of this decision?
2. Which are the most harmful in the short run? Why?
3. Which are the most harmful in the long run? Why?
4. Are there any positive unintended consequences?

Surveys at one week, four weeks, and three months should give a good picture.

What about all the time required to implement such follow-up?

That's the wrong question. The right question is: What about all that disaster if we don't? We should follow up, not because we don't have the right to make decisions, but because we want the decisions to be right.

We should always assume that "what goes around comes around," that what we do to others will someday be done to us. We need to train, develop, and discipline our employees by letting them experience the consequences of their actions. Speeches, pep talks, lectures, and reprimands seldom work as well as consequences—and often don't work at all or (even worse) backfire. "People don't change their behavior, unless it makes a difference for them to do so," said quarterback and motivational speaker Fran Tarkenton.

For example, guaranteed salaries or wages, automatic raises, routine bonuses, cost-of-living allowances, and standard-percent profit sharing are anticonsequence at the core and only serve to insulate people from the marketplace. The absence of a downside (poor performance can't result in a *lower* overall compensation) is also an anticonsequence. Businesses get neither guaranteed pricing or profits on the one hand, nor protection from losses or termination on the other.

We need to use:

➡ *Positive consequences*—achievement-related raises and bonuses, gainsharing for contributors only, comp time for efforts above and beyond, recognition and rewards for all legitimate suggestions (whether implemented or not), more responsibility (with relief from current work), public recognition

➡ *Negative consequences*—missed-goal-related reductions in compensation (on the variable portion), loss sharing, required redoing of preventable botched assignments on one's own time (at least for salaried workers), more of doing the same thing for people who complain instead of offering suggestions for improvement, reduced responsibility (and related compensation and privileges), and self-firing (i.e., a requirement that employees perform or resign)

This "letting people fire themselves" approach to handling employee performance or attitude problems, known as "discipline without punishment," demands personal responsibility from employees. "The greatest difficulty with the traditional punitive approach is that it asks too little. When an employee receives a warning or reprimand, he is simply scolded for what he has done and threatened with greater retribution should he choose to continue. No formal commitment to change has been asked or provided. . . . The Discipline Without Punishment system requires the problem employee to become one of two things: either a good employee or an ex-employee."[1] It puts the responsibility where it belongs.

A critical part of our responsibility is to avoid assigning people to duties they can't handle. Giving employees more than they can do is setting them up for failure, and the consequences of that failure should rest with us, not them. We've got to assign work that's demanding but not too difficult—and then let them enjoy all of the consequences of success and suffer all of the consequences of failure.

Discerning what people can and can't do is one of the most difficult tasks of managers, and too little thought is usually devoted to it. We'd rather dump work on them and illude that they'll get it done and done right. When they don't, we can vent our anger on them (when it's our own fault) and tell ourselves that people are just no good.

Making careful assignments is a real tightrope act. But we can do it.

People Responses

We can teach and encourage our employees to see the long-range consequences of current decisions and short-term behavior. President James Madison, when speaking of the early action of a group, said, "They saw all the consequences in the principle, and they avoided the consequences by denying the principle."

Beyond that, we can let our employees be taught and trained by the consequences of their decisions. As we discussed, the most effective corrective is not a lecture or tongue-lashing (which may not be effective at all or may have negative unintended consequences). The surest way to correct future behavior is to let employees live with the consequences of their decisions—and avoid the nastiness of an "I told you so" added on top.

The major response we should look for from people is a willingness to take responsibility, to own up to decisions they've made, and to accept the consequences. Excuse making and blame shifting have *no* place in a progressive, successful organization. If we listen to the first excuse, we'll start a "not me" epidemic that will probably spread to every person who works for us.

The three key questions to ask when someone attempts to fix blame are:

1. Forget about that—what's *your* part in this problem?
2. What are *you* doing to make it better?
3. How can you help the others involved make it better?

The goal is to fix the problem, not fix the blame.

Learning and Asking

Finally, we can be alert to the many consequences that can flow from the decisions of other people. Larry had founded and was president of a fledgling software-development company. He brought Cheryl in to provide management expertise and to assist in fund-raising. But Larry's wife, a jealous and vindictive person who was ostensibly the company's secretary but who in reality was calling the shots, stopped Cheryl's efforts in their tracks and pressed Larry to fire her. Larry agonized but finally conceded for the sake of "family peace." Cheryl was fired. Consequence? His company died in infancy.

We've got to become students of the decisions being made around us and how they could affect us. There are several unhelpful attitudes we can carry around that can bring indirect consequences down on our heads:

➡ *"It's not my problem."* If it affects the future of our organization or our ability to perform our roles to the maximum level of achievement, it *is* our problem.

➡ *"Nobody's paying me to worry about that."* We're not being paid to worry at all. We're being paid to anticipate negative consequences and avoid them wherever they occur in the organization.

➡ *"It's not the best, but we can live with it."* Living with second- or third-rate results is like dying a slow death. We can attack the mediocre directions and lose the mediocre results.

➡ *"This will sort itself out someday."* Someday is *not* a day of the week. Stop the consequences when they're small, by intervening now.

We owe it to ourselves and our stakeholders to learn what directions are leading to what consequences. We have to continually ask the hard questions:

➡ Is this the best we can do?
➡ Why are we doing that?
➡ Where is this taking us?
➡ Do we want to go there?
➡ Will we be able to live with the consequences?

Some people won't like it when we do this. Some people won't like *us* when we do this. Who cares? For the sake of excellence, we can live with their disaffection.

Understanding and applying the law of consequences—we reap what we sow—takes us out of a pretend world and into a small minority of organizations that are likely to be on top in the third millennium. A consequence-driven organization, focused on *all* outcomes, is (if it has a good product or service) very difficult to beat.

NOTE

1. Dick Grote, *Discipline Without Punishment: The Proven Strategy That Turns Problem Employees Into Superior Performers* (New York: AMACOM, 1995), pp. 33–34.

10

Comparisons: "We're Doing Better Than ———"

Always dream and shoot higher than you know you can do. Don't bother just to be better than your contemporaries or predecessors. Try to be better than yourself.

—Novelist William Faulkner

Peter, a division manager at TechnoKron, had been studiously measuring his group's performance for more than three years.

He tried to make sure that he was covering the major criteria for success—on-time delivery, cycle times, order fill rates, productivity, inventory record accuracy, inventory turns, scrap rates, and financial standards (cash flow, profit and loss, balance sheet). Using information from the chamber of commerce and from his national trade organization, he measured his group in two ways: against its own past performance over time and against other organizations in his city. By all measurements, his group was doing better than the norm.

So Peter was confused when market share and gross margins began to drop. He measured more things, in more detail. Performance stayed high, but the important numbers (results) kept dropping. Peter was even more confused. There was, in his mind, no reasonable explanation.

When he was transferred without comment—but obviously because of top management's dissatisfaction—he was stunned.

What had happened?

Two things obliterated Peter's plans. First, his comparisons gave the illusion of success, but they were too limited. Comparing current figures against his own past performance and against a mix of local and competitive compa-

106

nies was fine but insufficient. His focus was both too narrow and too broad. It was too narrow because it didn't take global competitors into account; it was too broad because it compared the organization to unrelated industries in the local area, using factors that weren't relevant to TechnoKron's market.

This led to the second problem. In part because of his acceptance of inadequate measurements, and in part because he was illuding that this would protect him from being beaten, he missed some major changes in the market that rendered his tools obsolete. He was no longer measuring what his customers needed.

The old saying is that "the numbers don't lie."

But very often, they do.

THE COMPARISON ILLUSION

Comparisons are a source of endless illusion. As long as we appear to be doing better than someone else, we can feel that we must be doing well, so we don't need to change. These illusions can begin when we compare ourselves with our own past performance (rather than simply learning from it) or with the performance of other organizations.

Nikita Khrushchev, premier of the Soviet Union from 1958 to 1964, was asked by President John F. Kennedy in the midst of a summit meeting if he ever admitted a mistake. "Certainly I do," said Khrushchev. "In a speech before the Twentieth Party Congress, I admitted all of Stalin's mistakes." An accurate and clever response, but it didn't keep Mr. Khrushchev from eventually losing his position of power.

Even benchmarking can become an illusion supporter. We rightly (up to a point) compare ourselves to our competitors to ensure that we're operating at an effective level of performance. However, we can end up measuring ourselves against others in areas that are peripheral to the main challenges or goals of our business, against organizations that themselves are not excellent, or against a standard that's about to be demolished by the market.

The business of comparing is fraught with dangers. At one point, when I was brought in to turn around a failing manufacturing operation, I was directed to focus on improving on-time deliveries. The company made dramatic strides in that direction, but we still saw little change in market share because our customers were primarily driven by price. In fact, the added cost of our improved efforts on customer service ended up making us less competitive and actually *lowered* our market penetration.

The companies we're comparing ourselves to may *all* be performing at lower levels than the market requires. They may *all* be doing it wrong. Since every organization is unique, another company's solutions may not apply to us. Imitating others may take too long or come too late.

This problem is compounded by the fact that we may not even know what those we're comparing ourselves to are really like. We can illude that we know what these other organizations are doing, but we may be basing our opinion on partial, incomplete, or erroneous information. People can "puff up" their performance on surveys or in conversations. They can lie. We could end up comparing ourselves to an illusion manufactured by an imposter.

In our volatile world, standards can change faster than our ability to improve against them. If we've grown at an annual rate of 15 percent compared to an industry average of 5 percent, we may be wildly successful—unless a new competitor from an entirely unexpected direction or unrelated industry finds a way to deliver our service at 60 percent of our cost. If we're getting eight inventory turns against an industry standard of five, we can win—unless some major competitor/ supplier alliances are about to go to just-in-time production and continuous replenishment and render the "standard" meaningless. We may copy something that is successful today but will be obliterated tomorrow.

Even if we try to copy the best, by the time we get there—if they're truly the best—they will have already re-created themselves and moved on to new competitive advantages. Imitation may be the sincerest form of flattery, but it makes a terrible strategic plan. "Comparisons are odious," says the old proverb.

Comparing can ultimately lead to disastrous illusion because it's looking at the *past* (maybe up to the present) rather than the *future*. The past and the present can be a useful guideline, but measuring against the future is where true success is found. Comparison can help us try to get a bigger piece of what we perceive to be the pie, but it can't show us how big the pie really could be or where there are other pies.

CAUSES OF THE ILLUSION

What leads us to the idea that comparing can be a successful way to run our business? Here are some possible factors:

➡ If we lack a vision of our own, we can get one on the cheap by borrowing it from others.

➡ Since from the time we're children many of us feel pressure to be like the "best"—the most popular, best-dressed, most athletic, smartest—comparing can become the "normal" thing to do.

➡ Many of us have an inherent fear of being left behind, so we constantly check to make sure we're keeping up.

➡ Because it's much easier to compare and copy than it is to lead and set our own standards, we can let our own lack of originality drive our plans.

➡ Since it's much easier to look at or analyze the past than to anticipate or create a future, we can easily allow ourselves to become immersed in the past.

➡ Many of us have a tendency to hero worship, which can lead to the erroneous conclusion that the big guys have already thought of everything and are doing it as well as possible.

HOW TO RECOGNIZE THE ILLUSION

Rate your organization from 0 (lowest) to 5 (highest) on the following statements:

_____ We work hard to develop our organization to be like no other.

_____ We focus on ways to make nonlinear adjustments in what we do and where we're heading.

_____ We focus more on how we *contrast* with, rather than compare with, the competition and work to leverage the gaps.

_____ We learn from everyone but imitate nobody.

_____ We spend more time asking questions like "How do we make a paradigm shift? How do we invent our own rules? How do we invent our own *game*?" than we do comparing.

_____ We measure ourselves on factors that are important to our customers and other stakeholders and to our future viability in a hypercompetitive world.

_____ We spend no energy on areas where we don't stack up to the competition *if* these areas aren't important to our stakeholders or to our bottom-line performance.

_____ We think more about the things that can't be easily measured (like organizational learning capacity and flexibility) than the standard measurements that everyone else is using.

_____ When we make comparisons, we look for the unusual items that can give a different, more meaningful, or more complete picture.

_____ We don't let difficulty of measuring prevent us from developing ways to check ourselves against the future.

_____ We compare ourselves against noncompeting organizations from a wide range of industries on *factors that are similar.*

_____ We are aware of, and absorb ideas from, organizations from a wide range of cultures.

_____ We encourage our people to innovate, rather than compare, on strategies, goals, processes, and methods.

_____ We do *not* believe we're superior because we benchmark well; we believe instead that someone's lurking out there ready to destroy our current competitive advantages.

_____ We encourage our people to be different, and criticize them for groupthink and following the herd.

_____ We insist that teams compare themselves to "stretch" targets and goals rather than to other teams.

_____ We insist that individuals compare themselves against personally established and agreed-upon goals rather than against their peers.

_____ We don't permit people to tout their own performance by comparing themselves with others.

_____ We don't permit people to excuse poor performance by comparing it with that of others.

_____ We compare ourselves first and foremost to where we need to be in six months, one year, and five years from now.

_____ TOTAL

SHREDDING THE ILLUSION

Organizational Viewpoints

Our action plan to shatter the comparison illusion begins with an organizational commitment to look for new paradigms, new rules, a new game. The most important question becomes "How do I lead?" rather than "How do I follow?" We have to find ways to create breathing room for ourselves, rather than just fight for a little bit bigger piece of an already divided pie.

In sports, the world-class athletes focus first and foremost on their own game. Great sprinters don't look over their shoulders. Top golfers don't fret over the leader board. The best wide receivers run their patterns and concentrate on the football rather than on the defender.

World-class organizations approach their work the same way. They focus on how they can best meet their customers' needs. They are aware of their competitors and other similar organizations, but they don't let others dictate their directions or practices. "Originality is the only thing that counts," said composer George Gershwin.

The survive-and-thrive goal today has to be to develop an organization that isn't exactly like any other—not just to be different, but because difference means something special to all stakeholders. The uniqueness needs to be both external (creative services and products, unusual and original responses to market conditions and customer needs, refusal to merely satisfy minimal trade or government guidelines) and internal (policies that promote rather than restrict freedom of movement, procedures that encourage rather than restrict flexibility of response, systems that measure and benchmark what no one else considers important—or considers at all). In other words, rather than comparing ourselves to "standard industry practice" or even "best of class," we are constantly asking ourselves the question, "What do we do (or what could we do) better than anyone else?"

This pursuit of uniqueness is what was missing from Peter's thinking and detailed benchmarking efforts at TechnoKron. Victory generally comes from successfully exploiting *contrasts* rather than from ensuring performance *similarities*. Marginal advantages in comparative categories have little power to open new doors. It's difficult if not impossible to copy others at a fast enough clip to ensure success or even survival. We need to follow analysis of market needs with the question "How can we meet this customer need in a way that no one else is doing—or even considering?"

It's the focus on the special that wins the prize. "By relentlessly driving themselves to deliver *extraordinary* levels of *distinctive* value to *carefully selected* customer groups, these market leaders have made it impossible for other companies to compete on the old terms. . . . No company can succeed today by trying to be all things to all people. It must instead find the *unique* value that it *alone* can deliver to a *chosen* market" (emphasis added).[1]

We don't, of course, want to reinvent the wheel. But we don't want to race down the competitive highway on retreads, either.

Leadership Attitudes

As leaders, we need to believe and spread the idea to our people that it's *contrasts*, not comparisons, that lead to breakthroughs and competitive advantages. Yes, we have to know the standards and how we're doing against them. And no, that's not enough. We have to know the competitive "rules," and then we have to break them—or find ways to render them obsolete.

We need to learn from, but not be content to be compared to, our competitors on processes and management methods. When we rely on comparisons to guide us, we're illuding at a very high and potentially fatal level. It's simply not wise to rely on comparing ourselves to others and to gain a false sense of security because we're doing "better" than they are.

The better route is to look for things that nobody else is doing or measuring, things that no one else may even think are important but that are, and then exploit these areas. Our competitors, for example, are focusing on price, terms, and delivery—so we watch those things, even as we focus our strategy on product value and service.

Traditional benchmarking can leave us chasing the wrong—or at least noncritical—things. Tom Peters calls benchmarking "the tendency to choose obvious rather than kinky/offbeat comparisons."[2] If benchmarking is measuring the obvious, then to be leaders (and even survivors) we're going to need to go beyond benchmarking.

This is really bench*breaking*: the focus on measuring ourselves against the contrasting, unusual, or critical—and often very difficult-to-measure—items that will really determine our future success, whether or not anyone else is measuring them.

The first part of benchbreaking involves measuring the differences between ourselves and others and looking for ways to exploit these differences. Rather than trying to close the gaps or ignoring the ways in which we're different, we try to find opportunity in the gaps and leverage the differences to the limit. In marketing and advertising, differentiation has long been the supreme guiding principle. Today, it has to be a way of thinking in everything we do.

A second key component of benchbreaking is looking for the unusual—what Peters calls the "kinky/offbeat" items. It's looking at employee turnover as a measure of how we and our competitors are doing on employee incentives and empowerment—key items for success in the twenty-first century. It's comparing ourselves to different kinds of organizations—like the concrete company, struggling with getting trucks on-site with the moisture content "just right," that compared its delivery process with a pizza delivery company. It's looking outside the culture for wisdom wherever it can be found.

A third major component of benchbreaking is focusing on the things that no one else is even thinking about or trying to measure. This includes issues like how thoroughly the corporate vision is understood or accepted or followed, acquisition or exploitation of unique market knowledge, the organization's learning capacity, new product and service innovation and success rates, percentage of revenue and profit from new products, the ease of information transfer (including bad news and mistakes), the number of new ideas and innovations generated by customers, suppliers, teams, and employees, and the time-to-market for these innovations. "Many of the things you can count don't count," said Albert Einstein. "Many of the things you can't count really count."

A psychiatrist reminded us of our tendency—seen even in the finest minds—to illude about analysis and measurement. "In regard to methodology, science has tended to say, 'What is very difficult to study doesn't merit study.' And in regard to natural law, science tends to say, 'What is very difficult to understand doesn't exist.' "[3] With conscious and extended effort, we can avoid this common but dangerous pitfall.

Benchbreaking can be complemented by bench*talking*—dialoguing openly with competitors and noncompetitors on best practices. Benchtalking involves establishing a group that can share information on future directions, process improvements, and reengineering strategies. This is different from the traditional benchmarking study, which is static—a picture in time that will soon be out-of-date. In benchtalking, there is opportunity for ongoing dialogue and for gaining more useful information, usually at less cost than benchmarking. Peter of TechnoKron could have benefited greatly from such dialogue.

We need to encourage our employees to dare to be different. Given the enormous diversity of human beings, and the truly odd behavior that exists out there, this can be a scary proposition. But anything else is routine and lifeless. We have to stand against groupthink, decision by committee, and the instinct to "do it like everybody else" that permeate so many organizations. The alternative? To tidily compare.

And to untidily disappear.

People Responses

We'll have to work hard to keep our employees from falling into the "comparison" mind-set, to get them to be more concerned about how they're doing against the future than how they're doing against Alex or Svetlana. We want them to be more concerned about how to innovate a process and invent new rules than how to tediously but faithfully follow a path that will eventually lead to the collapse of the organization.

To do this, we need to reward and recognize people for even small improvements and innovations, those where they have focused on building a better way in even a minor area of responsibility. Then we need to give these innovative people greater responsibility, because they've shown they can be faithful and creative in the small things that are never small.

We also want to encourage our employees to believe that avoiding the comparison mind-set includes avoiding the comparison of work-loads and the ducking—rather than the claiming—of responsibilities that don't belong to anyone else. We *never* want to get into the "who's doing the most?" argument (although we want work distribution to be fair). And we want to encourage people to adopt "orphan" responsibilities, with the conditions that "the orphan must make their own work easier or bring in additional revenue."[4] The work that nobody owns may determine the organization's future, and we need to encourage and reward those who courageously take it on.

We also need to welcome differences rather than glory in sameness. Groupthink—the tendency for people to compare their ideas and, if they don't match those of the group, to abandon them—is a deadly form of corporate mediocrity. Most people develop the herd instinct early in life, and watching what happens to mavericks only confirms them in their careful scrutiny and comparison of others. Effective teamwork, yes; groupthink (often disguised as teamwork), never.

When I worked for Hallmark Cards, a multibillion-dollar giant, fitting the corporate culture (homogeneous, territorial, and patriarchal) was everything. I was asked to build a department from scratch to manage a costly North American facilities expansion program. The assignment was big and the number of people I could hire was small, so I built a maverick, tough, results-oriented team that did high-quality work on time and at an excellent price.

A company officer called me on the carpet and searched his mind for a way to criticize the team. He didn't have any complaints related to performance (he ended up promoting me). So what did he come up with? "You're . . . You guys . . . are . . . *different.*" I thought about thanking him, but knowing it wasn't a compliment I held my tongue. A terrible corporate crime: He'd compared us to other departments and found us . . . different.

We need to minimize the ever-present human tendency to copy what others are doing and to compare our results with theirs. Competition and checking ourselves against others have a place. But it isn't first place. We must insist that people and teams compare themselves first to what they're capable of doing *before* they look at others. We can't allow ourselves to be impressed that team A beat team B if team A is only achieving 50 percent of what it's capable of achieving.

And we can *never* permit the "poor performance" comparison: "Sure we messed up, but that's nothing compared to _____." Rotten results are never excused because they're not as bad as somebody else's. Rotten is rotten. A rotting apple doesn't make a rotting orange any more edible. "It is not good to be better than the very worst," the ancient philosopher Seneca admonished.

Copying doesn't work very well in school. It isn't very effective in the workplace, either. We need to tell people, "Don't let us catch you copying!"

Learning and Asking

Comparing generally gets us focused on the wrong thing: yesterday's news, yesterday's results, yesterday's victories, and (at worst) yesterday's illusions. If we do finally beat the benchmark, we can end up in a truly fatal position: believing that we're superior and resting on our laurels. This kind of contentment is deadly. It's really a smug complacency in disguise.

This self-satisfaction gets compounded when we mix our all too easily acquired sense of "entitlement" into the picture: "We've earned this position in the market"; "we created this market—it belongs to us"; "we've got the best service in the business, and our customers know it"; "we've got the most educated and talented staff in town—nobody can beat them."

The only antidote is to remind ourselves and our workers *constantly* that there's someone out there, someone we don't even know, who's planning ways to wipe us out and take our "secure" position away. "When you're not practicing," said basketball great Ed Macauley, "remember that someone somewhere *is* practicing, and when you meet him he will win."

"Their trouble is that they are only comparing themselves with each other," said an ancient writer, "and measuring themselves against their own little ideas. What stupidity!"

The problem with comparisons is that we rarely compare ourselves to the only thing that really matters, which is where we ought to be—*need* to be—down the road. Ultimately, looking to the past or present (ours or others') can support illusions, while measuring ourselves against where we ought to be can produce effective thinking and lasting results.

We don't want to ignore history or experience. It's illusion to believe that what we're dealing with is totally different from anything anyone has ever encountered before, a completely brand-new problem or opportunity. There is truly nothing new under the sun. But a more deadly illusion is to think that we can build a future on comparisons and copying.

We need to be pulled by the future, not pushed by the past.

NOTES

1. Michael Treacy and Fred Wiersema, *The Discipline of Market Leaders* (Reading, Mass.: Addison-Wesley, 1995), pp. xiii–xiv.
2. As quoted in his newsletter, *On Achieving Excellence* (June 1996).
3. M. Scott Peck, *The Road Less Traveled* (New York: Simon & Schuster, 1978), p. 228.
4. Florence M. Stone and Randi T. Sachs, *The High-Value Manager* (New York: AMACOM, 1995), p. 106.

11

People: "Good People Can Be Successful in Jobs They Don't Like"

To business that we love, we rise betimes, and go to it with delight.
—William Shakespeare, *Antony and Cleopatra*

Jenny had it all: related degrees, certifications, intense industry-related experience, outstanding references. The two brief interviews went very well, and everyone was excited to get her into the fast-moving company. She was offered the role of vice president of Certicare Corporation.

Jenny took the position and hit the ground running. She impressed everyone—her boss, her peers, and, most of all, her subordinates. Before her first day, her boss had described her to her future colleagues as an intelligent, technically competent person who was going to help take the organization to the next level of sales, profits, and success. Jenny was meeting and exceeding his expectations.

Then, about three months into Jenny's tenure, the cracks began to appear. Several technical assignments, which hadn't been part of the interview and contract discussions and which required focus and attention to detail, lagged behind schedule. Jenny thought about objecting that she hadn't been hired to do this kind of project, but she felt uncomfortable about "trying to get out of work." She promised to get on top of things, but she continued to fall behind on these and other new assignments that she loathed. In spite of her technical background, Jenny was continuing to spend most of her time on teaching self-motivation and on team building, which she'd been hired to do and was interested in. Her subordinates liked her and appreciated her efforts.

Her boss didn't. The president was threatened by how well the employees

were responding to Jenny and had in fact given Jenny the technical assign-
ments as a way of isolating her.

Eventually, Jenny's position was "phased out." She wasn't surprised;
she'd seen it coming. She was frustrated with herself but hadn't been able to
make the adjustments to meet her boss's added requirements. What had
started as such a promising relationship had turned bitter for them both.

What went wrong?

THE PEOPLE ILLUSION

Everything about Jenny had been checked out except for the most important thing: Jenny, eminently qualified to perform in a technical position, hated dealing with technical details.

At core, Jenny was a people person, truly adept at inspiring people
and teams to high performance. Along the way, she had developed
formidable team-building skills. But her technical background, acquired because of pressure from family and friends to pick a college
major with a big payoff, had led her into a career path that she hated.
When her employer became jealous of her, Jenny's technical credentials provided a convenient way for her boss to undermine Jenny's position with the company.

Many people—perhaps even most people—in our economy are in
jobs for which they aren't completely suited. "I'm a very good man,"
said the Wizard of Oz. "I'm just a very bad wizard." This mismatch of
values and interests—even if the person has the technical skills and
capabilities to do the job—can lead to job dissatisfaction, poor performance, conflict, and *organizational* dissatisfaction.

This illusion—that people can be successful in jobs they don't
like—is deadly. In the long run, *no one* can be successful, either from
his own or from our point of view, unless he is reasonably well
matched with what he is expected to do. And this matching isn't just
a one-time event at the moment of hiring; matching values and interests with assignments is an ongoing process. It's pure illusion to think
that after we've made a good match, our problems are over and our
team is "set."

In a world where finding, retaining, and deploying excellent employees is such a critical issue, and we intuitively know it, why don't
we do the things that make it happen?

Because illusion can pile on top of illusion.

Illusions begin in the selection process, where so much is based
upon credentials and experience. Résumés can be deliberate illusion,
telling us nothing about who the applicant really is. Even if the résumé

does tell us, it may not tell us who the person really wants to be. Do we have to be psychologists? In a very real way, we do.

The interview process is often a "glamour shots" process. Both the organization and the person being interviewed can be putting their best (read: most illusory) foot forward. Jenny touted her technical background, and the company bought it as part of her package. The company touted its need for a people person, and Jenny bought it as part of its package. Interview misrepresentation—both ways—is as destructive as it is common.

Illusions about human beings in general can compound the problem. If we believe that all people are basically good and have potential, we can be led down a lot of paths to the organizational abyss.

The illusions also come out in our thoughts about retention. We know that money isn't the main reason people stay, but we constantly illude that it is because it's such an easy fix. So we try bonus programs, gainsharing, and retirement packages, which are great benefits but lousy hooks.

We illude that a better environment, more empowerment, and juicier assignments will do the trick. These are wonderful concepts. But if the person and the job are mismatched, we—and she—are destined for disappointment. Satisfaction is the hardest thing to achieve and, as far as truly innovative and excellent performance is concerned, the only thing that counts.

The illusions can carry forward when we assign and deploy people. Even though the market, the organization, and the requirements are changing, we can illude that people will, like water, seek their own level. We illude that training can make up the difference, but it can't make an apple into a banana. The right person in the right spot at the right time can save an entire organization. A top-notch person who is in that same position but who hates it might never even see the opportunity.

We can also illude that people can be effective without lots of ongoing, relevant training. Empowerment without training is the organizational equivalent of authorizing a premed student to do open-heart surgery. It might work—but we don't want to bet our organization (or our heart) on it.

People illusions show their faces in a lot of organizational paraphernalia: organization charts (which never tell us what's really going on, or what *should* be going on); job descriptions (almost complete illusions, usually inaccurate and quickly obsolete); coaching (which often doesn't explore the real reasons why the person isn't performing); and discipline (which usually begins *after* we've already "had it" with the employee and are simply taking the necessary steps to get rid of him or her).

Our illusions about people can be so pervasive that we carry them even as good people are leaving us. The "smart" ones tell us what we want to hear—the acceptable responses—in their exit interviews. We'd rather believe their explanations than face the fact that top-drawer matching on entry could have eliminated most of the exits.

CAUSES OF THE ILLUSION

We all *know* that we can't reach peak performance doing things we don't like. So what on earth leads us into the illusion that other people can? Here are some possibilities:

➡ Because making good matches is time-consuming, not black-and-white, and is often a frustrating process, we can look for the quick and easy fix, the superficially correct match to our people needs.

➡ Because seeing below the surface is so difficult, we can take the easier approach of buying the illusion that the interviewee or employee is selling.

➡ In a credential- and knowledge-crazed culture, we can be misled to focus almost entirely on the question of what people *know*, when the crucial question is how people *think*.

➡ Because it's easier to analyze the "facts," we conclude that the world and people operate in a rational manner, when in reality many (if not most) of people's decisions are based on nonrational (i.e., spiritual and emotional) or even irrational ideas.

➡ In spite of all of the empowerment stuff we've heard, if we're honest, we have to admit that the idea that people must be watched and controlled is still lurking about (and has great currency, in part because most people don't seem very interested in their work).

➡ It's more comforting (albeit more destructive) to believe that people are just rotten or worthless than to believe that we did a poor job of matching.

➡ Because thinking about beings who can be nonrational or irrational can seem overwhelming, we can easily fall into the habit of making people decisions on the basis of gut feeling (e.g., he reminds us of us; she's "easy" to get along with; she looks like a supervisor).

How to Recognize the Illusion

Rate your organization from 0 (lowest) to 5 (highest) on the following statements:

_____ We think of people as people and not as "human resources," "personnel," or "assets."

_____ We believe that finding the best people for our present and future needs is the most important thing we can do, and we spend all of the time necessary to do it well.

_____ We spend more of our time in interviews finding out how people think than finding out what they know.

_____ After hiring, accurate matching of our people to jobs and assignments is our top people priority.

_____ We don't believe or act on the idea that most people need to be watched and controlled if they've been hired, assigned, and trained appropriately.

_____ We refuse to hire or retain people who must be micromanaged or told what to do.

_____ We're comfortable with considering alternate organizational structures and refuse to be defined by our form of organization.

_____ We have minimized or eliminated the use of organization charts and job descriptions (5 for elimination, 4, 3, 2, 1 for degrees of minimizing).

_____ We focus more on people's values and interests than on their credentials.

_____ We methodically and consistently ask our people what they would *like* to do and then let them do it.

_____ We're careful to hire people with a complementary mix of values and interests so that everybody can do what he likes but everything still gets done.

_____ We offer and support training plans for each employee that target specific areas for education and hands-on training and with mutually agreed-upon times for completion.

_____ More than we're concerned that people might be mindlessly *breaking* the rules, we're concerned that they might be mindlessly *following* them because they just don't care or are afraid to take a risk.

_____ We believe that we as leaders and managers can't control all of the small (but crucial) decisions but that well-matched employees can.

_____ From their hiring and training through their exit interviews, we relentlessly ask people what they didn't like.
_____ Because we believe that it will lead to overall success, we use feedback to change our practices in order to enhance the pleasure people get out of their work.
_____ We consistently assign people to projects or teams on the basis of what they'd like to be involved with more than what they're "qualified" to do.
_____ Like a championship sports team, we don't bring people onboard or assign them to teams when we know they won't like the culture, even if they have tremendous abilities and credentials.
_____ We believe that a failure of an employee to perform is in most cases our failure to select, assign, and train people effectively.
_____ We perform postmortems to determine why every person who left did so and why every person who was terminated had to be.

_____ TOTAL

SHREDDING THE ILLUSION

Organizational Viewpoints

Few organizational platitudes have been voiced more often or stated more piously than this one: "Our people are our most important asset."

And few statements have meant less in actual practice.

It's not uncommon for organizations to spend much more energy, fervor, and concern on sales plans, hard assets (plant, equipment, inventory), and financial issues than on "human resources." The platitudes are voiced because people can be fooled, and hard assets just don't care.

First of all, people aren't "resources"; they're real, live, breathing, complex, incredible entities who put all the rest of our organizational sophistication to shame. But if we want to consider them resources or assets, we at least need to deal with them that way: lots of study and analysis before we "buy"; efforts to ensure that the assets' capabilities match up with organizational needs; careful handling; instruction and training on how to utilize; preventive maintenance; scheduled downtime; and capacity and loading analysis. If we don't make it so, fit will not just "happen." Jenny got none of this attention at Certicare.

It's paramount that we find the best people to help us, with best defined as "the most qualified people we can persuade to join us who will enjoy what we're going to ask them to do and think that it's important." We need to investigate the whole package: capability, interests, and values. All three need to say "go" before we bring the person in.

The reason is simple. If we hit on all three points, the person can be a source of delight, support, and innovation for many years in ways we can't even anticipate today. But if we miss on even one of the three, illuding that the other two (or money or benefits or whatever) will make up the difference, the person can sap organizational resources and be a source of discord and disappointment for many years—also in ways we can't even anticipate today. Because of these realities, we have to spend the time necessary to do hiring very, very well.

After people join us, they should have a hard time finding an organizational chart or a job description, preferably because we don't have any, preferably because we don't believe in these sanctified paper illusions.

We also should be unafraid to test the waters of ideas such as virtual organizations (we're all over the place), telecommuting (we're somewhere else), and flexible schedules (expect us when you see us).

An organization that needs to keep a close eye on its people is most certainly not ready for the twenty-first century.

Leadership Attitudes

Matching is everything.

"When men are rightly occupied, their amusement grows out of their work, as the color petals out of a fruitful flower," said English writer John Ruskin. From selection to project assignments to team membership, matching people to something that aligns with their values and interests is the crucial concern. Everything else is secondary. And when matching is done well, all other issues related to people are made much easier.

Interviewing

The first rule of interviewing comes into focus when we have the greatest need for help and the least amount of time to find or deploy it. This is when we need to take even more time than usual. It's almost guaranteed that rushing the interviewing process will lead to hiring results that are mediocre at best and disastrous at worst.

In interviews, we need to take enough time to find out how people *think*. This means that we don't ask leading questions where the desired answer is obvious. We don't ask questions with one-word answers; we always try to ask questions that call for narrative answers, out of which we can detect what the person cares about. We talk 20 percent of the time and listen the other 80 percent. We use the "ten-question rule": We have the prospect write out ten questions that she must have us answer before she'll take the job—not necessarily for us to answer right now but so that we can see what's *important* to her. We do anything we can to get a composite portrait of who this person really is.

At this stage, we're not interested in credentials. In fact, we should spend our time tearing up credentials and experience: "Why did you get this degree? Is that really what you wanted to do? If you had it to do over, would you do something different? If you could be doing anything you wanted, what would that be?" It's not that credentials are unimportant (although they often are); it's that credentials are distractions from the really important questions.

We're looking for what's important to our applicants, what their main interests are, what makes them tick. We need to have them take personality tests and go through interviews with numerous people so that we can find out who each person really is. We have to analyze applicants' values and interests carefully. We want to ensure that they not only *can* do the job but *want* to do the kind of work required by the position. And we're also looking for undeveloped but applicable skill sets, because we recognize that where the applicants can go is more important than where they've already been.

Exploring these issues takes a lot of time, partly because the applicants themselves may not know the answers. They, like us, can spend so much time illuding and projecting images that they forget who they really are. So if we do a really good job in the hiring process, we've done them a favor even if we don't hire them, because they'll have a great gift—they'll know better who they are and what they want to do than they did before they walked in our door.

The main traits I look for in job applicants are character (integrity and positive uniqueness), intelligence (mental and emotional), determination, curiosity, care for people, and passion. But even if those qualities all look outstanding, the answer is no if what we want the person to do doesn't match up with who the person is. It doesn't matter if it looks good on paper. Sports teams that look better on paper often lose, and people who look good on paper do, too. Games and careers aren't played out on paper.

Training

Illuding managers expect "someone else" to take care of the education and preparation of people. Leaders understand that there *is* no one else. Although we want our staff to take responsibility for their own training, we need to provide them with the appropriate opportunities. And we shouldn't resist training people even in the face of high turnover. As the maxim says, "Worse than training people and losing them is *not* training them and keeping them."

Part of our training program—a very *big* part—needs to focus on ferreting out the mismatches that snuck through our intensive interviewing and selection process. It's illusion to think that we can do a "pretty good" job of hiring and then fix any problems with good training and coaching. It's like making a bad match in a marriage and trying to fix it with counseling.

We have to constantly test not only whether our employees are learning how to do the job but whether they care about the job. We have to find myriad ways to ask them not just what they think but what they feel about what they're learning. What they think may be an illusion. What they feel is probably much closer to the reality of who they are.

We can learn this through a new round of interviewing. Asking questions and waiting for narrative answers can be helpful: "What are ten things you like about the company or your job that you didn't even know about before you joined us? What are ten things you *don't* like? What are ten things—even small things—you're doing that you think are a waste of your time? How could we rearrange things to alleviate each of the negatives?" An early 360-degree review (boss, peers, subordinates, others who interact) can help determine the person's passion level.

Caring about passion is simply recognizing that people aren't rational machines, that we just can't put person A into slot B. People are guided by reason but are often driven by emotion. The nonrational (spiritual and emotional values) and the irrational (illusions, biases, and out-of-control emotions) frequently dominate people's life view, and thus their performance over time.

A way to pull all of our training together and to shred the illusion that employees will magically be absorbed by the corporate culture is to establish a formal mentoring program. All new employees can be assigned a mentor for thirty to ninety days to make sure of two things: first, that the corporate vision and values are accurately communicated, and second, that all of the new hire's interests and capabilities are fully utilized.

Team Building

Matching, rather than "assigning," people to projects and teams is crucial for success. Sports teams regularly pass on a player with excellent abilities if he won't "fit" the team. They'll bring in a person of lesser skills because he matches the needs and the rest of the team so well.

Matching employees' values and interests with team objectives and other team members is an ongoing process. We need a mix of people—some analytical, some intuitive—in balance so that we can be both right *and* fast on decisions and new directions. This means we need to include team members who may not have the right credentials but who have great interest in the effort. They can bring not only necessary fire to their role but also a fresh perspective, because they haven't been locked in to what is "doable."

Disciplining

We need to begin any coaching by finding out whether the problem is the result of a mismatch between the person and the job. The same is true for any disciplinary process—we need to start by assuming we've made a mistake and have put a salt-water fish in a freshwater tank (or vice versa). The root of the problem may be that the person doesn't care about the work at hand, in which case the problem is a symptom—and an illusion not worthy of our time and energy.

Exit Interviewing

When people leave our organization, we need to ensure that we get more than the "standard" answers so that we can do a better job of matching people and jobs in the future. We need to find out where we mismatched, so a large part of our exit survey needs to center on this problem. If we really want the truth, we should allow people to mail in their answers anonymously some weeks or months in the future.

Then we need to sit down in a postmortem and thrash out what might have gone wrong. Although the person may have left for personal reasons or to pursue the opportunity of a lifetime, for analysis purposes we need to assume that the departure, whether voluntary or involuntary, is a clue that something in the system is broken. What did we miss? What illusions led us to this moment? How do we make sure that this never happens again?

Few organizations look at the loss of a person as a defining moment, a chance to reevaluate what they're doing, an opportunity to shred illusions and take a giant step forward. Be one of them.

People Responses

"To remove deep roots requires radical action, and that demands radical men and women. As never before, the manager must be a revolutionary, confident that anything and everything can be changed—for the better."[1]

If we do a great job of matching, we can allow some of our other people illusions to die: organization charts, job descriptions, policies, procedures, systems, checks and balances—all designed to control people who we fear won't do a good job otherwise. This massive waste of organizational resources can be avoided if we hire the best, put them in the right spot, drill them on the vision, and let them help us build it.

Written tools and measures offer us a false sense of security, stability, and certainty in a chaotic world. There are, to be sure, no little decisions, and everything must be managed. It's just that you and I can't do it; our influence over the "little" daily decisions flows from our influence over the matching process, not from our system of monitoring.

When we have excellent people doing what they really love, we can give up the spirit-crushing load of rule-encrusted legalism. We can stop worrying about whether people are breaking the rules, because we know that any rules broken by this bunch needed to be broken. And we'll begin to look at people who mindlessly follow rules not as loyal but rather as people who just don't care. "Any fool can make a rule," said Thoreau, "and every fool will mind it."

If we've got the right people in the right positions, we're ready to empower them. We can give up the hard-to-kill idea that people have to be watched and controlled. The only people who need to be watched and controlled are those who are either in the wrong place or who just don't care. The first group can be energized by better matching. The second group can be energized, if at all, by being able to think about its real life desires without the distraction of a job. Some turnover can be good, as long as it's from the misfits and not from the mismatched. Usually, it's the reverse.

Empowerment is a very good idea and a very bad idea. So much of empowerment is a panacea—"We'll fix things by getting everyone involved." Empowerment can be a cop-out—"We don't know what we're doing, so let's pass the buck down to the front line." Some organizations "downsize" (i.e., get rid of some very valuable people) and then "empower" (i.e., overload) the survivors, who don't have the time, energy, or creativity to think about today (much less the future).

And if we empower people who aren't happy with what they're doing, either they'll do no more than they did before or they'll do things we don't want them to do. If we empower chaos, we'll get chaos in spades.

We can't wait for performance reviews to ask people what they like and don't like to do (although asking then, too, is a good idea). We have to constantly be aware of their feelings. The seeds of dissatisfaction and poor performance can grow into a very large weed in a very short time.

Matching is so simple and important, but *organizations almost never do it*. The premise is simple—find out what they like to do and let them do it; find out what they don't like to do and work to find a way so that they don't have to do it. The goal is to have all employees spend as close as possible to 100 percent of their time on things that they care about and that are of interest to them.

Learning and Asking

It is important to create individual training plans that help employees develop *in the directions they want to go*. This is really quite an awesome task, and it's worth the time.

We have to seek feedback to make sure that our matching process is working, from hiring through assignment to promotions. We of course have the right to leave matching out of our thinking, but illusion-shredding leaders give up this right in order to make realizable the passions of their people and the ongoing success of their organization.

Finally, we have to force ourselves past our illusions and the projected illusions of others so that we see employees not as the clean, showered, "together" people that they are on the surface but as people who are often carrying emotional, personal, and career baggage. How does our speech about trusting each other sound to someone who's just been betrayed by a longtime friend?

We have to look at each person's whole life. Should we have to do this? No. What will happen if we don't? The organization will die a slow death when our resistance to learning what our people need keeps us from the cure of whole-life concern.

The world's economy is moving rapidly toward fluid, dynamic organizations and organizational forms. It has become an illusion to believe that the standard hierarchy with pigeonholed employees is a requirement for success. We need to learn how to take advantage of new organizational structures, including the virtual organization. One way to do that is to make matching people and jobs our number-one staffing priority.

NOTE

1. Robert Heller, *The Super Chiefs* (New York: Dutton, 1992), p. 14.

12

Openness: "We Can Run This Thing Without Sharing That Information"

Men cannot communicate their free thoughts to one another with a lash held over their heads.

—Thomas Erskine, 1792

Even though he was only in his forties, Bill insisted that everyone who worked for him call him "Mr."

He liked power and prestige. And to him, information was power. He was the only one at MSP, Inc., his 300-person, $20-million-per-year company, who knew all the facts. He parceled out information in a miserly and, at times, deliberately confusing manner. He reserved all major decisions for himself and would even use people's lack of information—not knowing what he knew—to humiliate them in meetings.

He said he operated on a "need to know" basis, an approach that many hierarchical organizations, from military to government to business, have used to frustrate employees and limit success. Bill's stated goals were to avoid wasting people's time with "unnecessary" information and to prevent the misuse of information by disgruntled (there were many) or exiting (there were very many) employees.

Like so many information misers, Bill was ravenous to get more for himself. His most devious effort was to bug the conference room, where negotiations with the union were occurring, so that he could listen in on the union representatives' private discussions when he was out of the room. This time, he got caught in his own trap. Right before negotiations were to begin, Bill had to "shush" people as they came into his office. He had just realized that the bugging had been done in reverse and his conversations were being transmitted to the conference room.

Bill was universally hated. When he retires or dies, few people will be genuinely saddened.

THE OPENNESS ILLUSION

Because information is power, the part of us that likes and needs to be in control can, like Bill, very easily—*very* easily—use it to try to control a living organization.

But the practice of control by withholding information is in reality a grand and fatal illusion. It's grand because it can work to some level; it's fatal because of its damaging impact on performance, morale, communication, and trust.

Impact on performance comes from several directions. First, people won't know everything necessary to make effective decisions, no matter how much we try to give them all they need to know but no more. No one is smart enough to know exactly what information is needed. Second, the illusion produces gross inefficiency, as people scurry to find the missing piece and expend great amounts of time trying to learn the organizational mysteries. Third, decisions will be made with an incomplete picture in mind, which will almost always produce less than optimal solutions. What Bill gained in control cost him dearly in poor decisions and, because people are often paralyzed by lack of information, nondecisions.

Impact on morale flows from the environment that this illusion produces. It's very difficult to feel motivated—and fatal to be open—in a cloak-and-dagger, secrecy-ridden organization. After they found out about Bill's conference room bugging, people began to whisper in their conversations and severely restrict what they said on the telephone.

Impact on communication proceeds from the negative version of the "golden rule": Do it to others as it's been done to you. When the "withholding information is control" illusion is believed and practiced, it shuts down sharing throughout the organization. Little versions of Bill cropped up in every department of MSP, Inc.

Impact on trust occurs because human beings can't be comfortable with people who are guarded, elusive, or misleading. Openness is always a two-way street. How can people feel secure when they don't believe we're telling them the whole story? People told Bill only what they had to, and turnover was exceedingly high as people fled to organizations where they could know what was going on. The people who remained were convinced that Bill had also bugged all of the offices and telephones, which eroded trust completely.

The openness illusion inhibits people and organizations. Not only does it prevent people from helping us; it paralyzes them. True empowerment means first and foremost removing obstacles that hinder performance. The systematic withholding of information is the opposite of empowerment, and no exhortations to "do your jobs better" can overcome its effects.

The openness illusion is often disguised by burying people in mounds of useless or incomprehensible information. We can illude that if we pump enough information into the system, somehow good decisions will come out the other end. Usually all this does is clog the system.

With the explosion of available data, a key to openness is the *selection* of what, when, and how much to share and the elimination of everything else. Like the historian who must choose relevant statistics out of a wealth of research (or else bury the reader), so we must work with our employees and systems to find and share only what will help us make better decisions.

This is very different from Bill's withholding problem. Bill withheld necessary information from people without their knowledge or concurrence. What we're talking about here is withholding *un*necessary information from people *with* their knowledge and agreement. Ineffective managers hoard the good and share the worthless. Effective managers share the good and shred the worthless.

Another dimension of the openness illusion is the notion that people will share with us if we give them the opportunity. Roger illuded this way. When he became president of the family business, he instituted monthly departmental and managers' meetings so that "everyone would know what was going on in the company and pull together as a team." Everyone in attendance was required to say something, which gave the impression that the employees had a forum to share issues and concerns.

But after people watched Roger ridicule any suggestion he didn't like and question the competence and loyalty of the person who made it, they were careful to report only safe news—or bad news where the blame could clearly be placed on others. Before the meetings, some departments even discussed what they would and wouldn't say. The forum as a place to share was theatrical illusion.

Another disguise of the openness illusion is having "open door" policies, which in themselves are illusions. An open door is not always an open door. An open door is not a function of making pious announcements or physically having our doors open. An open door, to be effective, has to have full flow of news both directions.

It has to be a revolving door.

Causes of the Illusion

In an age of telephones, overnight deliveries, fax machines, and E-mail, why would we hoard information? Here are some reasons:

➡ Since it can be very difficult to feel any sense of control in our topsy-turvy, rapid-fire world (whether we're talking about our personal or our professional lives), withholding news, or releasing it as we see fit, can seem to provide a sense of power.

➡ Since many people like to have influence with others, they can use gossip or slander ("I know something that you don't, and you want to know it. I'm a source. I have power over you. If I can tell you juicy morsels, and keep them coming, I've gained an ascendancy over you"), which provides a kind of power that's addictive—*very* hard to let go of.

➡ If we have disdain for other people, we can find ourselves talking down to them with statements like, "You wouldn't understand. It's very complicated."

➡ The need to build the illusion of control can come from damage we've suffered in our own lives, since most of us have been hurt by someone who learned something deleterious or embarrassing about us.

➡ When we've been hurt by what we've shared—what Tom Paine called the misery that comes from "furnishing the means by which we suffer"—it can easily lead us to the conclusion that we should bottle up everything we know.

➡ Since we sometimes get a delayed reaction (e.g., we share something with someone in January, and that person uses it against us in a meeting in July), we can become cautious even when we see no immediate threat.

➡ We can operate under the idea that life is war, that information is intelligence, and that everyone not openly for us is against us (when the reality is that most people don't care about us one way or the other).

➡ We can blame misuse of information on people's inability to deal with truth, when the reality is that they didn't understand what we were saying or were reading our tone and body language (or that *we* didn't understand what we were saying).

➡ If we want to appear optimistic or avoid negative responses, we can find ourselves sharing only good news.

➡ Because of our concern about its effects on morale, we can reverse the "good news" problem and avoid telling our people the bad news, or repackage it as better than it really is.

➡ Because of our desire to protect people from fear, we can forget that it's the sharing of bad news that allows people to help us, that it's the *not* sharing it that scares them to death, and that if we present only good news—long enough and strong enough—it can discourage our employees from saying anything negative to us.

➡ Because of our desire to avoid pain, we can develop an appetite for good news, causing people to share only what they think we want to hear. ("Corporate executives get hooked on good news, as do scientists, publishers, physicians, performers. It keeps them in a state of bliss. At the same time it destabilizes their inner compasses, and heightens their vulnerability to the big dumb mistake."[1])

➡ We can develop an openness illusion because we want to appear knowledgeable or learned, even though acting this way is almost always a total turnoff for other people (who know that true experts are those who are humble, know how much they don't know and how much they've learned from others, and who know they haven't gotten anything on their own out of the blue).

How to Recognize the Illusion

Rate your organization from 0 (lowest) to 5 (highest) on the following statements:

_____ We provide information to our employees that disagrees with management's decisions and theories.

_____ We don't try to send the message to our employees that "all is going well" but tell them the bad news.

_____ Our first question is, "Is there any compelling reason why we shouldn't share this?," not "Why should we share this?"

_____ We don't try to impress or manipulate our people with the information we share.

_____ We stop and reevaluate what we're doing when we

find ourselves tempted to color what we're about to share in order to make it look better than it really is.

_____ We are careful with the information we share so that it doesn't unnecessarily frustrate or discourage listeners.

_____ We consistently encourage people to be open to new ideas from many sources and reward them for sharing what they've learned.

_____ We regularly and methodically investigate the reasons people might withhold information in our organization.

_____ We spend consistent effort on breaking down functional, departmental, and other unnatural barriers to open, two-way communication.

_____ We discourage the withholding of information by individual employees and departments.

_____ We assume that it is management's fault when people won't share information.

_____ We systematize the sharing of information so that no valuable data are stopped from getting to the people who could use them.

_____ We work with our employees to establish screening processes that can keep them from drowning in useless or distracting information.

_____ People regularly and comfortably take advantage of our "open door" policy (ask them).

_____ We don't criticize or abuse people for admitting mistakes or sharing bad news.

_____ We work very hard to get all the bad news on the table fast.

_____ We are determined to find ways to get people to be honest about everything they believe to be counterproductive or useless.

_____ We make listening a valued skill at all levels of the organization and provide the time and opportunity to do it.

_____ We thoroughly train our people in critical listening skills.

_____ We train our people to communicate their needs clearly and to be assertive without being aggressive.

_____ TOTAL

SHREDDING THE ILLUSION

Learning and practicing "shrewd vulnerability" is the starting point for a cure to this immobilizing illusion.

Organizational Viewpoints

Open-book management isn't a system; it's a philosophy.

> To be successful in business, you have to be going somewhere,
> and everyone involved in getting you there has to know
> where it is. That's a basic rule, a higher law, but most compa-
> nies miss it. They miss the fact that you have a much better
> chance of winning if everyone knows what it takes to win.[2]

We shouldn't share information openly because it's a fad; we
should share it because it's the right thing to do, produces better decisions and more creativity, motivates our staff, and lets them help us
manage the business. In his lust for control, Bill at MSP, Inc., missed all
of these advantages.

We need to commit our organizations to sharing information immediately unless there's a compelling reason not to share it. There can,
of course, be occasions when it's necessary to hold information tightly
to our chest. Possible reasons are these:

➡ The information is useless because it's totally unrelated to
anything this person is doing or interested in.

➡ The timing is wrong because receiving the information at this
moment will affect in a negative way how it is received and
used.

➡ The data are incomplete or possibly inaccurate, and we
haven't had the time to verify them.

➡ The quantity is overwhelming because we haven't established
mechanisms to effectively select, summarize, and disseminate
information.

➡ The information is related to our competitive advantage, and
sharing it could cause us loss.

Leadership Attitudes

Shrewd vulnerability means that our basic orientation is to share
news—good news, bad news, comforting news, terrifying news.

To be *shrewd*, though, we must thoroughly analyze the potential
impact of the news. What are the possible ways in which it could be
misinterpreted? How could it be misused? What might be the unintended consequences of sharing it? We must tell not only what we *know*
but also what we think it *means*. This includes giving our interpretation

(where it fits) of how the news affects us in light of our vision statement.

But even telling people what we mean isn't enough. We also have to tell them what we *don't* mean. People tend to fill in the blanks. Since no sharing of news is likely to be complete on all points, the blanks can be filled in with amazing things. Sharing specifically and in detail what we don't mean or what the data do not touch on can focus the listening and prevent destructive speculation.

Being shrewd also means that we select the appropriate timing, form, and audience for our sharing. Sometimes waiting even a few hours can make the news more palatable and hearable. The form—passing the news through channels, making an announcement, sending a memo, having a chat—is more critical than we might expect and must be selected carefully. And the audience—everybody at once, managers first, certain departments before others—can often determine not only how the news is received but how it's utilized.

In one company where I worked as a project manager early in my career, top management, without warning, took everyone at the end of the day to a meeting in a church building across the street. Some people kidded that we were heading to a funeral, and they weren't far wrong. Management announced a 10 percent across-the-board pay cut. Everyone (correctly, as it turned out) assumed that this was the precursor to mass layoffs. The abruptness of the announcement and the incomprehensibly discouraging way it was made left us all mumbling as we left the meeting. The best people left the company even before the layoffs began.

Sharing unpopular data, including those that disagree with a pet management theory or strategy, is critical—and rarely done. We have to encourage contrarian thinking before we can expect to get contrarian viewpoints. If we only give information that supports management's perspective, people won't have enough of a perspective to do anything but agree with us.

We have to break down existing barriers to openness and prevent the growth of new ones. Poor, deficient, ineffective communication is perhaps the biggest time-waster in organizational life, and provides high-octane fuel for the spread of illusions. *Anything* that stops the ready flow of information of any type has to be scrutinized and quickly demolished.

One of the best incentives we can give to encourage openness is to develop effective listening in ourselves and throughout the organization. In a very real way, openness starts with *listening*, rather than talking. Wise managers use words with restraint and know that, surprisingly, the person who listens in a conversation is the one who actually controls the conversation.

Listening is as gracious a thing as a leader can do. "It is impossible to overemphasize the immense need humans have to be really listened to, to be taken seriously, to be understood. No one can develop freely in this world and find a full life without feeling understood by at least one person."[3]

True listening takes a lot of work. "They think they are truly listening when all they are doing is pretend listening, or at best selective listening, but this is self-deception, designed to hide from themselves their laziness. For true listening, no matter how brief, requires tremendous effort . . . it requires total concentration."[4]

Active listening is fed by a dedication to asking incisive questions, nonleading questions that lead to narrative answers. We need to ask questions that stir the passions, stir the creativity, and stir the discontent. People listen especially closely "to those who advocate new or different images of emerging reality."[5]

People Responses

The key question about sharing anything flows out of the Golden Rule: "What would *I* want to know if I were in their shoes?" It has a corollary: "What would I *not* want to know if I were in their shoes?" A not uncommon problem in many organizations is that employees are overwhelmed with useless data while being unable to access the two pieces they need to make a solid decision. We have to help our people both *access* and *select* appropriate information.

The use of scoreboards for basic performance data puts a lot of valuable information into a form that people can easily read and understand. Sales, number of units shipped, on-time performance, order fill rates, inventory turns, number of customer complaints—all of these and more can be put on accessible scoreboards around our facilities. We should, of course, train people in how to read and use the data, and not illude that it's "obvious." This public display of core information can dramatically affect morale and can work to retain and motivate our employees.

Openness with our staffs will build trust, inspire them to improve the numbers, improve their sense of self-worth, and encourage them to bolster other people as well. It builds trust, because we as human beings are naturally drawn to those who take us into their confidence and seem to have no hidden agendas. It inspires people, because it makes them feel as if they're really an important part of what's going on. It improves their sense of self-worth, as access to knowledge often does. And it encourages them to be open with others, because people usually follow examples and have now seen firsthand how valuable openness can be.

After we've shared information, we have to do everything possible to help people share with us, because it's one of the most difficult things for people to do. The place to start is by assuming responsibility not only for our own sharing but also for creating an environment where openness is the norm. It won't happen overnight. It involves eliminating fears and other obstacles, on the one hand, and creating incentives to share, on the other.

One of the biggest fears employees face is that the messenger who brings bad news will be killed. We have to send the signal that it's not only all right to share bad news, it's positively *welcome* (except, of course, for willful and repetitive dumb mistakes). We have to assure people that we'd rather hear bad news than good news (and really mean it). And rather than getting hooked on good news, we need to let people know that it's the *good* news that's going to be received with skepticism ("Really? How can you be so sure?").

We need to recognize that the problem of being "burned" is a reality for everyone. We have to understand that our employees may not even *want* to share, even if we give them the opportunity, because of a fear of loss: of power, of prestige, of importance, of control, or of job. For many people, opening up takes a very long time and requires very great patience on our part.

If the measure of an excellent organization is the speed with which bad news (not gossip or slander, but *news*) travels to the top, then it follows that we have to reward the sharing of bad news (and not just penalize the cover-ups). Track bad-news reporting—number of times reported, timing, effectiveness, willingness to accept responsibility for it, positive solutions offered—and encourage it with incentives. If we only reward good news, we shouldn't wonder when that's all we get. (We don't have to worry that these incentives will cause people to deliberately commit mistakes so that they can admit them. Admitting mistakes will still be unpleasant, and none of us is going to offer *that* large an incentive!)

But beware of the person who brings slime rather than news. People with destructive motives and hidden agendas can use an open environment to further their own aims. We have to listen below the surface, because people can be deceitful and can learn to play to our illusions. We can think that what they're saying is good, helpful, and right because they present it that way. People who never take personal responsibility for the bad news they're sharing should be suspect. So should those who take only a little responsibility to make us think they're being humble and honest, while what they're really doing is cleverly setting us up for gossip, slander, or blame-shifting.

We have to break down the power illusion, which can cause people to cling to what they know. From the gourmet cook who won't share recipes to the engineer who won't share technology, the "I'll be stronger if I know more than you" approach to life is severely limiting and organizationally destructive. Once again, we have to recognize and reward those who make sharing, helping, and mentoring a career style.

Tying openness into performance reviews is critical. We need to know what new ideas people have discovered, what books they've read (from a suggested reading list or on their own), tapes they've listened to, seminars or meetings they've attended, and with whom they've shared what they've learned. We can find out who has led a reading group and discussion of a book. We should have a section on the form for voluntary recording of when they've reported mistakes and bad news. And we need to make the results of all of this an important part of their compensation package.

Learning and Asking

We have to learn what information will really affect the daily decisions of the people in our organization. "It is not the quantity, but the pertinence [of your words] that does the business," said Seneca.

We have to make sure, if we're driving for an open culture, that we're actually getting it. "Since managers rarely get honest feedback on their behavior, they don't realize how often they use traditional command-and-control management. They treat people as another set of assets with skin wrapped around them."[6] We have to be open about our openness.

We have to ask.

Information control is, in the end, an illusion. Sooner or later, people will find out the truth anyway, or they will fill in the blanks with their own assumptions and conclusions. We can't run things successfully without sharing information, widely and constantly.

The right information needs to flow like the oil in a piece of machinery. All of the parts need it, all of the time, or something is going to wear out or break. We have to decentralize and send information to all levels constantly. Boundaries—department to department, facility to facility, store to store—are the kiss of death in a hypercompetitive economy.

In the end, we have to develop our own organizational communication style. Companies, like people, have individual styles, and it's an illusion to believe we can learn to copy that of a competitor. It's got to be our own style.

And it's got to be open.

NOTES

1. Mortimer Feinberg and John J. Tarrant, *Why Smart People Do Dumb Things* (New York: Fireside, 1995), p. 98.
2. Jack Stack, "That Championship Season," *Inc.*, July 1996, 27.
3. Paul Tournier, as quoted by Bill and Nancie Carmichael, *The Best Things Ever Said About Parenting* (Wheaton, Ill.: Tyndale House, 1996), p. 195.
4. M. Scott Peck, *The Road Less Traveled* (New York: Simon & Schuster, 1978), p. 125.
5. Warren Bennis, as quoted in *Bottom Line/Personal*, July 1, 1996, 14.
6. Jim Clemmer, as quoted in *The Lakewood Report*, May 1996, 12.

13

Incentives: "In This Economy, They Should Be Happy to Have a Job"

Understanding how to motivate and the practice of motivating don't seem to be directly related in the real world.

—Ken Matejka and Richard J. Dunsing,
A Manager's Guide to the Millennium

Lori was at the end of her rope with Sean.

Once a model employee, Sean now seemed listless throughout the day. He dragged through meetings, was behind in all of his assignments, and hadn't contributed a creative suggestion in more than six months. Two of ATAB's clients had already complained about Sean's attitude and shoddy work.

Lori tried to coax Sean out of his malaise. She used soft approaches that had worked with others. She encouraged him, complimented him even when he didn't quite deserve it, and tried to ask him about his outside interests. Lori was frustrated when these attempts had no impact on Sean. Surprisingly, he began to react to her with a subdued resentment that she hadn't seen before. Unknown to her, he complained to his friends about his lack of recognition. His work continued to slip, and nothing Lori said seemed to register with him. She felt like a failure as a motivator.

Finally, after several more customer complaints, Lori's patience gave out. She received a memo from Sean that contained a number of typos, and she exploded. She shouted at him in front of three coworkers, then called him in to her office and laid it out for him: thirty days to mend his ways and do what Lori wanted. "It's my way or the highway," she said as he turned to leave her office.

Sean made some minor, short-term adjustments.
And he spent his lunch hours tearing Lori down to her other employees.

THE INCENTIVE ILLUSION

The incentive illusion begins with one of the greatest myths of management: that we as managers can motivate our employees.

To say it again, differently: We as managers *cannot* motivate our employees. "If high performance is going to be sustained, motivation must ultimately come from the inside out, rather than the outside in."[1]

Any book that promises to show us how to motivate people is an illusion from the get-go. It implies that we can just push the right buttons and get people to do what we want. But people are much more complicated than that. "The door to change is opened from the *inside*," goes an old French saying. People can choose to be motivated, but we can't make them choose.

If we illude that we can motivate people, we can end up placing on ourselves and on the managers who report to us a terrible and unnecessary burden: that we, not the employees, are responsible for employees' motivation and morale. It's the "caretaker" management model, which lifts responsibility for performance from the shoulders of the performers. It isn't real, it causes headaches, and it doesn't work.

We can't be motivators, but we can be "door openers." We can find ways to knock on the doors of people's minds and hearts and invite them to "open up" to the possibilities that exist for success. Some employees will answer the door. If we knock in just the right way, many may answer the door.

But other pieces of the illusion can cause us either to knock too softly or to come crashing through the door. We illude that people will be effectively motivated when we "soft knock"—for example, try to reach everyone the same way, use means that people don't care about, or continue plans that have lost their impact. We can also illude with the "hard knock"—for example, use fear and play on people's insecurities, announce the newest "big deal" performance plan, or focus on monetary incentives (and their withdrawal if behavior doesn't measure up) as the answer.

The problem with the "soft knock" is that many people just won't hear it. We can stand outside the door and whisper, trying to coax people to come from behind their dead bolts and join the battle. They'll ignore us and carry on with whatever they're doing (or not doing), as Lori found out with Sean.

The problem with the "hard knock" is that most people will resent the heavy-handedness of it all, even if they in part deserve it. They can smell manipulation and coercion from a mile away, and they will have an instinctive reaction against these power tools. Lori's attack on Sean in front of his peers and her threats to terminate him only increased Sean's negative influence on the organization, while doing nothing to improve his performance.

Even while we're feeling responsible for motivating people, we can also carry the illusion that people should "just be happy to have a job." Given the facts that job security is many employees' primary concern and that we can often get ever more qualified people to do ever less demanding work, we can illude that people will perform at their best because they *have* to. This was the attitude of the captain on the slave ship in *Ben Hur:* "We keep you alive to serve this ship."

But human beings are never moved to open the door to higher performance by insecurity and fear. Ironically, the reverse often occurs. People *lock* the door, because they fear that creativity and risk taking can lead to career-limiting moves and general disaster. The normal reaction to being controlled and dominated is to resist and build up defenses, to protect ourselves rather than move ahead positively into a new future. For a while, fear works. Fearful people won't.

Our incentive illusions can be compounded by the illusions of our employees. Many still illude that organizations are offering lifetime employment. Many illude that organizations "owe" them—jobs, money, benefits. This conviction can cause them to settle in and, in some cases, assume that showing up is enough—which is a difficult position from which to motivate oneself. But in a market-driven world, no organization is owed further business from its customers, and no employee is owed further "business" (employment) from his or her "customer" (employer).

The reality is that the new "employment contract"—which states that the employees owe their employer labor and creativity and the employer owes employees remuneration and growth—is here to stay. The fact that some employers and employees don't live up to their ends of the contract doesn't change that reality.

The Industrial Revolution is dead, and so are the organizational form and approaches that went with it. The very term "employee," in a day of virtual organizations, contract and temporary workers, consultants, and transients, is on the way out—of meaning, if not out of existence. People are going to have to take responsibility for their careers and manage themselves as if they were their own small businesses, whether they like it or not. We have to tell them so, because it's not fair to them or us to let them live in illusion. If we do the telling well, they might even come to appreciate standing on their own instead of being helpless dependents.

We, however, are going to have to live up to our end of the bargain—and, frankly, even more, as I discuss later in this chapter—if we want to build an organization that will prosper, because high turnover is very shaky ground. As I write this, unemployment is at a six-year low, but people are still scared to death. What's going on? Part of it is the fact that many of us have been downsized or know someone who has been. Part of it is the reports about massive downsizings that still come out regularly.

But a huge part of it is that people don't really believe that they'll be dealt with fairly and given new and marketable skills and kept on by their current company if at all possible. In short, they feel usable and used. People who feel like disposable commodities aren't very likely to commit their hearts and minds to the future of an organization.

But it would be as bad as trying to do too much or doing it the wrong way to illude that we can do nothing to inspire people to self-motivation. We *can* knock on the door. We *can* tap into high performance and extraordinary results. And we *can* build a new, mutual loyalty—not the loyalty of a feudal lord with serfs and vassals but the loyalty of two living organisms that profoundly respect and need one another.

CAUSES OF THE ILLUSION

Since we want to do so well in this area of management, what causes us to take too much responsibility, use the wrong methods, or not try at all? Here are some possible reasons:

➡ Since so much of our training—education, on-the-job, books, articles, seminars—drills home the point that it's our responsibility as managers to motivate people, to make something happen, it's hard to get away from this idea (and we feel guilty if we don't try).

➡ Because of uncertainties about what we can expect from or offer to people, we can find ourselves coaxing them like little children rather than meeting them on mature ground.

➡ Because of increasing pressure to get results, we can forget that the path to high performance is indirect (knocking and waiting) rather than soft-direct (manipulating and hoping) or hard-direct (banging and demanding).

➡ For many of us, a less than stellar view of people ("People are lazy"; "People only want to get their paycheck and run") can convince us that we need to light fires under recalcitrant employees.

➡ Propaganda about the success of motivational programs (aided by the fact that they seldom tell us about the *downside* of the programs, the disgruntlement they cause, or what happens when they run out of steam) can lure us into illuding that motivating people is our job and that it's doable.

➡ In frustration, we can remember that fear and insecurity have worked on us, forgetting that "worked on" and "inspired" are two very different things.

➡ Because knocking on individual doors is so time-consuming, we can ignore it because we don't think we have the time or don't want to spend the energy.

➡ Because many people want someone to take care of them, meet their needs, and fix their problems, we can be pressured by their demands into trying to do so.

➡ If we're not certain of who we are or what we're capable of doing, we can be lured into the role of "motivational messiah" by expectations from above and below.

➡ Although the "contract" between employer and employee has changed and "corporate security" is gone, the illusion of job security can be kept alive because people want it so badly and fight to make it a measure of our success as their leader.

At best, we can create an environment where people can hear the knocking and, by their own choice, open up and come out. In the right setting, many will be self-motivated when given the opportunity to improve their own situations. In the long run, that's the most we can hope for. But it's enough.

How to Recognize the Illusion

Rate your organization from 0 (lowest) to 5 (highest) on the following "door knocking" statements:

_____ We provide fair wages (i.e., competitive with our industry, competitive with our local economy, enough to live on) that we'd be unembarrassed to post publicly.

_____ Our pay scale is based on merit and is as objective as we can make it.

_____ We offer additional monetary compensation that is tied to results (e.g., customer satisfaction) rather than performance (e.g., perfect attendance record).

_____ The people who are affected have been consulted and agree with the criteria used for compensation (ask them).

_____ We have a program of consistent, deserved recognition for both short- and long-term results.

_____ We look and plan for many nonmonetary ways to reward people.

_____ Our reward and recognition plans have both general components and components that have been individually tailored to reach employees where their needs are.

_____ We collaborate with people to provide clear, challenging, individually tailored goals that require growth and risk.

_____ We are willing to let people "intrapreneur" (i.e., exercise true business initiative in-house), and we provide time and resources to support them in doing so.

_____ We provide incentives both for coming up with new ideas (whether implemented or not) and for the implementation of those ideas.

_____ We provide continuous feedback to individuals and teams on results, and they are free to do the same with us.

_____ Our people would rate our organization high on the issues of ownership and empowerment (ask them, take the average, and enter that number here).

_____ Our teamwork (task, problem-solving, project, cross-functional) is effective and provides incentives to belong and work toward common goals (again, ask the people).

_____ We have structured our incentive plan to spur individual performance where that is needed and team performance where that is needed.

_____ We provide "inside information" to people so that they will be motivated to make informed decisions.

_____ We provide thorough, deep, broad-based, ongoing training and reward people for learning as much as possible and turning it into something of value.

_____ We do not use fear as a motivator.

_____ We have a strong culture of dignity and mutual respect (ask your people to rate this one; if the average score is less than 4, you're in deep trouble).

_____ We have taken the time to make sure that our organizational vision is a shared vision with our employees that inspires them to extraordinary effort.

_____ We regularly ask our employees what incentives are important to them and then structure general and individual incentive plans to meet those needs and desires.

_____ TOTAL

Shredding the Illusion

Organizational Viewpoints

A critical and underutilized incentive is shared vision. The first step, of course, is to develop a compelling vision as described in Chapter 4. Then we have to fight to *keep* it compelling by making sure that it permeates the rest of the incentive plan down to the smallest details.

Incentives will fail if they aren't in line with the real values of the people on whose doors we're knocking. We have to do the hard work of determining exactly, individual by individual, what will move them to open the door. Some incentives have general application and should be pursued generally. Other incentives—perhaps at times the most important ones—must be tailored to the actual human being sitting in the chair in front of us.

In our opening example, Lori's first mistake in dealing with Sean was to take him and his role in the organization for granted until his performance began to slip. If she had knocked on his door before the problems began, she might have figured out what would make him open it, and the entire disciplinary situation could have been avoided.

After the problems began, Lori mistakenly assumed that the approaches that she had successfully used with others would work with Sean. But Sean was different from the others. Lori's "soft-knocking" methods not only didn't spur him on; they actually annoyed him and led him to lose even more interest in his work. Sean was living by his own set of self-motivational rules, rules that Lori not only didn't understand but didn't even realize existed.

Leadership Attitudes

The best way to shred illusions about incentives is to ask our employees—openly if there's trust, anonymously if there isn't—what it is that would open up the door for self-motivation. We should ask them once every two or three years to list their top ten motivators in priority order.

Then we need to analyze their responses to determine our action. Common responses can be addressed with common incentives. Individual responses can and should—no, *must*—be addressed with an individually tailored incentive plan (and no, we're not talking necessarily about money here). All people are alike. And all people are different.

With wages, we need to list everyone by salary order and then ask the question "Is each person on this list really contributing more value to the organization than everyone lower on the list?" If the answer is yes, we're operating with an illusion-free payroll. If the answer is no, we can take steps over time to rectify the unrealities.

We also need to make sure that we're paying people enough so that they won't think about looking around. "If you pay peanuts, you get monkeys," someone once said. Skimping on salaries is like waiting for the paperback version before buying a book that could show us how to save $100,000. I'd rather have one high-priced dynamo who can't quite get everything done than two half-priced helpers who do mediocre jobs. "We're overpaying him," said American movie mogul Samuel Goldwyn, "but he's worth it."

Rewards are an indispensable tool that have immense power to draw people out from behind their doors. "What gets measured gets done; what gets rewarded gets done well," says the management maxim. The English clergyman George Herbert reminded us that "service without reward is punishment." To believe otherwise is to live in illusion.

Added monetary compensation (e.g., merit increases in pay, bonus programs, gainsharing) that isn't tied to specific results isn't an incentive at all. Effort- and performance-based compensation is focused on the wrong goal. Instead, is our added compensation tied to customer satisfaction? Customer value? Improved quality? Number of innovations? Profitability and increases in profitability? Measurable process improvements (technical or business)? Or is it tied to salary level, number of years with the company, or title?

Whatever the approach, it's absolutely mandatory that the people who will be rewarded agree with the criteria for the rewards. "You have to be careful with the way you manage gainsharing. The programs cannot be run by management; they must be run by employees."[2]

Consistent and deserved recognition is a wonderful and underused way of getting people to open their doors. Bob Townsend told us that "Thanks" is "a really neglected form of compensation."[3] Recognition programs that are fairly administered (as understood by the employees) may open up doors for many of them faster than anything else. Again, a mix of short- and long-term recognition is best.

"Hero/heroine boards" can be very effective. When people go the extra mile, write them a short thank-you on company letterhead, and then copy it to the "board" with another copy to the employee's personnel file. People will read these boards, be thrilled that they're on them, and want to get on if they're not (try to catch everyone doing good during the year). Then group the letters by month. Ask the employees to select the most notable *achievement* on a given monthly list for inclusion on a permanent plaque. It's harder not to perform, and harder to leave, when you have a legacy displayed permanently in a very prominent place.

Nonmonetary rewards are becoming ever more important to the "baby boomers" and "Generation Xers." These rewards can include comp time/personal time, more opportunity (not more work) as a reward for a job well done, and greater visibility (e.g., attending meetings with upper management, participating in a presentation).

These were the rewards that Sean craved. If Lori had given him more freedom to plan his own schedule and a more visible role in the department, Sean's creative energies could have benefited the organization. Instead, he used them to alienate others while he planned how to get out of the company.

Because they demand that we become better than we are today, clear, challenging goals will bring people outdoors (or drive them away). If the goals are doable, the best people will respond. We need to applaud and reward risks taken to meet or exceed goals whether or not the risks paid off fully. A must-have section of the performance evaluation should ask employees to list the risks they have taken in the preceding time period, the results (favorable or unfavorable), and what they learned from taking the risks.

Continuous feedback will make people more comfortable with "stepping out." When we don't know how we're doing, it's a lot harder to keep doing it. Feedback starts with open-book management; we let employees know how we and they are doing, and they let us know how they and we are doing. The two keys to the feedback employees need from managers are *value* ("you're an important part of our future") and *honesty* ("you may not like it, but this is the way things are").

Another section of the performance evaluation should ask employees to list other forms of feedback: bad news they reported fast and their good ideas that were nurtured quickly by management.

When they see that we're serious about incorporating their views and ideas, the stage has been set for a steady flow of helpful suggestions and innovations.

Because most people want to feel that their efforts count for something, a terrific incentive is to give people ownership of their jobs and the empowerment that makes the ownership meaningful. This doesn't mean dumping more work and responsibility on people who have neither the time nor the resources to do a decent job. It does mean involving them in goal setting and then letting them set the methods to achieve the agreed-upon goal. It means fighting like anything to get the organizational obstacles out of their way (we'll have to ask them what they are).

One of the less obvious but most valuable incentives to grow out of true ownership and empowerment is that we no longer waste people's time. Orchestra members, when asked why conductor Sergiu Comissiona was so outstanding as a leader, gave a single response: *He doesn't waste our time.*[4] People will appreciate us in the same way.

If at all possible, we can bolster employees' sense of ownership by giving them *real ownership*. If properly structured, stock ownership can be a tremendous incentive to produce results and to stay with the organization. It gives much more of a sense that "this is mine" than bonuses or gainsharing.

Whenever possible, we should even let people "intrapreneur" (i.e., start their own business within our business). Why let their dreams and ideas die? Or let them take these possibilities to our competitors? Or let them *become* competitors? A design firm allowed one of its designers who wanted to work on projects outside the firm's scope to become an independent contractor while continuing to use the company's office and equipment. The result? The appreciative designer's most creative work was on the projects he did for his old firm.

Effectively structured teams (as opposed to "teams" that are really just groups) can be a tremendous incentive in their own right. With teams, we can appeal to the sense of belonging that most people need, rather than the ever present competitiveness. It's a matter of "motivating one another by appealing to our needs for attachment rather than to our pathological fears of separation."[5]

We can also provide team reward and recognition. It's an illusion to think that we can have effective teams if we only reward individual performance, and vice versa. Organizations that have a mix of individual and team incentive programs are the closest to achieving the organization's full potential. "If people serve together on teams, they must ultimately be paid as team members or they won't work together as a team."[6]

One outstanding way to encourage openness among team members is to reward those who enhance creativity and synergy rather than those who come with and defend their "positions." And we can recognize and reward those who develop teams or develop individuals in a mentoring (two-person team) relationship.

Thorough, deep, broad-based training and learning shred cherished assumptions, in addition to providing an excellent tool for self-motivation and retention of employees. "Training and education are fundamental; if you lose workers to the competition, it's your fault," says Roger Ackerman of Corning Inc.[7] Books, tapes, seminars, plant and office visits, travel—we need to use anything and everything to stir people's imagination and give them a way to see a bigger reality, a more complete truth. Rewarding employees for turning the learning into a value-add to the organization makes the learning even more appealing to them.

We can sit down with each person once a year and do a career evaluation in which we talk about where the person wants to go in his career and what he needs to do to get there. We can then research both training and advancement opportunities for the employee. This is an excellent way for us to fulfill our side of the new "employment contract" in which we promise the employee personal growth.

Our goal here should include giving people a different perspective on "employment security." We need to let them know that as the market changes, the organization must change and along with it the people who make it up. Security for employees comes first from knowing who they are, doing what they want to do and doing it well, and learning constantly. It also comes from adopting and applying new skills even as they drop now unneeded tasks that they are currently doing. Finally, it comes from getting ahead of the curve—innovating, broadening the organization's offerings, and essentially helping to create their own future. Job security, no. Creative employment security, absolutely.

Another piece in shredding the incentive illusion is building and fighting to keep a culture of dignity and mutual respect. We need to recognize how little it takes to affect morale. "A little criticism makes me angry, and a little rejection makes me depressed," said Dutch priest and author Henri Nouwen. "A little praise raises my spirits, and a little success excites me. It takes very little to raise me up or thrust me down." We must pay attention to all the little things, because it's only an illusion that they're little. Bad morale, like good morale, is produced by 10,000 "little" things.

Mutual respect also means recognizing that we're all adults and taking personal responsibility where appropriate, collaborating effectively as it fits. "He treats us like men," said one of the world champion Chicago Bulls when asked what made Phil Jackson such a great coach.

This also means we don't hold people back because "they're too valuable where they are." At its best, we should even be willing to tell a great employee about an opportunity elsewhere that beats what we can offer. When word of *that* gets around, we'll be an even bigger draw for highly self-motivated people.

And you never know. Someday, they might even be our customer.

People Responses

It is very important that we understand what our people are looking for so that they will (we hope) respond properly. When I worked for Hallmark Cards, it was known as a lifetime employment company with a no-layoff orientation. It was a prestige employer (tying in only with excellent concepts like the television specials on *Hallmark Hall of Fame*). The facilities were great, and the benefits, including an extremely generous retirement plan, were extraordinary. Few, it was said, could leave because of the "golden handcuffs" they had on our career wrists.

Right after getting a promotion and a raise, I left.

Why? The incentives the company had in place couldn't overcome the disincentives it also had in place: stifling paternalism; maddeningly slow pace on instituting new ideas and change; procedures for when to breathe and cough; interdepartmental jealousy and warfare; and intracompany politics that could rival those in Washington, D.C. After the enjoyment was gone, the "handcuffs" part of "golden handcuffs" was the part that stood out.

We want to get an inspired response. We need to be careful to determine what specific responses we need as an organization, and then structure our incentive program to knock on the door of those responses. We need to have both individual and team performance incentives. We can't let ourselves illude that one will get the other.

These incentives can be extended to collective compensation for broader groupings than teams. "[The] apparently simple device of pooling compensation is probably the single most powerful instrument for promoting cross-boundary and cross-border collaboration—and learning."[8]

Learning and Asking

In many ways, the biggest incentives need to be offered for creativity. Ideas are difficult to quantify but impossible to live without. We need to reward and recognize people for good ideas, whether or not we can implement them at the moment. A separate incentive plan can be offered for implementation, whether it's done by the original creator or someone else.

So we knock and wait for the door to be opened. We stop illuding that we can whisper through the door or knock it down. We're willing to structure not an incentive program, but an incentive *philosophy* that is so coherent and complete that it becomes compelling to the person on the other side of the door.

And we're willing to put our time, energy, and resources into the plan. If we want something, we'll have to give it.

NOTES

1. Dean R. Spitzer, *SuperMotivation: A Blueprint for Energizing Your Organization From Top to Bottom* (New York: AMACOM, 1995), p. 19.
2. "An Era of Wrenching Corporate Change," *Management Review*, July 1996, 45.
3. Robert Townsend, *Further Up the Organization* (New York: Harper & Row, 1984), p. 224.
4. Reported by Warren Bennis in *Bottom Line/Personal*, July 1, 1996, 14.
5. Jerry B. Harvey, *The Abilene Paradox and Other Meditations on Management* (Lexington, Mass.: Lexington Books, 1988), p. 101.
6. Steven E. Gross, *Compensation for Teams: How to Design and Implement Team-Based Reward Programs* (New York: AMACOM, 1995), p. 5.
7. "Empty Promises," *Management Review*, July 1996, 18.
8. Matthew J. Kiernan, *The Eleven Commandments of 21st Century Management* (Englewood Cliffs, N.J.: Prentice-Hall, 1996), p. 209.

14

Cooperation: "Just Give People a Chance and They'll Work Together"

We are divided anyway and always have been, as any independently minded people should be. Talk of unity is a pious fraud and a politician's cliché. No people worth its salt is politically united. A nation in consensus is a nation ready for the grave.

—Barbara W. Tuchman, *Practicing History*

Michael came to the meeting more prepared than he had ever been before.

He had been asked to lead a design-review team that was supposed to evaluate the current design on an architectural skylight system. The stated goal was to reduce the weight (and cost), streamline the installation, and improve the aesthetics. Michael was prepared to present a plan that, with relatively modest up-front costs for design and retooling, would reduce the weight by 30 percent, simplify installation, and produce a much greater glass-to-metal ratio (which was considered preferable from an appearance point of view). Structural engineers had already approved the design. Michael was excited about the plan.

Barry, his boss—a man with a commanding personality—opened the meeting by saying, "I've thought a lot about this redesign idea. Although it has some appeal, I think the changeover time and costs are going to be gigantic no matter what up-front estimates might show. I'm also very concerned about safety, since we know the current system works but have no idea what'll happen when we go to this underweight system." Barry looked straight at Michael. "We've got a good thing. Why mess with it?"

Several others around the table nodded in agreement. After brief comments from a number of them supporting Barry's ideas, Michael was asked

what he thought. He looked down at his files and drawings, rifled through
them briefly, and made some mental calculations.
   "I agree with Barry," he said quietly.
   Ah, cooperation.

THE COOPERATION ILLUSION

Few things in life are as much of a mixed bag as the idea of "cooperation."

   On the one hand, we should know from experience that we can
often accomplish much less by ourselves than we can when we find
others who'll work alongside us. Few important things in life are done
totally solo. Most great projects require the cooperation of many people to make them a success.

   But we can illude that we can go it alone, as individuals or as
organizations. Our job, our function, our department, our division, our
company, our industry, our economy, our country—all can be thought
of as stand-alone and self-sufficient. Too often we illude that we can
pull ourselves up by our own bootstraps (once we literally try it, we
can see how absurd the idea is).

   We can also illude that competition is the answer to our needs for
growth and change. We can believe that setting people in an environment of fierce me-versus-you confrontation is all that is required to
generate ideas, sales, and productive effort. Forgetting that competition carried to its extreme is called "war," we produce a culture that
devours itself. Competition has a place—but that place isn't the throne.

   Just as we can illude that individuality and competition are sufficient to produce a dynamic enterprise, we can illude the opposite: that
we can get—and should want—continual harmony and near-perfect
cooperation. In this utopian organization, decisions are driven by consensus, and working toward a common goal is the respected mode of
operation.

   But cooperation is a double-edged sword.

   As in the case with Michael and Barry, cooperation is often a superficial mask for compromise and avoidance of conflict. It's the harmony that comes not from working together like a symphony
orchestra to bring numerous virtuosos into a common goal, but rather
from silencing the discordant notes.

   So, although this piece of the cooperation illusion says that cooperation and teamwork are always desirable, cooperation can in fact be
deadly. Dissent—constructive, encouraged, and considerable—may
often be more valuable. "There are discordant sounds within a com-

pany. . . . You must orchestrate the discordant sounds into a kind of harmony. But you never want too much harmony."[1]

In fact, cooperation and dissent may be a powerful one-two punch. It's often a question of timing. We should normally want dissent to predominate during the "forming" and "storming" (brainstorming) phases of a project or team and, although not predominant, still to be active through the later stages to keep us moving in the right direction. We should expect cooperation to predominate through the "norming" (standard-setting) and "performing" phases and, although not predominant, to be active in the earlier phases to keep us from devouring each other.

People understand the importance organizations place on harmony. In a 1996 survey by Dale Carnegie Training, employees rated "getting along with others" as the skill most essential to success.[2] Is this good or bad? Yes. If this answer means "I'm willing to lay aside nonessential differences to get on with it," it's a good response. If it means "I'll sacrifice what I believe in to go along and get along," it's a terrible response. Why is it that "willingness to stand up for my ideas and principles" seldom or never ranks high on skills essential for success?

So we can have the illusion of harmony when what we really have is bogus agreement, a consensus based on fear or avoidance of conflict. This illusion arises partly because "listening to what you don't want to hear is *not* a natural skill."[3] And many managers haven't learned how to listen. People won't try to talk to a person with illusion-based deafness.

A related illusion is that people will work to implement a decision or plan just because they don't disagree with it. But the silent disagreement won't just evaporate. It can come out in many ways: lowered morale, less creativity, resistance to implementation, sabotage of the selected path. Few ideas are as deadly as the assumption that we're all working together on a common goal when forces below the surface in fact oppose it.

The worst form of "false harmony" cooperation may be agreement on "the reality" of one of the fatal illusions. If we agree that we have an open-door policy when we really don't, if we're illuding without dissent that our employees are talking to us about the real problems when they're not, we're finished.

Another piece of the cooperation illusion is that people, given the opportunity, will more or less automatically work together. But telling people that they're assigned to a team and that they'll work in teams not only doesn't guarantee teamwork, it doesn't even guarantee a better performance than if everyone worked alone. "A committee is a group that keeps minutes and loses hours," said Milton Berle.

The reality is that if we give people the opportunity to cooperate but no training, support, resources, encouragement, or correction, they will often work contrary to one another's—as well as to the organization's—goals and needs.

Only taking off the blinders of illusion and realistically looking at human nature and its true potential to cooperate (and at those times when it's not realistic to expect cooperation) will allow teamwork to produce effective results. Only a well-trained, illusion-free team can be a synergistic, effective team.

Illusion says that people like to cooperate. Reality says that we all have our own agendas. Organizations that try to get cooperation when they think it's the natural thing won't do the hard work it takes to get true, powerful, expansive cooperation. Breaking down barriers to needed cooperation is the first and most crucial piece of building a cooperative enterprise, but we won't do it if we're illuding that there are no barriers.

If our whole organization is geared toward individual performance, results, evaluations, rewards, and recognition, we shouldn't illude that we can get a cooperative culture simply by speech making, posters, and sensitivity training. What we get from people is what we tell them—in the daily operational details and in the management processes—is important.

We also can avoid facing the reality that many people don't care as much about close cooperation as they do about tearing others down. They can respond more zestily to gossip, slander, and bad news than they do to truth, harmony, and good news. The absurd magazines at the checkout counters in stores sell huge numbers of copies based on P. T. Barnum's motto, "You'll never go broke underestimating the taste of the American people." Mark Twain said, "A lie can make it half way around the world before the truth puts on its shoes." For all of us, if we're not careful how we listen, it's very easy to believe the ugly things that destroy people's willingness to *sit* next to each other, much less work together.

Speeches by upper management about how "we're all family here" and "I know we all want to pull in the same direction" are pious drivel—at the worst lies and at the best fatal illusions. Saying it won't make it so. It's even worse if we're telling people at the same time that they're on their own in keeping afloat careerwise. You don't create a "survival of the fittest" mentality and get a collaborative enterprise.

This form of the illusion can spill over into our relationships with suppliers and customers. Building true alliances that will work effectively over time is *incredibly* difficult, primarily because each company has its own agenda and would—given the right opportunity or conditions—probably abandon the alliance and watch its former partner sink. Alliances may be the best way, but in the actual world in which we live, they're more often than not a myth.

In some ways, the best partner in an alliance might be a competitor. Here, at least, there would probably be no illusions.

CAUSES OF THE ILLUSION

How can an idea as good as cooperation end up so misapplied and mishandled? Some possible reasons:

➡ Because we live in an age of rapid change, we can conclude that the only stable or trustworthy things are ourselves and the part of life we can totally control.

➡ If we're too proud, on the one hand, or too broken and wounded by others, on the other, we can resist the concept that we need people to help us achieve our goals.

➡ If we've been steeped in the concepts of "rugged individualism" and "competition is king," we can feel that cooperation is sissy stuff, unfitting for a vigorous person or organization.

➡ If we're in an atmosphere of fear and insecurity, we can do all we can to avoid making waves, while at the same time putting a mask (e.g., "team spirit") on our acquiescence in an attempt to keep our image of ourselves intact.

➡ Because so many of us hate conflict and don't know what to do with it, we can end up agreeing *not* to disagree.

➡ If we believe that people are generally and basically good, generous, unselfish, and altruistic, we're almost guaranteed to think that groups will automatically turn into teams.

➡ If we believe that people are generally and basically lazy, worthless, selfish, and self-centered, we won't value their dissenting views, and our demands for "cooperation" can really end up becoming a false front for tyranny.

➡ Because it's such hard work to build a truly cooperative enterprise (in many ways going against the natural grain of many people), it's enticing to believe the things we read and hear about "just getting out of the way and letting people collaborate."

➡ We express a desire to have effective alliances with suppliers, but down deep we believe we can't trust them and that we'll have to fight to get what we need out of them.

➡ We say we're seeking long-term relationships with our customers, but our inner reality is that we're constantly trying to figure out how to make more profit at their expense.

HOW TO RECOGNIZE THE ILLUSION

Rate your organization from 0 (lowest) to 5 (highest) on the following statements:

_____ We plan and work to create a culture where individuality and dissent are in balance with teamwork and cooperation.

_____ We establish clear criteria for determining when decisions will be made by individuals and when they will be made by teams.

_____ We don't permit individuals to build personal empires or use our organization to advance personal agendas.

_____ We encourage and celebrate individual risk taking and maverick behavior that break us out of unhelpful habits and crippling mental models.

_____ We encourage healthy (i.e., constructive and pointed toward organizational goals) competition and discourage unhealthy (i.e., destructive and pointed away from organizational goals) competition.

_____ We carefully identify core limitations and explore ways to let other organizations (internal or external) fill in the gaps with competitive alliances.

_____ We recognize how difficult it is to get effective cooperation, so we spend a lot of energy to get just the right amount of it.

_____ We value constructive dissent and take every opportunity to encourage it.

_____ We deliberately assign dissenters and people of widely differing perspectives to every team or problem.

_____ We dramatically reward and recognize dissent that "saves our bacon."

_____ We stop the presses and reevaluate the project, problem, or idea when we realize that no dissenting or doubting questions are being asked.

_____ We avoid hiring people who don't think they need help and don't value cooperation, or are driven by the desire to win at the expense of others in the organization.

_____ We avoid hiring people who rate too high on "desires to get along with others," who are looking for a "job," or are driven by the desire to be accepted.

_____ We ingrain into new hires our devotion to the balance between the two living ideas of cooperation and constructive dissent.

_____ We find many ways for people to tell us what we *don't* want to hear.

_____ We realistically and regularly assess our people's ability and willingness to effectively cooperate (e.g., by questioning peers and subordinates, measuring results of teams led).

_____ We understand that some people are going to clash, so we find out where this is happening and remix rather than waste precious organizational energy trying to get people to like each other.

_____ We ensure that our value system and our reward and recognition systems are geared toward cooperation with constructive dissent rather than either dog-eat-dog competition or cooperation at all costs.

_____ We teach people in an ongoing way how to manage dissent (not let it get out of hand) and how to manage agreement (not let it get out of hand).

_____ We quickly assess whether conflict is either healthy or destructive, and we take immediate steps to encourage the former and resolve or eliminate the latter.

_____ TOTAL

SHREDDING THE ILLUSION

Organizational Viewpoints

The first thing to work on in shredding the cooperation illusion is to recognize and embrace the dissent that already exists in our organization.

The United States was founded in large part on the principle of dissent—the right to do it, the *need* to do it. We're at our weakest when dissent is stifled. When dissent is embraced, nurtured, encouraged—and, of course, directed and restrained—it is one of the most powerful tools in the manager's arsenal for making things better.

We'll need to work hard to keep from becoming a consensus-driven organization. It's easy for people to give up the fight and just start showing up each day. Coming to work without our hearts is crippling. Without some fire, our organization will freeze.

At the same time, we don't want an organization of isolated, alienated individuals whose contact with others is distant and unmeaningful. This is the seedbed for the growth of destructive dissent and "crush you" competition.

The solution is to balance teamwork and consensus with individual initiative and decision making. Both of these are needed to have a healthy and powerful organization. We can have both by developing clear guidelines about when decisions should be made and/or implemented by teams and cooperative methods and when decisions should be made and/or implemented by individuals and personal accountability methods.

In effect, we need a two-tier system for decision making, in which the first critical decision is how we should make the decision: team decision after dialogue or individual decision after discussion. My experience says that in most cases, the split should be about 10 percent team and 90 percent individual.

One of the key factors in favor of a team decision is the existence of significant core limitations (the opposite of, and corollary to, core competencies) *in* ourselves or in our organization. If we can't get the job done excellently on our own, we'd better collaborate with those who can make the difference.

Leadership Attitudes

We've got to get past the illusion of perfect cooperation and harmony. We don't *want* perfect cooperation even if we could get it. We'd have to give up too much of our fire. We would stagnate. We'd miss the powerful management tool of constructive dissent.

In daily interchanges, the key to utilizing this dissent is to insist that it all be expressed *out in the open*. We have to let people know that if they disagree it's all right to say so. It's *more* than all right; it's critical for the life of the organization. And we have to let people know—over and over and over—that "hidden agenda" or "backstabbing" dissent will be neither appreciated nor tolerated.

In meetings, we have to ask—positively *insist*—that people express their dissenting opinions and the assumptions that lie behind them. The opposite environment prevented Michael from expressing his concerns on the skylight decision. We have to know when to use *discussion* (in which everyone expresses and defends his or her positions for the purpose of coming to a decision) and when to use *dialogue* (open-ended, group "thinking out loud," questioning everything for the purpose of coming to a whole new viewpoint or paradigm).[4]

If we're going to get cooperation from people, we're going to have to eliminate much of the internal competition that so often paralyzes organizations. This can include jockeying for position, trying to get noticed, and backstabbing. Much of this competition comes from the patriarchal, family-style way in which many organizations still operate. If our organizations treat those at the top as fathers (or mothers), how can we not expect sibling rivalry throughout the rest of the organization? Hierarchies *promote* sibling rivalry, while lean, flat organizations with empowered workers promote achievement—and cooperation, *when it supports employees' goals.*

We'll get true cooperation not when we believe that everyone wants to be one big, happy family but when we recognize that we all have our own agendas, our own goals. Then, without illusion, we can devise ways to get people to cooperate on common team and corporate goals by showing them (this showing must *always* be done) how working toward these goals will help them achieve their own.

This means we also have to "trust but verify." The fact is that many people *aren't* trustworthy and are uninterested in cooperation. If we're managing without illusion, we'll have a natural and healthy skepticism that will keep us working on—rather than illuding about—teamwork and cooperation. But since many people *are* trustworthy, and many of the others can be called to a "better self," we need to keep our skepticism ("I'm not sure if we're getting the right kind of cooperation") from turning into cynicism ("I'm sure everybody out there is a selfish pig").

We'll also need to have an effective plan for resolving the often present and brutal conflict that can tear our organization to pieces. In open warfare between individuals, we need to give up the adversary illusion—"Bill, you give your side," followed by "Susan, you give yours." This is a formula for entrenching people in their current positions and can build even more animosity (even if they end up reluctantly agreeing to a compromise).

Instead, we can use the five-question rule. We can have each party ask the other five legitimate, respectful questions that require narrative answers. The other person writes down the questions for answering later. Then each of them privately gives us their answers. At this point, we're in a position to analyze their positions, decide on a recommended plan, secure their agreement to it (in writing, copy to their personnel files), and follow up the implementation. The same process can be used to settle warfare between functional departments (if you still have departments).

One of the best ways to negate unhealthy competition or withholding of information between organizations is to share the rewards of success or the losses of failure.

We also have to ensure that we're not agreeing on a superficial or less than useful path because we've been unwilling to do the work necessary to uncover a *deeper* level of genuine and useful agreement. If everyone down deep agrees that Product A is the best direction but we never get our true feelings out, we can end up "agreeing" that Product B is the right way to go. Less than optimal decisions are made way too often in organizations that won't tolerate (much less encourage) dissent.

We have to realize that one of the biggest cooperation destroyers is the reduction in force (i.e., downsizing, rightsizing, reengineering, streamlining). We can't get people to cooperate with us when they think we're the enemy (because we might sack them at any time) or that their fellow employees are the enemy (because they might outlast them in a shrinking workplace).

If we must cut the workforce, we need to do two things: First, to show we're really a team, we need to cut our own salary (as Lee Iacocca did when he took $1 as an annual salary in the short term and looked for his gain further down the road); and second, we need to do it ourselves. That is, we need to hand all 5,000 people their final paychecks *personally*, watch them cry, and cry ourselves. It might slow us down. And it'll surely make us be *very* cautious before we start adding people pell-mell again.

In his book *Mean Business*, corporate butcher "Chainsaw" Dunlap talks about his "tough" move of ordering a manager to fire someone Dunlap thought to be unnecessary. That's mean, but it isn't tough. In fact, it's downright cowardly, as well as abusive to the manager in the middle. We can expect supervisors to terminate people for performance problems, and we should insist that they do. But if we're just cutting people and it's our decision to do it, we need to do it ourselves. (I also think generals should have to visit the families of every soldier killed following their orders.)

With external organizations, we have to move, at least selectively, from the usual concept of "competitive advantage" to the often more useful "cooperative advantage." We have to make an important part of our communication an openness about who we are, what we agree with, what we don't agree with, what we'll *never* agree with. We have to say, "Here's a place where we can work together," but also "Here's a place where our two cultures are too far apart for cooperative advantage to occur."

Shrewd managers know that the path to success includes balanced doses of healthy competition and healthy cooperation. They know that they need harmony between competition and cooperation, not harmony without competition.

People Responses

People do have some level of need for acceptance and belonging. They respond to initiatives that let them feel like they're part of something that has meaning and purpose. We can create an environment of cooperation that provides for these needs.

At the same time, we don't want them to get too comfortable with belonging. At times we need people to respond as mavericks. We'll need to show them by our own example that success often comes from breaking with the past or present rather than plodding through and bowing before the faddish god of consensus. All too often the crowd agrees but is very, very wrong.

One important way to encourage maverick behavior is to create structures where everyone is forced to exercise some form of leadership (e.g., in projects, teams, work cells). Periodic leadership will prevent the tendency of people in groups to become followers of the strongest personality and regress to an immature level.

Expecting and putting the maverick response to work is doing the best we can with reality. As human beings, we can be very competitive; in countries like the United States, this competitive spirit is woven into the national and individual character. Telling us to be "nice," to forget all that competition and get along, will not work as a general rule and allows all that competitive energy to come out in intraorganizational warfare. With careful direction, we can convert this energy into productive effort.

Learning and Asking

Individuals have their own unique blend of need for competition and need for cooperation. We need to dig deep to find out what the best mix is for each person and make team and project assignments on the basis of that knowledge.

When we learn that people are clashing, insisting that they cooperate is feeding an illusion. Some people just don't like other people. Remixing of relationships is often a low-cost solution to conflict that may never otherwise be resolved, even if we possess good conflict resolution skills.

In this business of cooperation, there are a number of pitfalls we want to avoid:

➡ *Lone Ranger "I don't need anyone else" individuality*. Result: Empire building. Solution: Insistence on common goals.

➡ *Fierce competition*. Result: Internal warfare. Solution: Structured, compensated cooperation.

➡ *Conflict* (fed by illusions about people's "better" side). Result: Mis-spent passion. Solution: Careful assignments and a nonadversarial resolution approach.

➡ *Buried dissent*. Result: Phony agreement or cooperation. Solution: Abandonment of compromise as a first tool.

➡ *Buried agreement*. Result: Superficial agreement on a less than optimal path. Solution: Abandonment of conflict-avoidance strategies and unearned harmony.

When our illusions are gone, we know that the goals are cooperation (earned by honesty, constructive dissent, and effective dialogue) and harmony (the kind that comes from every voice being heard). At best, cooperation can provide the means to accomplish great goals. At worst, cooperation can nullify critical dissent and drown us in an ocean of warm maple syrup.

NOTES

1. Taleo Fujisawa, cofounder of Honda, as quoted in Matthew J. Kiernan, *The Eleven Commandments of 21st Century Management* (Englewood Cliffs, N.J.: Prentice-Hall, 1996), p. 46.
2. *HRFOCUS,* July 1996, 6.
3. Eileen C. Shapiro, *How Corporate Truths Become Competitive Traps* (New York: Wiley, 1991), p. 48.
4. For an excellent discussion of discussion and dialogue, see Peter M. Senge, *The Fifth Discipline: The Art & Practice of the Learning Organization* (New York: Doubleday/Currency, 1990), pp. 237–249 (I have all team members read these pages even if they don't read the rest of this book).

15

Passion: "We Don't Need Passion If We Have a Good Plan"

We may affirm absolutely that nothing great in the world has ever been accomplished without passion.

—Georg Wilhelm Hegel, *The Philosophy of History*

The merger was going to accomplish so much.

Now the company would be able to reach a larger customer base, derive synergy from the combined skill sets of the two organizations, consolidate and streamline functions, lower costs, and even improve quality. Leaders in both organizations, even those who were initially skeptical, had become excited about the possibilities.

So Vic, CEO of the larger of the two organizations, approached the meeting where the merger would be announced to the troops with much anticipation. He thought the move would inject new life into an old, staid team. He was sure the response would be strong, even overwhelming.

And he was right.

The people hated it, loathed it, laughed at it, couldn't believe it. The other organization had been a fierce competitor. It had always been considered "inferior," an opinion that had been nurtured by management. One key member of Vic's management team had left the other group years before with much turmoil, and he had been a consistent and respected voice against it for years.

The reaction was swift and passionate. People who had grown lethargic worked against it exuberantly, both openly and behind the scenes. Vic was lambasted for his role in advancing the merger. He had stirred up so much animosity by this act—as well as by his authoritarian and moody management style—that the fury was directed against him personally, especially after

people realized they couldn't do anything to stop the merger. The new man-
agement, led by an outsider, offered Vic a major demotion—and, when he
turned it down, the door.
　　Vic had learned that passion is a double-edged sword.

THE PASSION ILLUSION

All organizations have passion.

The passion may be active or latent, positive or negative. Vic's
company had no active, positive passion, but it did have a reservoir of
latent, very negative energy. Vic, who couldn't find a way to the positive variety, stumbled into the fierce and vengeful negative passion.

There are many illusions about passion. Our opening story illustrates a number of them: that passion is always a good thing (it isn't);
that actions intended to improve things will evoke positive passions
(not always or even usually); that negative passions won't last in a
professional organization (the half-life can outlast uranium); and that
we can trust our instincts on what people will get passionate about,
either positively or negatively (we're usually not that emotionally
savvy).

Even in the face of intensely negative emotions, we can illude that
we're on the right track, that people just don't "get it." We can believe
that people are, in fact, acting irrationally. But negative passions (e.g.,
anger, rage, disgust, frustration, sarcasm, cynicism) evoked by changes
or new information are a bad but helpful sign, one that we need to
heed rather than attempt to squash or manipulate—and one that often
precedes a revolution.

An increasing level of negative passion is usually telling us that at
best we're not taking the time to present the facts, and at worst we're
showing our hardheadedness in being unwilling to modify or discard
an unworkable mental model. We're illuding at a high level when we
believe we can squelch a roaring fire of negative passions—especially
when we're doing things that add fuel to the fire because we don't
believe there is a fire (or at least won't acknowledge its size).

We make another fatal error when we illude that passion is in
itself bad, that we don't need passion if we have a good rational plan.
This philosophy has led to the creation of many organizations—some
titanic in size—that are so boring and mind-numbing they can make
us long to be back in grade school.

The reality is that many organizations simply won't condone passion. The great homogenization of business and social life that occurred in the 1940s and 1950s held that good strategic and tactical

planning was sufficient to build a successful enterprise. In the 1960s and 1970s, this process was further entrenched by business-school thinking, scientific management methods, and a reliance on cognitive and statistical skills. Only since the 1980s have we seen any widespread attempt to build organizations on a foundation of passion—and still the rational planners live on.

The Soviet Union was, perhaps, the ultimate example of an organization built around rational planning (remember the five-year plans?) and had the ultimate supporting tools of totalitarian power and control to enforce it. The result? Total failure, total collapse, bankruptcy. The only thing the Soviet Union was ultimately successful at was unleashing the angry passions of the people who brought it to its knees.

Just as it's important to match people to assignments that align with their values, so we have to match our organizations with—and stick to—products, services, and directions that we and our people are *passionate* about. It's illusion to believe we can build something enduring with cold rationality. "Genius is initiative on fire," said the English writer Holbrook Jackson. People may not remember the facts of a speech or sermon, but they *will* remember the story that made them laugh or cry. We use facts, but we're driven by passion.

Many organizations seem to draw people who want to be "taken care of," people who don't want to grow or take risks, people who resist being creative or innovative. "Many organizations favor predictability over maverick and innovative behavior because people who do not take risks do not make expensive mistakes."[1] Or at least no new (and obvious) mistakes.

The problem with "filler" people is that they may make the biggest mistakes of all: perpetuating an ineffective or dying system and contributing nothing to future victory. In our efforts to make sure we hire no one who will violate the system, we can protect ourselves from those who can invent our future. We can, very effectively, kill passion at the front door.

This mistaken focus on rational planning at the expense of passion can lead to micromanagement, an approach that by its nature usually kills passion. "Organizations that are overmanaged but underled eventually lose any sense of spirit or purpose."[2] The passion in people has to be harnessed, not annihilated or used up in endless efforts to avoid blame. People need an incredibly high level of freedom and trust in our response before they'll release the passion that can lead to exceptional achievement.

So we illude as leaders and managers when we tell ourselves that we don't have to be aware of or concerned about the passions of those

who work for us and around us. We deceive ourselves when we conclude that it's a waste of time to learn how to interpret and deal with
their emotions and hidden "drivers." The reality is that statistics come
and go, but passions endure to the grave.

This ties in with a corresponding illusion that we can go to the
other extreme and manage or control people's passions. We can manage inputs that will excite positive passions or control negative ones,
and, to a certain extent, we can manage outputs that flow from those
passions, but we can't manage the passions themselves. It's a gross
mistake to try to tap into those passions if we're not ready for what
may erupt.

This is hard to acknowledge, but we also illude when we think we
can really get most people's "loyalty." Most of our employees—
perhaps all of them—would leave us in a minute if they received a
huge inheritance or won the lottery. We can misspend a lot of our time
trying to earn their loyalty, while the path to getting their passionate
commitment to goals is shorter, more achievable, and much more rewarding. In fact, real loyalty can't be gotten directly; in large measure
it's a by-product of a long relationship of mutual passion about common goals.

Every organization has passion in some form. The only questions
are what kind, what degree, and in which direction it will go.

CAUSES OF THE ILLUSION

We can observe and admire passion in actors, public speakers, and
athletes but try to ignore it or crush it in our organizations. Why do
we fear passion at work?

➡ Since passion by its nature is not controllable by others, it can
scare us (whether or not we understand its sources or its potential
value) and keep us from acknowledging its existence.

➡ To many of us, passion and emotion look like signs of weak-
ness or even mental imbalance, which make us uncomfortable and lead
us to avoid or suppress them.

➡ From childhood on, many of us have been laughed at, ostracized, or abused when we exhibited a passionate response or strong
emotion toward a person, project, or goal, so we've learned to keep our
feelings bottled up.

➡ If we have some basic understanding of our own passions on
an issue but fail to recognize the passions of others, we can transfer

our own feelings onto others and illude that they will respond the same way.

➡ We can avoid uncovering negative passions (which continue to grow anyway) because we don't want to spend the time or face the pain it will take to deal with them.

➡ Because positive passions can't be systematized but plans can be, we can choose to take the easy road and rely on what can be documented.

➡ Because people can seem so beaten down, lethargic, and uninterested, we can assume (incorrectly) that there's no fire in the belly.

Passion is *always* present. To deny it is to allow the negative and destructive passions to grow and to permit the positive and enhancing passions to waste away or (at worst) turn sour.

HOW TO RECOGNIZE THE ILLUSION

Rate your organization from 0 (lowest) to 5 (highest) on the following statements:

_____ We are fully committed to understanding the underlying passions that are driving our employees, their decisions, and their behaviors.

_____ We believe that all new ideas and change initiatives unleash strong passions (positive and negative), and we work to understand them in advance.

_____ We are careful not to transfer onto people our assumptions of how they will react.

_____ We don't assume that a nonpassionate response means that there are no passions.

_____ We find ways to harness the positive passions in people.

_____ We constantly search for latent positive and negative passions in people by asking them how they *feel* as well as what they think.

_____ When we uncover or become aware of what people are feeling, we take the time to understand and respond to these feelings.

_____ We have structured our recruitment process to quickly find people with positive passion and to relentlessly weed out those with no discernable passion (or who have negative passions that are immutable).

_____ We work to recognize and quickly respond to negative passions, which can tell us where the organization is sick (and which, if left unchecked, can cripple it).

_____ We give people a passion for victory by focusing only on doing things that we're passionate about and by continually recognizing and passionately celebrating successes, both small and large.

_____ We give people a passion for excellence by never doing or permitting anything that isn't excellent and by avoiding everything that would embarrass us.

_____ We give people a passion for uniqueness by clearly differentiating who we are, what we do, and what we believe in.

_____ We give people a passion for versatility by challenging them to develop all of their potential values, interests, and abilities in a broad amalgam of projects and assignments.

_____ We give people a passion for new things by exposing them constantly to new people, ideas, cultures, books, tapes, seminars, workshops, and assignments.

_____ We give people a passion for effectiveness by letting them be intrapreneurs, build their own successes, earn their own recognition, and leave their own legacy.

_____ We give people a passion for productivity by letting them share in all of the fruits of their labors.

_____ We give people a passion for detail by focusing only on details that are important and by giving people the resources to attend to these details well.

_____ We give people a passion for understanding by making mutual respect, dignity, listening, genuine dialogue, and constructive dissent hallmarks of our culture.

_____ We give people a passion for people by finding ways to make them take responsibility for the development and encouragement of a broad range of their coworkers.

_____ We spend our energies trying to get passionate commitment to goals rather than trying to earn loyalty.

_____ TOTAL

Vince Lombardi said it well: "Those who have invested the most will be the last to surrender."

Shredding the Illusion

The passion illusion may be the quintessential illusion. If we have it, we probably won't be able to generate the organizational energy to shred any of the other fatal illusions. If we shred it, there's a real hope that reality will prevail. "None are so old as those who have outlived enthusiasm," said Thoreau. May none of us live that long.

Organizational Viewpoints

We do need to have good (i.e., creative, intelligent, participatory, and flexible) plans, but plans aren't sufficient to ensure success in our hypercompetitive world. We have to learn how to evaluate and use people's passion, enthusiasm, interest, and "emotional intelligence," as well as their intellectual and learned skills.

Without the passion of the people who will implement our plans, the plans will fail—or at least not achieve all that they can potentially accomplish. This means that we need to build our vision and goals around ideas that all of us can get excited about. "Top-flight performance is not dry and deadly; it is spirited, it is emotion-filled."[3] If people are true believers, they'll fight to win in spite of huge obstacles that block their way. If they don't really care, they'll run when the going gets tough.

We can develop anonymous questionnaires to determine the level of passion our people have about our current products, services, plans, and goals. Anything that doesn't register a collective 8–10 on a 1–10 scale needs to be seriously remodeled or abandoned. The dead weight of unimpassioned plans will drop us to the ground and keep us there.

We can also use questionnaires to uncover negative, festering passions. What people hate can be an incredible driving force and a major destroyer of morale. If these passions are about real problems with our goals, structure, and treatment of people, we can use them as gut-level guidelines for improvement. If we also involve people in a genuine "fix" of the problem, all of that negative passion can be converted to the solution.

We've also got to be very careful not to *introduce* negative passions into our organization. The CEO of one large organization began every meeting with his frontline sales and customer-service people by saying, "Well, business is really lousy" (the business was profitable). Needless to say, the people weren't exactly inspired to go out and give passionate, world-class service to their customers. Many were too busy worrying about their futures.

More than almost anything else, we've got to create a passion-friendly organizational structure. Decentralization, ownership, open-book sharing of information, openness to—no, *seeking out*—new ideas and challenges to the status quo are vital if we're going to avoid being slaughtered. Passion is nurtured by structured empowerment and killed by powerful structure.

Leadership Attitudes

The key ingredient we've got to incorporate at the working level if we're to shred the passion illusion is freedom.

People can't be passionate unless they're free. The only thing fearful, beaten-down, enslaved people can get passionate about is getting their freedom. They'll do this directly, by leaving the organization and encouraging others to do the same. And they'll do this indirectly, by "black market" behavior—flouting company rules, sabotaging plans, and tearing down the company whenever we're not watching. People have died to get their freedom. They've killed to get their freedom. We aren't going to stop that desire—not at the core, not in the long run.

With intelligent questioning, we can determine what our people's passions are and where they align (or don't align) with the organization's vision and goals. Once we understand the passions—which is a *very* time-consuming process—we can find creative and freedom-inducing ways to harness that passion.

For example, we should always select the person who is the most passionate about a project, a new idea, or a change to lead it. Passion will make up for technical inadequacies. If the person is really passionate, she'll probably devote the time necessary to erase the inadequacies.

If a passion is negative, we need to take the time to locate its source, bring it out into the open, and fix the cause or rechannel the passion into fixing the problem. If we really understand that negative passions can only destroy us if we illude that they don't exist or don't matter, we'll *want* to get them out in the open. If we understand how the energy of these negative passions can be converted to solutions, we'll welcome getting them on the table.

This is no Sergeant Friday "just the facts, ma'am" kind of activity. People don't operate just from the facts. If the passions are strong enough, the facts can become irrelevant. And often the "facts" themselves aren't real, aren't accurate, are in reality cognitive illusions. Facts don't stir passion, and facts are usually helpless in trying to stop passion.

Although it is time-consuming, determining people's passions doesn't need to be a complicated process. Simply ask people questions: "What do you hate? What drives you crazy? What would make you do anything to try to change it? What are we doing that's boring our customers? What turns you on about your job or our organization? What *could* turn you on about your job or our organization? What are we not doing that would thrill our customers? What makes you want to start breaking things?"

The passion is there. In a recent study of U.S. managers, although 46 percent said they felt more overwhelmed in their work than they had two years earlier, 63 percent still said they were enthusiastic about their jobs.[4] We just need to open up and throw out our projected illusion of calm, quiet reserve.

The time has come to welcome passion into the workplace. Let it begin with us.

People Responses

It's as essential to find out what people are *feeling* as it is to find out what they're thinking. In a world where a less-talented team with passion can beat an unimpassioned one that on paper ought to win, understanding those feelings may be even more important. This kind of outcome happens all the time in sports. It happens all the time in business, too—just not as obviously, since it takes longer and isn't on television.

We have to accept the fact that a large part of people's responses to questions, ideas, or change initiatives isn't rational. That doesn't mean that it's irrational; it may be, but it's more likely that it's nonrational (i.e., emotional and passionate). This is what Vic got when he announced the merger: a gigantic, explosive, nonrational response. To say that people aren't responding "rationally" is often to say nothing at all. Of *course* they're not. Neither am I. Neither are you.

We need to look at these responses as opportunities, not nuisances. It will require time and patience to hear these passions out, understand them, and provide answers and changes to deal with them. But most or all of that negative energy can be dealt with. Much of it can be converted to something useful.

If we're doing even a modestly successful job of finding talent compared with our competitors, passion can make all the difference. Spending time trying to build loyalty is a fool's errand—we can kill ourselves implementing programs, benefits, techniques, tricks, and semantics, and still get a "9 to 5" mentality and people who'll leave us with little warning and even less regret. But spending our time trying to evoke passion—by finding out what people care about and then getting out of their way—can lead them to real commitment.

Learning and Asking

We have two directions to take in the creation of a passionate environment. On the negative side, we need to find out—continually, persistently, almost obsessively—what negative passions are seething in our people. We need to be ready for a flood of negatives (e.g., they hate the office layout, can't stand one of our key customers and the abuse that customer deals out, feel that firing Stephen was a gross betrayal, are disgusted by all of the boring meetings). We need to give up the illusions that these feelings aren't there or that they aren't important. They are there, and we'll end up dealing with them in one way or the other: directly, by learning what they are and addressing them, or indirectly, by ignoring them and wading through the turnover, internal wars, sabotage, terrible morale, and reduced inefficiencies that are sure to come.

One of the most critical "negatives" to explore is to find out what people are afraid about. Fear always kills passion—except, at times, the passion to kill.

On the positive side, we need to find out what excites people— what will make them come in early, stay late, do research on their own. What do they dream about? Laugh about? What will they fight for? Few forces on the planet are as powerful as passion and desire. We ignore them at our own risk.

What's needed today are organizations and leaders who can balance two competing demands: the need to take enough time to make sure they're not operating out of irrationality or visceral reactions, and the need to throw themselves passionately and without a second thought into meeting the demands of a hypercompetitive environment. We need intelligent people who are willing to fight for—and, in a figurative sense, die for—their ideas.

Notes

1. Manfried F. R. Kets De Vries, *Leaders, Fools, and Imposters* (San Francisco: Jossey-Bass, 1993), p. 76.

2. Lee G. Bolman and Terrence E. Deal, *Reframing Organizations: Artistry, Choice, and Leadership* (San Francisco: Jossey-Bass, 1991), p. xiii.
3. Tom Peters and Nancy Austin, *A Passion for Excellence* (New York: Random House, 1985), p. xx.
4. Reported in *Management Review,* July 1996, 10.

Section III

Shredding Illusions Before They Shred Us

16

Good Medicine for Bad Ideas

When the delusion fades, reality emerges.
—Averil Marie Doyle, *Delusional Relationships:
How They Are Formed, How They Falter and Fail*

*In one of my very early career assignments, I worked for the Lee Company
(the large apparel company) as a production and inventory control analyst.
Although I had a lot of responsibility for someone so young and so early in
his career, there still were three layers of management between me and "ma-
hogany row."*

*So I was stunned when, early in my tenure, the executive vice president
of operations came down to the large, open office area where many of us were
working, walked over to me, and invited me to come up to his office. Visions
of pink slips and lengthy personal time off began running through my mind.
As it turned out, what he wanted to do was to put me on the path of reality
and shatter any management illusions I might be carrying.*

*"Tell me your philosophy about communication with subordinates," he
said, intently staring into my eyes.*

*"Well," I said hesitatingly, "my philosophy [please remember that I had
only one employee reporting directly to me at that time] is to tell her what she
needs to know and only what she needs to know on each project she works
on."*

*His eyes seemed to bore more deeply into mine. I started to squirm.
"Wrong," he said.*

*If this was a test, I had obviously flunked. It was a test, but only a test
of what I believed to be true about managing and dealing with people. It
wasn't a survival test. He went on to graciously explain that people would
only be as knowledgeable and capable as the information that was given to
them and would only achieve their highest potential (and thus help me the*

most) by being trusted as a colleague and seen as an intelligent part of my team.

I got the message.

Several years later, when I had given notice and was preparing to leave for a different career assignment, this same executive vice president called me back to his office one more time. I was astonished (and still am) that a man of his position and responsibility in the company would want to do an exit interview with someone so far removed from him in the chain of command.

But that's what he wanted to do. With no sense of pressure, frustration, or anger, he patiently probed to find out everything that I knew about the organization, both good and bad. He set the stage by his approach, tone, and form of questioning, and I relaxed to the point where I was able to share openly, freely, and without any "bite" to my comments.

It was a phenomenal experience. Somehow, this man knew that if he took the opportunity and handled it properly, the point of exit was an exquisite opportunity to learn a tremendous amount about his organization. This exceptional man didn't want any glowing reports, "acceptable" answers, or "feel-good" comments about his organization.

All he wanted was the truth.

UNDERSTANDING OUR NATURAL BIAS TOWARD ILLUSION

Before we can begin to shred illusions, we need to understand the power of the everyday cognitive illusions that surround us—ways of thinking that give us a natural, built-in bias toward illuding that we can only overcome by tenacious intellectual warfare and soul sweat. Let's look at several of these barriers to facing reality.[1]

Problem Presentation

We can have a hard time getting past illusion on many problems because of the way the problem itself is presented. Operating in illusion, we tend to go to work on a problem and try to solve it *as the problem was originally presented to us.* In other words, the way we first think of the problem is how we try to solve it. This is one of the illusion-causing difficulties of surveys and polls, in which people are asked to respond to a carefully framed question or statement without reference to anything else. The wording becomes supremely important.

Consider the example of doctors responding to the question, "Would you recommend a particular surgery?" If they were told that 7 percent of the patients died within five years of the operation, the doctors hesitated to recommend it. But if they were told that 93 percent of the patients were still alive after five years, the doctors were more inclined to recommend the procedure.[2] The question is the same; it's a 93 percent survival rate either way. We get a different answer just by presenting the problem differently.

This barrier to viewing problems as they really are is compounded by another cognitive illusion called "segregation," where we separate the problem from its contextual setting as we focus on it to the exclusion of all else. The cumulative effect is either to cause us to be frozen in inaction because we don't have enough information or context to give us the confidence to try to solve the problem, or to take only limited action to solve the problem as we've come to understand it.

The solution is to reframe the problem. In their book *Reframing Organizations*, Lee Bolman and Terry Deal suggest that we need to look at any major organizational change from four different perspectives: the structural frame (how we meet organizational goals and needs), the human resource frame (how we fit our people and organizations together interdependently), the political frame (how we distribute power and scarce resources), and the symbolic frame (how we use images and stories to give the organization meaning).[3]

From an individual perspective, the questions we need to ask about a problem with which we are wrestling are as follows:

"Do I agree with this problem as I understand it or as it's presented?"

"Is this a fair representation of the problem?"

"Are there any other ways that this problem could be presented?"

"What are the underlying assumptions that lead to this definition of the problem?"

"What is the core issue that is causing my uneasiness or discomfort?"

"Could others help me frame this problem more realistically?"

As we look at solutions, we need to question further how this particular problem is tied in with other personal or organizational issues:

"What else is affected by this problem?"

"What other issues could or should affect the solution?"

"Who cares about this problem as much (or nearly as much)
as I do and will help me to solve it?"

Solution Standardization

Solution standardization means that we base our judgments on what
we believe to be standard or the norm, based on whatever evidence we
have in our possession. This can lead us to draw conclusions from the
flimsiest of evidence. We see someone driving a beat-up car, and we
draw conclusions about them based on our experiences with (or at
least our impressions of) the kind of people who drive beat-up cars.

We need to avoid words like *standard, general, usual,* and *typical.*
Standard assumptions lead us to generalize, stereotype, and draw conclusions that may be completely absurd compared to the reality of a
particular situation. We shouldn't want to know what's "usual"; we
should want to know what's "real." Ultimately, I shouldn't care if anybody else is struggling with the ethics of a decision that I need to make;
I am.

Categorization

We tend to illude quickly by putting things into categories as soon as
we come across them. It gives us an easy—if illusory—way to deal
with mounds of new data and stimuli. This is the problem of "first
impressions." The old saying "You'll never have a second chance to
make a good first impression" is true. The problem is that first impressions can be both terribly, terribly incorrect and very hard to undo.

As a seminar leader, I've found that first impressions can be
deadly. The person who looks so unapproachable at first sometimes
ends up making the best connection with me throughout the day,
while the person who seems friendly and interested can end up sub-
mitting a low evaluation of my presentation. Sometimes the person
who seems completely "out of it" ends up making the most profound
comment to come out of the audience, while the person who seems so
alert asks a stunningly simplistic question.

We need to suspend judgment for as long as possible. There's no
way we can avoid forming impressions early on, but we can work to
suspend conclusions based on those impressions, and we can continue
to challenge those impressions as we go more deeply into the problem
or relationship. Where possible, asking others what they think of the
situation or person in question can be a tremendous help in broadening our perspective. Then we need to force ourselves to believe what
the reality, the facts, is telling us, in *spite* of our first impressions.

Cause Oversimplification

This problem is common to all of us: We look back only so far to find the cause of our problems. Rather than going back to a primary or first cause, we stop at an immediately preceding secondary cause.

A classic example of this barrier is the reports made regularly on radio and television that go something like this: "The stock market was trading lower today on news that XYZ Company had announced substantial layoffs for the fourth quarter." Are these future layoffs really the reason stocks traded lower on that particular day? The fact is that many traders may not have even known of this particular bit of information, and most or all of the ones who did probably didn't make any buy or sell decisions based on this singular piece of news.

Cause oversimplification can bring great harm to our organizations in the form of resources wasted on noncauses or symptoms. It makes us ripe for any new fads that offer to fix the noncause. This is especially appealing if the noncause is located somewhere else inside or outside our organization. My experience as a consultant is that half or more of all change initiatives are not even directed at root causes or problems.

The solution to this barrier is to wrestle past the illusions of secondary causes to the reality of primary causes. People are leaving our company. Is the reason that people are just no good? Is it that people today just don't stay in one place very long? Is it that they've left because of better pay and benefits somewhere else? Or is it that people simply don't feel that they're treated with respect or listened to on a daily basis?

If we have a struggling and problematic relationship with someone at work or home, is the problem that the person is just expecting and demanding too much? Or is it that we just don't like her? Is it that we're rubbing each other the wrong way because we haven't taken the time to sit down and work out the relationship? Or is it because we feel guilty about something we've done that concerns this person, something we don't want to sort out but that makes us feel embarrassed to be around him?

I try *never* to initiate or authorize a fix until I know what I'm fixing and agree that it's what's really broken. This process includes a rigorous definition of the problem, broad exploration of all of the possible causes, prioritization and examination of the causes, and finally, selection of the causes most amenable to "fixing." Every time I try to shortcut this process, I regret it.

Finding root causes will take us into deep soul searching. The closer the causes are to home and the more determined we are to get the answer, the more difficult it can get. "Ah, what a dusty answer gets the soul/When hot for certainties in this our life!" said the English poet George Meredith.

Certainty and Uncertainty Traps

We can draw erroneous conclusions in our lives on the basis of things that seem certain but aren't true or that are uncertain but unimportant and unworthy of effort.

Before reading on, please read and answer the following question: "How many times taller is the Saint Louis Gateway Arch than it is wide?" (Please round off your answers to the nearest 0.5 times).

I grew up in Saint Louis, and as a child I watched the Arch being built. My answer, whether standing and looking at it, studying a picture of it, or thinking about it, is always the same: 2.5 times. The actual answer? It is exactly as high as it is wide. Exactly. But no amount of measuring and reasoning can change my perception of this gigantic optical illusion.

The same kind of illusions can occur in our minds. We're often at one of the most dangerous possible points when we're the most certain about a particular situation or solution.

We can also be paralyzed by uncertainties *that have no bearing on the problem.* For example, after completing extensive studies, we decide to build a facility somewhere. Then we hear that a competitor may be building a facility very near the location we've selected. We delay our decision and spend time and energy trying to find out what the competitor is going to do, even if we're going to go ahead regardless of what the other company decides. Uncertainty, even when irrelevant to our decision, can become a paralyzing illusion.

At the two extremes of certainty and uncertainty, when the need for a decision is at hand, we need to wrestle. We need to wrestle with our certainty, asking ourselves why we are so sure and asking others to challenge our certainty. One of the greatest areas of danger here is, surprisingly, our own area of expertise; the more we know about a subject, the easier it is for us to illude that an erroneous idea is absolutely correct.

When we are uncertain, we must choose to stop wasting time and move ahead, after verifying that the missing information has no bearing on our decision, even though doing so will produce uneasy feelings in our souls. If we recognize that these feelings stem from a normal cognitive illusion, we can proceed in the face of uncertainty and queasiness to make timely decisions without the expenditure of unnecessary resources to track down information that has no bearing on our decision.

"What If" Roller Coasters

In fiction, "what if" thinking, supported by lots of poignant details, is desirable. The process is called verisimilitude—making it seem real—and it's what good novelists do to give us the feel of a setting or situation. In real life, however, this illusion can cause us to make very bad decisions and go in very unhelpful directions, all because of a problem that exists in no other place than our minds.

We don't have to play the game. We can wrestle with the information given to us and ask the necessary questions: "What part of this scenario is true? Which of these details are real? What's the real probability of any of this happening?" The solution isn't to look for hard data on everything to disprove "what ifs"; in fact, for many of the decisions we have to make in life, hard data are very hard to come by. No, what we're talking about here is refusing to illude by ignoring data that are no data at all.

THE CHALLENGE

Reality doesn't come ready-made and unchangeable. We create our own future reality by our decisions in the present. If our decisions are based on illusion, we'll build a house of cards that reality will eventually knock down. The greater the illusion, the greater the collapse.

Our first step to growth is to commit ourselves to the truth—its validity, its value, its importance for our success. This means that we agree in advance to acknowledge the truth, whatever form it takes and whoever the messenger is who delivers it.

The second step is to face the reality that exists all around us, exposing and abandoning our illusions. This is not an easy task, because we and those around us can build up tremendous defenses against the truth, especially painful truth. In general, the more painful the truth, the greater our resistance to seeing it. Facing reality includes uncovering the perceptions (even the "harmless" ones) that don't align with reality and then working to align them (rather than pandering to illusion with a "perception is reality" mind-set).

Our third step is to build our own future reality, as much as possible, by our own illusion-free decisions in the present and our reality-based plans for the future.

We now look at these three steps in more detail.

Step 1: Committing to Truth

Only truth leads to freedom, correct decision making, and success. An immense amount of organizational energy can be spent avoiding and suppressing the truth. This is surely the essence of folly.

It's critical to build a commitment to truth into our organizational culture, but it takes more than words to do this. Here are six ways to ensure that we commit ourselves to truth:

1. Stop and analyze any time we find ourselves getting angry or resentful over a new idea, a question, or a thought that's contrary to (or that violates) an existing truism. Emotions can be a terrific subconscious clue that something is amiss, and wise leaders listen to the clues.

What's making us respond so strongly? Why are we so tense? If our position is right and logical, why are we feeling so emotional and defensive? Are we defending ourselves against reality?

2. Exercise special care when dealing with major concepts and thoughts that don't fit long-established plans, directions, or goals in which we've made big investments of time or money. Having made an investment can drive us on to "firm up" the illusion and continue to make investments. Discomfort may be pointing the way to a life-saving change. Good scientists search for the facts that disagree with their hypotheses, and we should do no less. The bigger the prior investment, the more vulnerable we are to having a mind closed to changing directions.

Why are we uncomfortable? What can we learn that will make us even more uncomfortable? Whom can we talk with who thinks this is a bad idea? Should we spend even more energy and resources on an idea we've got questions about? Wouldn't it be better to abandon this at the point of 80 percent of full investment rather than get killed at 100 percent?

3. Make a practice of always pursuing the lone fact, the single piece of data that doesn't quite fit, the persistent nagging question. This may be the direction in which reality lies. It may even be where there is an outstanding opportunity that we can exploit. These facts are easier to ignore than the major discomforting concepts, but they may be just as important to our success. The executive vice president I reported to looked at every departure as one of those unsettling facts.

Why can't we talk about this? Are there other data out there that support this? Shouldn't we find out? Is what we're doing so shaky that it can't stand up to scrutiny?

4. Rather than look for consensus (in a world where reality is so hard to see and can change so fast), get very nervous when there isn't even a minor dissenting voice to a decision or direction. Even good ideas can be improved. There is no perfect plan. The ideas or information that can derail a disastrous decision or action often already exist right in the room. All too often, however, they never see the light of day.

How can there be perfect consensus? How can so many unique personalities be looking at this thing in exactly the same way? What do I have to ask or do to break through this obvious illusion? How can we consistently honor those who throw a fit rather than silently acquiesce to a bad idea?

5. Be wary of people who have no questions or doubts about what we or they are doing. Principles endure, but nobody knows everything. "It's what you learn after you know it all that counts," said former professional baseball manager Earl Weaver. Overconfidence always sets organizations up for fatal illusions.

How can you be so sure? Is there nothing that could make you change your mind? Is there no possible and believable scenario where this thing could blow up in our face? Whenever we're in a position where something seems either totally safe or totally risky, we should stop and reevaluate. As human beings, we tend to see things as either risky or not risky, and we can miss the huge continuum between those two points. We may accept either extreme because we haven't pursued possible outcomes far enough or gotten enough insight into the plan. Nothing is totally safe; everything can have unintended negative consequences. And things are seldom if ever totally risky; there may be an unbelievable opportunity hiding under the illusion of disaster.

If this plan is so safe, why is nobody else doing it? Could its appearance of safety mean that there's no real payoff for doing it? Is there really no risk? Could this direction look so scary because we're missing something that would explain or negate some of the risk? How can we reduce the risk? How can we share the risk? Would more thought and analysis make this safe idea seem risky or this risky idea seem safer?

6. *Always* have questions when we're hearing only one side of an argument or one perspective on an issue. An old proverb says, "The first to give his side seems right until somebody else starts asking questions." We've got to be very careful here, because we often will like one person more than the other and will be tempted to give the one we like more (but perhaps illusory) credibility.

Have you talked with anyone who disagrees? What are other conclusions that could be drawn from your data? Would you be comfortable presenting this idea again to a group that may be skeptical?

Commitment to truth should shine through all of the daily details of our work as well as through our vision statement. An organization committed to truth is virtually unstoppable.

STEP 2: FACING REALITY AND EXPOSING ILLUSIONS

There are a number of things we can do to help us face reality and expose illusions in our organizations:

1. Go through Chapters 4 to 15 of this book (which outline the twelve fatal illusions), discuss the causes, and take the "How to Recognize" tests (using them as a starting point for change). Don't rush through the lists. Consider doing one per week (or even one per month) so that people have time to think deeply about each one and really take your organization apart. Think of it as a twelve-step plan for recovery from the drug of illusion. It could be a critical turning point.

2. Use the power of anonymity—questionnaires, surveys, evaluations of ourselves and others, exit interviews—to get at the bad news, the limiting myths, and the fatal illusions. This unbelievably effective tool is almost rusty from underuse.

3. Have an adviser inside the organization who can learn what's true independently (not just from what we tell them) and who is committed to telling us the truth about ourselves. This will help us to avoid the devastating effect of hubris. We need a sentinel of reality. Such a person will be very, very hard to find; once found, he will be worth his weight in gold. We'll need to take steps—including addressing the person's career security—to make sure he won't fudge on the truth.

4. Also have an outside adviser who can evaluate the organization from a different perspective. This has to be a "no baloney" person who is free to get her own information and draw her own conclusions. The power of the "outside look" is incalculable. Boards of directors are supposed to do this, but they aren't usually involved frequently or deeply enough to break through the projected illusions. The outside adviser can be a trusted friend, a fellow leader, or a retired executive. She should be well compensated (in a variety of ways). It will probably be best if she is from a different industry—often we illude that the longer someone has worked in an area the easier it is to see the reality, when in fact it usually becomes harder.

5. Form "Anti-Illusion" (or "Truth") teams on either the company's general direction or on specific projects to force the truth to the surface. The teams can be a clearinghouse (perhaps anonymously) for questions, doubts, and concerns, and they can ensure that all of these make it to our desk. Their goal is to look down the road to see what unreality threatens to make the results ineffective or damage the company. They can be a subset of the larger management or project team as long as they are really free to do their work. It's better to have them operate as a parallel or "shadow" team, an internal advocate for the unpleasant idea. These are *reality* advocates, not devil's advocates—they disagree to expose the truth, not just to disagree. Their reports can be made to the team proper or, if we want the most open input, directly to us. In any case, they have to be independent.

6. Within individual project, task, or problem-solving teams, always give one person the prime responsibility for exposing illusions. Let the person know that you don't expect him to be arrogant, cynical, or obstructionist, but you do expect him to raise all issues and get all questions and concerns on the table with the team. Have him report these things independently to you (don't just rely on the meeting minutes). Don't keep this person's role a secret or let him operate as a spy. You can rotate this assignment so that no one gets singled out or ostracized and everyone learns how to be an illusion shredder.

7. Give up on credentialitis. As we've discussed, credentials are often pure illusion. They prove nothing; in fact, they may mean that the person is locked in to certain knowledge or assumptions that keep her from seeing things in a fresh (i.e., realistic) way.

8. Use one of the most powerful tools in our arsenal to expose illusions: humor. Humor can suggest ways to point out illusion and cut through layers of unreality. It can point out bad (or potentially bad) decisions or directions in a way that serious commentary sometimes just can't do. The wisest kings had a court jester who could (usually) safely point out the things that would lead to stupid decisions, injustice, or revolution. We should be as wise. The importance of having someone on our staff whose primary (perhaps sole) responsibility is to get us to see our illusions through humor isn't always obvious. The humor, of course, should be tasteful and morale building and never tend toward cynicism. This person can exercise his skill in private or—if we're really bold—in a column in the internal organization newsletter or in a section of meeting minutes. We should be *very* leery of people who can't laugh at themselves or at our organization's foibles (and all organizations have foibles).

9. Last but not least, continually ask how current success could lead to failure in the future. Confidence is a very useful attribute, but pride *always* leads to destruction. It's always easier to ask what went

wrong when something doesn't work than to ask what could go wrong in the future when something does work in the present.

Illusions are crouching at the door, waiting to barge in and take over the house. We'll have to be proactive to expose their presence and their intentions.

STEP 3: BUILDING A FUTURE REALITY

We can build our own future reality by shredding the illusions that we expose. We can do this in the following six ways:

1. Go through Chapters 4 to 15 on the twelve fatal illusions, discuss the Shredding the Illusion sections with our team, and evaluate how to implement these sometimes very unsettling changes. This should only be done *after* a thorough review and discussion of the Causes and How to Recognize sections, as outlined in Step 2. You won't fix it if you don't think it's broken.

2. Recognize that illusion will almost always be comfortable and truth will almost always make us squirm.

3. Insist that we all be accountable for our own areas of responsibility, including mistakes—*especially* mistakes.

4. Ensure that victimization and blaming others (the "there's nothing we can do" attitude, which actually disempowers us) have no place to hide in our organization.

5. Resist the pressure—external or internal—to shade the truth in order to give ourselves relief from the pain of reality and of making necessary changes.

6. Value truth as the starting point in every dialogue, discussion, decision, meeting, and announcement.

It's a normal part of being human to buy in to the illusions of others and to build our own illusions from scratch. At the extreme, we can lose all contact with reality, *by our own choice,* and require the strong medicine of spiritual and psychological intervention. The only truly curative medicine at this point is the truth—that we've been living in a world that doesn't exist—and the medicine at this point can be pretty hard to swallow.

But long before we get to this point, the percentage of the time we're living in illusion will determine the percentage of the time that we will be unsuccessful. The medicine is still the truth. It still may taste bad. But it's a lot easier to swallow.

NOTES

1. I received much helpful insight into the cognitive illusions discussed in this section from Massimo Piattelli-Palmarini's groundbreaking book *Inevitable Illusions: How Mistakes of Reason Rule Our Minds* (New York: Wiley, 1994). I recommend it if you want more detail and are ready for a somewhat technical read.
2. As reported by Piattelli-Palmarini, pp. 56–57.
3. See Lee G. Bolman and Terrence E. Deal, *Reframing Organizations* (San Francisco: Jossey-Bass, 1991).

17

Soul Sweat: Winning by Facing the Truth

And see all sights from pole to pole,
And glance, and nod, and bustle by,
And never once possess our soul
Before we die.

—Matthew Arnold, *A Southern Night*

"The trouble is," sighed the Doctor, grasping her meaning intuitively, "that youth is given up to illusions. . . ."

"Yes," she said. "The years that are gone seem like dreams—if one might go on sleeping and dreaming—but to wake up and find—oh! well! perhaps it is better to wake up after all, even to suffer, rather than to remain a dupe to illusions all one's life."[1]

At perhaps several crossroads in our work, we will face the possibility—even the probability—that one or more of our directions are not rooted in reality.

It's the thought that comes back to our mind for the hundredth time and fights to be recognized. For a long while, we've dismissed it or laughed it off. And then, it comes once more. Relentless. Challenging. Offering mainly pain and change, perhaps mixed with a generous serving of regret. Little recommends permitting the thought to linger, much less pursuing it.

This situation represents a kind of crossroad. It confronts us with a choice. We can step out onto the steep and thorny path of honesty and take a huge risk, or we can choose the descending and rose-colored path of illusion. The decision to wake up is critical, much more so than would be apparent based on the speed—mere seconds—with which it can be made or avoided. Depending on which direction we choose, we will find ourselves either facing even greater demands for honesty or facing the much more difficult job of shattering a more deeply held illusion.

As leaders and managers, our greatest calling is to soul sweat: to face the discomforting thought—to pursue it, flesh it out, dissect it, study it, and embrace it as a friend (however unwelcome it may be).

We promote Manny. We like him—he's bright, articulate, humorous, and hardworking. We're high on Manny. And then a thought comes: His numbers aren't quite what we'd expected. It's just a thought. It comes, seemingly, from nowhere. It doesn't fit our picture (read *illusion*) that Manny is a great manager, so we dismiss it. Then, weeks later, another thought: The environment in Manny's department feels a little . . . well, oppressive. People seem sullen. Another opportunity for dramatic organization-enhancing change, but it doesn't seem like it. It's just a feeling, an impression. We dismiss it as well.

When we're finally sitting across from Manny at his termination meeting, we'll have to ask ourselves how many opportunities to face reality at a less costly point (to him and us) we passed up because we weren't willing to soul sweat.

What Is Soul Sweat?

To soul sweat is to say, "Enough."

Enough of what? Enough of letting others define us, enough of living up to the expectations of others, enough of playing games, enough of projecting images, enough of scrambling and clawing for a piece of the pie.

Soul sweat is an exercise in authenticity. To soul sweat is to want to learn who we are, what's important to us, what *isn't* important to us, what things we really want to spend our time and life on.

To soul sweat is to say, "No more charades!" It says, "I'm ready to take this thing called life apart and find out what it really is." It says, with John Greenleaf Whittier, "The windows of my soul I throw wide open to the sun." To soul sweat is to be through with a small view of life, the world, our organization and its possibilities, and our own dreams and potential. It says that skills, abilities, education, and credentials aren't enough. It agrees with L. R. Akers that "Life's greatest tragedy is the man with a 10 × 12 intellect and a 2 × 4 soul."

People who are ready to soul sweat are ready for the rest of their careers and they work to have more impact and leave a greater legacy than what has gone before.

Soul-Sweat Questions

Warning! Don't start on this section unless and until you are ready to sweat.

To soul sweat is to ask ourselves tough questions and give ourselves a lot of time to answer them. These ten questions are the most important (and the toughest):

1. *Is this what I really thought I would be doing five years ago?* One step leads to another, and in many journeys it can be years before we look up and ask, "What? Where am I? I never intended to be here!" It might be very hard to even remember what our dreams were five years ago. It's worth the effort.

2. *Is this really what I want to be doing today?* Once we've answered the first question, we're ready to compare where we wanted to be with where we are. "Is this home? Or am I mismatched?" It doesn't mean I have to leave the organization. But I may need to adjust some goals, lose some responsibilities, delegate others, and create what I always wanted right here. Matching is as important for us as it is for our employees.

3. *Who am I, really?* Each of us is an amazing conglomeration of many experiences, decisions, personality traits, interests, and abilities. "Who is the person under all of that? Whom do I like (list them)? What do I hate (list these, too)? What am I able to do, and what would I like to do that I'm not doing? What is it that I am able to do but hate to do and find myself doing?" Success is in large part determined, and measured, by the pleasure we find in our work. It's okay to enjoy it. It's *critical* that we enjoy it.

4. *What are the values that I hold dear?* "What's really important to me? What am I doing that makes me feel worthwhile? How can I do more of those things? How can I extend these values into the organization? How can these values connect with, and inspire, others in the organization?" At the end of our lives, values are the only thing still standing.

5. *What unmet needs are causing me to do the illusory things I'm doing?* Unmet needs are powerful undercurrents, driving us along but largely unseen. "My children are acting in a rebellious way, and it hurts. Could this be why I'm instituting so many rules at work and spending so much time on issues of control?" "I don't really feel cared about by my family and friends. Could this be why I'm so anxious to have people in my organization like me and why I'm so unwilling to have conflict—even if it's constructive?" "I feel like a failure in my personal life. Could this be why I'm driving the people in my organization so relentlessly toward perfection?" "I feel like I have to achieve before people will like me. Could this be why my feelings for people in our organization rise and fall based on their performance?" Think long and deep about your unmet needs.

6. *What have I contributed to my own problems and dissatisfaction?* "Am I really ready to break out of the blame game and take responsibility for solving my own problems? Am I ready to admit that satisfaction isn't something that happens when the world straightens itself out, but instead comes both from deciding to solve my problems and from having them faced and solved?" I remember clearly when I came to the conclusion that, although others certainly had contributed to my difficulties, I was the one who had to solve them. They were mine to resolve. I didn't like the feeling at first, but reality started feeling pretty good after a while.

7. *Do I have the right combination of interests, skills, and background to be able to do what I need to do well?* Admitting deficiencies is never easy or enjoyable (although I've come to feel that one sign of maturity is the ease with which we can do it). "Maybe I *don't* really know what drives people internally; well, I *ought* to, so . . . Stop! Who cares what the 'oughts' are? If I don't know, I don't know. Maybe taking a course in psychology at the junior college will help. But *wait!* I'm almost forty-five . . . Stop! Who cares?" (As my daughter said to me, "You're going to be forty-five whether or not you take this step.")

8. *What am I doing that makes me feel awful?* "Awful" is a clue. Whether it's a destructive relationship, an addiction, or a ruinous habit, if we end up with an empty or sinking feeling, it's probably taking us down a road that leads to the disintegration of our personality. This is far different from "if it feels good, do it"; this is "if it feels bad, stop"—unless it feels bad because it's a painful truth. In that case, keep going. The awful feeling will pass.

9. *How do I respond to pressure?* I have come to see this as one of the most crucial questions of life. Answering it honestly can give us an unimaginably deeper perspective on our lives. "Do I crack? Do I become angry or abusive? Do I pass the pressure along, crushing others? Do I escape through some less than helpful means?" Few questions will give us more helpful insights into who we are and what makes us tick.

10. *Is our organization a representation of what I believe, value, and care about?* I have worked with and for organizations that I, in truth, did not respect. The right answers are either:

➜ Fight like the dickens to make this organization worthy of staying around.
➜ Get the dickens out of there.

The first is always preferred, because we're there and owe the company an opportunity to become a reality-based organization.

Coming up with the right (i.e., nonillusory) answers to these questions will take soul sweat, but you'll like the look of that person in the mirror when you've shed all those layers of unreality.

SOUL-SWEAT PATHWAYS

There are some pathways that we can take in the process of soul sweating, of finding our way to the deepest level of reality in our own lives, as we cast off illusions.

1. *Nurture, but question and hone, emotions.* Many of us grew up being taught (and believing) that feelings are untrustworthy. Others swing the other way and make big decisions (sometimes spontaneously) on the basis of their feelings. The first group produces teachers and writers who like rational planning and scientific management. The second group produces teachers and writers who like gut instincts and intuitive management. The reality—as with most things—lies in the middle. Emotions are that subterranean, visceral, this-is-who-I-really-am voice that needs to be listened to. They are an incredibly valuable tool. But they are unformed and, in some cases, misformed. We need to pull them up on the screen, where we can question them, refine them, draw them into a realistic picture of ourselves. If we follow and explore any emotion, we'll learn a lot about who we are. We'll also be helped to shred the illusions about who or what we aren't (e.g., we think we're quiet and understanding, but we follow the trail of impatience and inner rage and . . . oh). Emotions aren't bad. They just need some work—and sweat.

2. *Toss things overboard.* A willingness to suffer loss is a key tool in effective soul sweating. We can be easily derailed in a quest for an illusion-free existence by the fear of what we'll lose if we're honest. But if we can hold on to something only if we live an illusion, how real is it, anyway? Is it really going to benefit us in the long run? Are we probably going to lose it anyway (since it isn't based in reality)? Giving it up will cause us to sweat. But the end result will be peace.

3. *Give up victimhood.* Giving up victimhood means getting out of the blame game and trying to find reasons "out there" for why we're in the position we're in, doing the things we're doing, or relating to the people with whom we're relating. *It's our choice how we live.* To be a victim is to be disempowered. We've talked about empowering our employees; it is just as critical to empower ourselves. We do this by assuming responsibility for our own lives from this point forward and by choosing to stop waiting for other people in our organization or personal life to _____ (change, leave, have a change of heart, die). If it's their fault, I can only cry; if it's my fault, I can sweat.

4. *Talk less, listen more.* If we want to learn more so that we can grow more, the key is listening and asking questions, not talking. As any person who has been interviewed knows, the person asking the questions controls the conversation. We actually are more in control of the learning process when we're asking questions and listening than when we're talking. The fact is, average people say what they know, fools say more than they know, and wise people say less than they know. Listening allows us to detect the errors that can lead us into mental tunnels and deep illusions. If we listen deeply, we'll spend a lot of time sweating.

5. *Read more and differently.* Exquisite knowledge is available to us if we'll only search for it. The key isn't to read what confirms us in what we already believe (many book clubs make a living telling us what we're already illuding about) but rather to read what makes us uncomfortable. To soul sweat, we need to pursue and explore the thoughts, ideas, and information that make us uncomfortable, that force us to rearrange our mental models, that cause us to remap the way we look at our lives, organizations, and the world. The goal is to eliminate the bondage of seeing things from only one point of view. I try not to read anything anymore unless it makes me rethink, rearrange, redo—and sweat.

6. *Find a friend who will make you sweat.* Try to sit down at least once a week with someone who is willing to ask you the kinds of questions that will make you sweat. Even if you agree not to answer all the questions, you should free this person to ask every question that comes into her mind. Honest wrestling with these questions—especially the ones that do things like infuriate us, make us feel self-contempt, or fill us with regret—is worth pursuing in our own quiet times. It is not for nothing that someone once said, "Write down the advice of him who loves you, even though you like it not at present."

Better than one friend would be several, so that there's less chance we can either successfully project an illusion or be trapped by the illusion of another person. This personal board would be "like a set of tribal elders that you turn to for guidance at times of ethical dilemma, life transitions, and difficult choices, people who embody the core values and standards you aspire to live up to."[2]

7. *Give up taking credit.* The fight to be noticed and to get the credit that is due us can consume a lot of energy that could better be spent on self and organizational development. It causes a lot of sweat, but none of it really advances our souls. Freely give the credit for successes to others. One president had a sign on his desk that said, "There is no limit to the amount of good a man can do if he doesn't care who gets the credit." Warren Bennis says, "A good leader never takes credit. I have found that the people who most quickly gain trust, loyalty, excitement and energy in an organization are those who pass on the credit to the people who have really done the work."[3]

Or, as Paul "Bear" Bryant, the legendary football coach at the University of Alabama, said: "If anything goes bad, I did it. If anything goes semi-good, then we did it. If anything goes real good, then you did it. That's all it takes to get people to win football games." If I give up taking credit (or trying to figure out *how* to take credit), I can focus my attention on the really important issues. Being noticed, at long last, doesn't amount to much and isn't very soul-satisfying. Being real— being authentic, being generous? That's worth everything.

THE PROCESS OF SOUL SWEATING

There is a process that can be used to facilitate the asking of the soul-sweat questions and the proper taking of the soul-sweat pathways. This process includes these steps:

1. *Retreat.* For years, I never took a concentrated period of several days to get away from the stress and pressures of everyday life in order to ask and answer the important questions. My experience is that this process needs to occur at a minimum once a year, although twice a year or even once every three months would certainly not be too much or wasted. The time frame probably needs to be at least three days: the first day to unwind and begin to think in deeper terms; the second day for really digging in to the questions and getting some early answers; and the third day for drawing some tentative conclusions about changes and new directions. Plato said, "The unexamined life is not worth living." What good will it do us to miss those possible retreat times and just keep growing further in our illusions?

2. *Meditate.* There is nothing spooky or mysterious about meditation. It simply means that we take the time to get quiet and ask ourselves the hard questions about the hindrances in our lives. These hindrances can be illusions about our philosophy, relationships, circumstances, or habits. Meditation will have its best effect if we decide in advance not to dodge a single uncomfortable thought.

3. *List.* We can make a list of all the things that we suspect may be illusions in our own lives, our relationships, and our ways of thinking and doing. At this point, we need to write everything down, regardless of where the thought comes from or whether there's really a problem. This is a time for total honesty with ourselves. We especially need to pay attention to those subterranean feelings that may represent discomforts or fragments of an idea.

4. *Review.* We can go back through our list of questions and thoughts and begin to write down possible reasons these things may be illusions. At this point, we're not trying to produce a report; rather, we're trying to produce information in written form on which our minds and hearts can feed.

5. *Prioritize.* After we've spent some time reviewing our list and analyzing it, we should put the list in priority order, based on the illusions that are causing us the greatest harm. This is not an exact science, so we don't have to be too concerned about whether all of the details are in exactly the right place.

6. *Study.* Next, we can take the first item on our prioritized list and review resources (e.g., books, audiotapes, videotapes, magazines, novels, Internet information) that can give us more insight into it. If we're at home, we can use our own personal library as well as the public library and bookstores. If we're at a quiet retreat, we can, in advance, carefully select and bring along a stack of books with the understanding that we may not ever look at a large percentage of them. We can also make notes for further study when we get back home. So many illusions, once listed and prioritized, can begin to be seen for what they are after quiet study with authors—experts who have studied the particular illusion, and people who have suffered to break free from it in their own lives.

7. *Write.* We should make sure that we have a notebook where we can list the first item on our prioritized list of illusions and then begin to jot down our findings. The goal is to write things down as we think of them, not try to make it read like a book for somebody else. We can list not only the illusion and its causes but also describe the consequences, including the pain, that we see this illusion working into our lives. We should leave some room to add the specific ways that we will need to change our thinking and actions to shred the particular illusion.

8. *Share.* We can take our prioritized list and our notebook to our trusted adviser (or adviser board) and share what we've learned. This probably should happen very shortly after the retreat, perhaps as early as breakfast on the morning after the end of the retreat. We can ask the adviser to be honest with us about our blind spots—anything we've left off our list, our prioritization, the thoughts that we've accumulated in our study, or our proposed changes to shred the illusion. It is very critical that we do all of the earlier steps before we begin to share with someone else. We have to sweat first.

Few efforts in life—perhaps none—are as important as this process of soul sweating.

To sweat or not to sweat?

Soul sweating is time-consuming, difficult, painful, and at times unpleasant. It requires a commitment to the truth, a willingness to shred even long-held and cherished illusions, and a decision to build our lives based on reality.

It's not easy, but the alternative is fatal illusion.

I'll take the sweat.

NOTES

1. Kate Chopin, *The Awakening* (1899; reprint, New York: Barnes & Noble, 1995), p. 157.
2. Jim Collins, "Looking Out for Number One," *Inc.,* June 1996, 29.
3. "Lessons in Leadership From Superconsultant Warren Bennis," *Bottom Line/ Personal,* July 1, 1996, 14.

18

Dealing With the Illusions of Others

Most of us are not very skilled at detecting deceptions or the underlying motivations for actions; perhaps even more troubling, most of us are not nearly as good at such detection as we think we are.

—Howard Gardner,
Leading Minds: An Anatomy of Leadership

Sarah's boss had really blasted her.

Sarah had been crossing swords with Jean for days, as they worked together to keep the office functional during a major renovation. Jean's temper, always on the verge of going off, had been going off continually.

Sarah had asked for the afternoon off to tend to some personal business. She gave Jean an update on office activity before leaving. When Sarah got home, she found a raging message from Jean on her answering machine. Jean accused her of leaving when she was needed (in spite of Sarah's having gotten clearance), not being responsible, and (in the lowest blow) not being honest about the work that needed to get done that afternoon.

Sarah was rightly furious. She saw the illusion that Jean was operating under, the illusion that she could treat people badly and still have them stay around, much less stay around with good morale. The turnover rate in the organization had, in fact, been astronomical. Sarah now understood why.

Sarah stormed around her apartment. She intended to call Jean that evening to fight the thing out, or at least to ask for a meeting to do it the next day. She was sure the truth would wake Jean up. Sarah called a friend, told her the story, and expected sympathy. She got the sympathy but also something she hadn't asked for.

A reality check.

"I wouldn't do it when you're so angry," her friend advised. "And I wouldn't do it when she's so angry, or during the workday when the tensions

are running so high. You could both say and do things you'll regret later. I
suggest you catch her for coffee over the weekend."

Sarah started to protest but then began to see that Jean hadn't been the
only one operating with illusions. She took her friend's advice and lunched
with Jean on Sunday. She not only got the problem cleared up but reached a
whole new level of understanding and connection with Jean.

Although their relationship after that still required hard work, the pattern had been set: no illusion.

THE WAR

The quest for an illusion-free existence is not an easy one. In many
ways, it's a war—complete with sabotage (of self), ferreting out the
enemy (illusion), and shredding the enemy by constant and costly attack.

We have to begin this war with ourselves, as we discussed in
Chapter 17. We have to ensure that we ourselves aren't operating under
crippling illusion before we'll be ready to take on the illusions of others. Sarah's friend had to deal with Sarah's illusion before Sarah could
effectively handle Jean's. Sarah's own illusion about the best way to
handle confrontation with Jean was the obstacle she had to overcome
before she could tackle Jean's illusions about the best way to handle
people.

But we do have a responsibility to tackle these illusions. We have
to try to keep the views of others based in reality—for their sakes, as
well as ours and the organization's. We should go in expecting a war,
expecting others to disagree with us and to fight against reality, expecting a lot of pain (both ways) in the process. If we don't understand that
it's a war and act accordingly, we'll give up as soon as people's resistance seems too strong or their pain too intense. But allowing people
to remain unchallenged in their illusions may prove disastrous for our
lives and careers.

We also need to count the cost of fighting the illusions of others
and decide if we want to pay it. The cost can be very high. At the same
time, we have to count the cost of *not* fighting people's illusions. The
cost of inaction may take a different form, but it could be just as
high—or higher.

Jack could see that it was time to sell the business. He had stopped
the organization's long downward slide, but the market had changed,
and SRP Corporation didn't have the internal resources to meet the
changing demands. Jack, the general manager of SRP, went to the
owner and laid out his concerns.

Jack told Mr. Edwards, who was nearing retirement age, that SRP wasn't in a position to keep up with the market, retain current customers, or acquire new customers in new fields fast enough to remain profitable and viable. He also indicated that there would have to be substantial reorganization with new people in new slots if the corporation was going to try to meet these new conditions.

Mr. Edwards protested. He thought the organization was viable, wanted to carry on with it until he retired, and had long dreamed of passing the business along to his successors. He told Jack that he was way out of line. Jack, who had analyzed and agonized over the numbers and possibilities for months, persisted in the face of the owner's certainty, which was out of touch with the actual situation the company faced.

After more intense dialogue, Jack told Mr. Edwards that he would personally be looking into other opportunities and that if Mr. Edwards wanted to continue to operate the business, he would need to find a new general manager. Due to their long-standing relationship, Jack gave indefinite notice so that Mr. Edwards would have plenty of time to find a replacement. If Mr. Edwards wanted to sell, Jack offered to handle the negotiations.

Mr. Edwards decided to sell. Jack began the process of seeking out buyers and ended up with three legitimate offers. The negotiations went well, and Jack sold the corporation for a princely sum twenty times more than Mr. Edwards's family had told him they hoped he would be able to get. With their retirement secure, Mr. Edwards and his wife were able to travel and enjoy other amenities that they hadn't previously been able to afford.

Jack hadn't negotiated any fee for handling the sale of the business, but he had assumed, on the basis of other discussions and of their relationship, that Mr. Edwards would pay him somewhere between 8 percent and 12 percent of the proceeds of the sale. Jack oversaw the transition to the new owners, served as a consultant to the business for several months, and then moved on to other opportunities. He was stunned, after quite a period of time had passed, to realize that Mr. Edwards wasn't going to pay him a brokerage fee—or even give him so much as a simple thank-you.

Years later, Jack learned that Mr. Edwards was telling mutual acquaintances that Jack had "forced" him to sell the business by threatening to leave unless the business was sold. Worse, Edwards was telling people that it was Jack's fault that the business had been struggling. Edwards was portraying the sale as essentially a theft of his life-long dream, and his resentment toward Jack showed. Jack tried to discuss the reality of the situation with the Edwardses, but they refused to listen. The anger and slander eventually reached such a level that Jack began avoiding social gatherings where the Edwardses might be present.

The chasm between the two men's views eventually led to a complete rupture in their relationship. Mr. Edwards's illusions were that he was a victim, that he hadn't agreed to sell the business but rather had been forced, that he would rather have had a failing business and a small salary as he and his wife grew older than a huge payout upon completion of the sale, and that Jack had done all of this to hurt him. Mr. Edwards was illuding at high levels, even though Jack's pushing through Mr. Edwards's illusions had given Mr. Edwards a security in retirement that he would never have otherwise attained.

Jack learned the hard way that other people's illusions can have a devastating impact on our lives. Although he was upset that Mr. Edwards had turned the truth upside down and was slandering him, he still knew that the steps he had taken were the right ones. He also learned from analyzing his own illusion that he should not optimistically but unrealistically assume that an illusion-filled person was going to pay him or thank him for shredding those illusions. In his future negotiations, Jack always had what he expected written into a signed agreement.

Although there's no guarantee that others will ever be willing to shred their illusions, we need to do what we can to point them toward reality. There are a number of steps we can take to do this.

STEP 1: RECOGNIZE WE'RE NOT IN CONTROL

We have to recognize that we can't make people give up or even modify their illusions. People will change only if they choose to do so. They may act as if they agree, but if they don't really want to change, their agreement to discard an illusion will *itself* be an illusion—to us.

We'll be able to accept this fact if we understand that there is no "out of the blue" in the thinking and acting processes of human beings. Everything we say and do is either an overflow of what's going on inside us or a reaction to an external stimulus *based* on what's going on inside us. Illusions take a long time to develop. If we can only try to see how long an illusion might have been in the making, we'll see the deep and painful process that will be required to address it. "It isn't that they can't see the solution," said G. K. Chesterton. "It's that they can't see the problem."

As part of this first step, we have to accept the fact that our desire to see people change has to be balanced with our respect for their right to make their own decisions. Jack, for example, left the decision to sell or continue with Mr. Edwards.

To laugh at the illusions of others and their inability to quickly shred them is to not only deny what it means to be human but also to express incredible arrogance—since we, too, can tightly clutch illusions that others could perhaps easily shred.

STEP 2: MAKE SURE WE'RE NOT CO-ILLUDING

The second step in helping to rid people of their illusions is to make sure that we ourselves aren't joining in the same illusion. For example, it's all too easy to illude that fear is an effective long-term motivator for high achievement. But to threaten a subordinate as a way of stopping him from threatening his subordinates because "fear isn't the way we do things" is a hypocritical participation in the very same illusion. We can very easily share in illusions and not see that we're doing it.

This is a human and everyday phenomenon. We shout at a child to stop shouting at a sibling because it's disrespectful. We tell a friend that someone's a terrible person because she speaks negatively about other people. We say that we wouldn't put up with an intolerant person for even a minute. "There are two things I hate," one man said, "people who tailgate me and people who go so slow I have to tailgate them."

The fundamental question to ask and answer honestly is this: "In what ways is what I'm doing similar to what they're doing?" The details may be different, but often there are core similarities. We've got to sort those illusions out and stop buying into them before we're ready to tackle them in others. (As a parent, I've been long convinced that the things that drive me the craziest about my children are the things that so—unfairly, of course—remind me of me.)

We've also got to acknowledge that others can draw us into their illusions. Illusions are seductive; therein lies their power. It's the truth that usually looks nasty.

This sharing of illusions can come by invitation. The frequent call to "work together," be a "team player," "learn to get along," and "labor toward a common goal" can add the avoidance of loneliness and separation to the avoidance of confrontation and pain. We've got to learn to dread quick assent rather than thoughtful dissent.

We have to be especially careful when people are giving us sob stories and excuses and generally acting like helpless victims. They're setting us up for a purchase of their illusions. Early in my career I hired people who would wax on about how awful and abusive their last boss was. After managing them, I could understand what it was that might have driven their previous boss to abuse.

This "sharing" of illusion is at its worst when it becomes part of the landscape, a permanent set of stereotypes. We "agree" that hierarchical decisions are the best way, so you don't challenge what we're doing after I've made a decision, even if you think it's wrong. We agree that we can't expect too much of those who work for us, so I don't challenge you to your best efforts and you don't even try. "One stereotype is dependent on another to maintain it."[1]

STEP 3: PICK OUR SPOTS

We've got to take enough time to correctly decide when to intervene and when to hold back. We can't take on every illusion of every person with whom we come in contact. Illusions are too prevalent. We've got to take the time to determine which illusions are potentially *fatal* and devote ourselves to those.

Key questions to ask (but *never* as a cop-out):

➡ "Does this illusion really warrant intervention?"
➡ "What's the worst thing that can happen if I don't intervene?"
➡ "Is this person really ready to hear what I have to say?"
➡ "Would this be better handled by someone else?"
➡ "What's the best way to present this?"
➡ "Am I sure I'm not doing the same thing?"
➡ "Am I really ready to fight this war?"

STEP 4: DEVELOP A BATTLE PLAN

We've got to have a battle plan that looks something like this:

1. Approach the person one on one. Attacking an illusion in front of others is a counterproductive and illusory approach. It usually entrenches others in their illusion and causes them to stoutly defend themselves. The private approach, if used with patience and respect, can shred many illusions. It's important that we go into the meeting open to the idea that we ourselves might be dragging illusions into the room. The best tone for this meeting is humble, patient, caring, and soft-spoken. "A compassionate word can break a bone," says an old proverb.

2. If that meeting fails, we should take along one or two others to meet with the person. The selection of people to bring is critical—they have to be people perceived as neutral (i.e., not there to help us hammer the other person) and fair. The attitude with which we approach the conversation is also very important; the atmosphere has to be cordial, rather than accusatory or judgmental. Our purpose is to let the person see his or her illusion from as many different angles as possible.

3. If the first two steps aren't successful and the illusion really is fatal, it will be necessary to take major intervention steps: in-depth discussions at team meetings, removal of the person from all related decision-making roles, and possibly even termination. It makes a lot more sense to let people go because they're carrying an illusion that's fatal to the organization than because they've missed a performance goal or been absent too many days.

At each of these three steps, we have to remember that our advice will be *very* easy to ignore. We'll have to avoid the lecture and work with probing questions, such as these:

➡ "Do you agree that this might be an illusion?"

➡ "What parts of what we're saying don't you agree with? Why not? What parts are you uncertain about?"

➡ "What about our comments makes you the most uncomfortable? Why?"

➡ "What in your reaction do you think is coming from old mental models or an emotional response based on past negative experiences?"

➡ "If you agree that this could be an illusion, what are the three main things that would keep you from admitting it or shredding it?"

➡ "What's the worst thing that can happen if you don't change direction?"

➡ "What's the best thing that can happen if you do change direction?"

Again, we've got to remember that we can't shred the illusion. We can, if we're not careful, shred the *person*, but only the person can break the power of the illusion. Our care and truth are catalysts, necessary but insufficient ingredients in a very important process. But it will work only if the person is ready to listen.

STEP 5: ENCOURAGE PROACTIVITY

In this final step, we should suggest to people that they take some proactive steps to shred fatal illusions. This includes:

➡ Reading this book as a team and together taking the "How to Recognize the Illusion" test in each chapter.

➡ Having a "truth partner" (someone who cares about them enough to make them uncomfortable) both inside and outside the organization, as discussed in Chapter 16. The insider should be from some other department.

➡ Periodically assigning people to doable work that isn't within their normal range of duties.

➡ As opportunities arise, assigning people to work that is demanding, challenging, and difficult for them to relate to (given their current mental models) and refusing to bail them out if they get stuck. The goal is to force them to approach an assignment without any of their current grids (or illusions) there to support them as crutches.

➡ Developing training based on the "How to Recognize the Illusion" test in each chapter in order to establish an illusion-shredding environment with all new hires.

➡ Rotating people in monthly or quarterly stints as your organization's "anti-illusion monitor."

➡ Assigning readings (articles, books) that will broaden their perspectives in general or challenge suspected illusions and having them report in writing the major points, what they agreed with (and why), and what they disagreed with (and why).

➡ Taking time to share with them what you're dealing with and why you're having to make the decisions you're making. A dose of your reality might help them see the organization's challenges and opportunities much more clearly—and they might even have some good ideas for you.

➡ Having people share their outside experiences with the group, with the additional requirement that they make practical application of what they've learned to some current situation in the organization. (For example, "We ordered room service and they told us it would take fifteen to thirty minutes. It was almost an hour and a half. In that last hour, all of the goodwill went down the drain. We started bringing up other negative things that hadn't even seemed to register with us before. We could hardly say anything nice about the place. It was all I could do to give the guy who brought our meal a tip. Then I remembered how one of our primary customers got so mad at us when we were late on one shipment and threatened to take his business elsewhere. We all thought he was a jerk, but now I understand.")

➔ Making "student exchanges" with other managers—sending some of your staff for several weeks into another department and taking some of the other department's staff into yours *to do actual work.* You'll hear a lot less about how "stupid" or "incompetent" people in other areas are. Any loss of productivity in your department should be more than offset by the loss of illusion in the people who'll come back to you and the fresh ideas you'll get from the staffers loaned to you. And *don't* wait for the organization to initiate this or adopt it as a program (just do it and watch the illusions die).

➔ Doing the same with your customers and suppliers. Agree on educational and informational people exchanges, with the purpose of making both organizations more intelligent and more collaborative. "The people we send over there might leave us!" you say. But think how much better your customers and suppliers will be. And how much more understanding of you and your needs, assuming the people who leave are strong contributors who care about your organization (if not, you shouldn't be sending them). Go one better. If a customer or supplier can offer one of your people a better opportunity than you can, consider the radical approach of letting your employee know about it. But agree with everyone on a lengthy transition period so that the move doesn't cripple your organization. Respect for your organization will go through the roof.

➔ And one more time, if you're really courageous: Do it yourself with customers and suppliers for a few days. Trade places. (Afraid they might take your job? If you're willing to do something like *this,* long before they get your job, you'll have been promoted.)

This problem is worth getting radical over.

● ● ● ● ●

Helping others to shred illusions is in some ways easier than shredding our own, because ours are so "personal," and in some ways harder, because it can be so difficult to understand what's driving another human being.

But the rewards for doing it well are magnificent.

Note

1. Averil Marie Doyle, *Delusional Relationships: How They Are Formed, How They Falter and Fail* (Westport, Conn.: Praeger, 1995), p. xix.

Epilogue

I'd like to make a motion that we face reality.
—Bob Newhart, *The Bob Newhart Show*

As we've seen together, although information, education, and experience can all contribute to wise and healthy decision making, they alone won't move us to change. We can know what the right way is, and may have observed it working for others, and still not be moved to do it ourselves. Examples illustrating the disastrous outcome of our current direction can leave us still fundamentally unchanged.

If we know the right way and still don't do it, the problem isn't one of knowledge, and it won't be solved by more information or more education. There must be something deeper, more woven into the fabric of who we are and how we think, that is keeping us from productive change.

These deeper reasons are illusions, false beliefs about the reality of who we are, how other people are thinking, and what our organizations are like and where they are going. Even if these illusions originally came from bad information, training, or experience, they have become part of who we are.

We can hang on to these illusions and fiercely resist giving them up, even in the face of mounting evidence to the contrary, for many reasons. Perhaps our view of business took years to build; we're comfortable with it and don't want to give it up. Or perhaps the illusion fits our own personal view of life and people; change would require modifying our entire worldview.

The basic driving force is usually avoidance of pain—the pain of facing poor past decisions, the pain of having to admit error, the pain of giving up a comfortable known for an uncomfortable unknown, the pain of abandoning an idea that we once defended with passion, the pain of making a necessary but difficult decision.

213

But this pain is nothing compared to the real misery that lies at the end of a fatal illusion. Months and years of pain avoidance can lead to organizational suffering and strife, massive downsizing, financial chaos, and, ultimately, organizational death.

Just as individuals who avoid reality end up mentally unhealthy, so our organizations can end up in a netherworld of confusion and sickness. But they don't have to stay there. We can face the problems honestly and realistically and can "schedule" the smaller pain now rather than be swamped by the illusion-cloaked, gargantuan pain later.

We can't do this alone. We'll need the help of others—bosses, colleagues, subordinates, consultants, customers, suppliers, competitors, friends, foes, authors, philosophers, theologians, poets, historians. But the answers we need most in a knowledge-filled world are not about how to "do it," but rather about how to clear out the illusions that prevent us from doing what we know to be right or effective.

My hopes join yours as we bring this piece of our journey to an end. I want to be illusion-free, living in reality. I believe that you do, too.

We can do it.

Suggested Readings

One way to support your shredding of the twelve fatal illusions is to read the books listed here. Many reading lists are too general and aren't worth the powder to blow them up; I wanted to give you one geared to the specific topics in this book. I've arranged them within each chapter in the order in which you should read them to get the full illusion-shredding effect.

Chapter 1

Crossen, Cynthia. *Tainted Truth: The Manipulation of Fact in America.* New York: Simon & Schuster, 1994.
Coontz, Stephanie. *The Way We Never Were.* New York: HarperCollins, Publishers, 1992.

Chapter 2

Feinberg, Mortimer, and John J. Tarrant. *Why Smart People Do Dumb Things.* New York: Fireside, 1995.
Piattelli-Palmarini, Massimo. *Inevitable Illusions: How Mistakes of Reason Rule Our Minds.* Translated by Massimo Piattelli-Palmarini and Keith Botsford. New York: Wiley, 1994.
Key, Wilson Bryan. *The Age of Manipulation.* New York: Henry Holt, 1989.
Schmookler, Andrew Bard. *The Illusion of Choice: How the Market Economy Shapes Our Destiny.* Albany: State University of New York, 1993.
Sun-Tzu. *The Art of War.* Translated by Ralph D. Sawyer. New York: Barnes & Noble, 1994.

Chapter 3

Shapiro, Eileen C. *How Corporate Truths Become Competitive Traps.* New York: Wiley, 1991.

Downs, Alan. *Corporate Executions: The Ugly Truth About Layoffs: How Corporate Greed Is Shattering Lives, Companies, and Communities.* New York: AMACOM, 1995.

McNamara, Robert S. *In Retrospect: The Tragedy and Lessons of Vietnam.* New York: Times Books, 1995.

Chapter 4

Albrecht, Karl. *The Northbound Train: Finding the Purpose, Setting the Direction, Shaping the Destiny of Your Organization.* New York: AMACOM, 1994.

Gardner, Howard. *Leading Minds: An Anatomy of Leadership.* New York: Basic Books, 1995.

Drucker, Peter F. *Innovation and Entrepreneurship: Practice and Principles.* New York: Harper & Row, 1985.

Ohmae, Kenichi. *The Mind of the Strategist: The Art of Japanese Business.* New York: McGraw-Hill, 1982.

Chapter 5

Covey, Stephen R., A. Roger Merrill, and Rebecca R. Merrill. *First Things First.* New York: Simon & Schuster, 1994.

Minkin, Barry Howard. *Future in Sight: 100 Trends, Implications, and Predictions That Will Most Impact Businesses and the World Economy Into the 21st Century.* New York: Macmillan, 1995.

Treacy, Michael, and Fred Wiersema. *The Discipline of Market Leaders: Choose Your Customers, Narrow Your Focus, Dominate Your Market.* Reading, Mass.: Addison-Wesley, 1995.

Florida, Richard, and Martin Kenney. *The Breakthrough Illusion: Corporate America's Failure to Move From Innovation to Mass Production.* New York: Basic Books, 1990.

Chapter 6

Brown, Mark Graham, Darcy E. Hitchcock, and Marsha L. Willard. *Why TQM Fails and What to Do About It.* Burr Ridge, Ill.: Irwin, 1994.

Walton, Mary. *The Deming Management Method.* New York: Perigee Books, 1986.

Sewell, Carl, and Paul B. Brown. *Customers for Life: How to Turn That One-Time Buyer Into a Lifetime Customer.* New York: Pocket Books, 1990.

Hart, Christopher W. L. *Extraordinary Guarantees: A New Way to Build Quality Throughout Your Company & Ensure Satisfaction for Your Customers.* New York: AMACOM, 1993.

Chapter 7

Senge, Peter M. *The Fifth Discipline: The Art & Practice of the Learning Organization.* New York: Doubleday/Currency, 1990.

Kanter, Rosabeth Moss. *When Giants Learn to Dance.* New York: Touchstone, 1989.

Chapter 8

Matejka, Ken, and Richard J. Dunsing. *A Manager's Guide to the Millennium: Today's Strategies for Tomorrow's Success.* New York: AMACOM, 1995.
Hammer, Michael, and James Champy. *Reengineering the Corporation: A Manifesto for Business Revolution.* New York: HarperBusiness, 1993.
Thompson, LeRoy. *Mastering the Challenges of Change: Strategies for Each Stage in Your Organization's Life Cycle.* New York: AMACOM, 1994.

Chapter 9

Kierman, Matthew J. *The Eleven Commandments of 21st Century Management.* Englewood Cliffs, N.J.: Prentice-Hall, 1996.
Heller, Robert. *The Naked Manager: Games Executives Play.* New York: Truman Talley Books, 1985.

Chapter 10

Stone, Florence M., and Randi T. Sachs. *The High-Value Manager: Developing the Core Competencies Your Organization Demands.* New York: AMACOM, 1995.
Smith, Martin R. *Contrarian Management: Commonsense Antidotes to Business Fads & Fallacies.* New York: AMACOM, 1992.

Chapter 11

Goleman, Daniel. *Emotional Intelligence: Why It Can Matter More Than IQ.* New York: Bantam Books, 1995.
VanGundy, Arthur B. *Idea Power: Techniques & Resources to Unleash the Creativity in Your Organization.* New York: AMACOM, 1992.
Adams, Scott. *The Dilbert Principle: A Cubicle's Eye View of Bosses, Meetings, Management Fads, & Other Workplace Afflictions.* New York: HarperBusiness, 1996.

Chapter 12

Stack, Jack. *The Great Game of Business.* New York: Doubleday, 1992.
Heller, Robert. *The Super Chiefs: Today's Most Successful Chief Executives and Their Winning Strategies for the 1990's.* New York: Dutton, 1992.
Ralston, Faith. *Hidden Dynamics: How Emotions Affect Business Performance & How You Can Harness Their Power for Positive Results.* New York: AMACOM, 1995.

Chapter 13

Spitzer, Dean R. *SuperMotivation: A Blueprint for Energizing Your Organization From Top to Bottom.* New York: AMACOM, 1995.

Nelson, Bob. *1001 Ways to Reward Employees.* New York: Workman, 1994.

Matejka, Ken. *Why This Horse Won't Drink: How to Win—And Keep—Employee Commitment.* New York: AMACOM, 1991.

Gross, Steven E. *Compensation for Teams: How to Design and Implement Team-Based Reward Programs.* New York: AMACOM, 1995.

Chapter 14

Harvey, Jerry B. *The Abilene Paradox and Other Meditations on Management.* Lexington, Mass.: Lexington Books, 1988.

Lewis, Jordan D. *The Connected Corporation: How Leading Companies Win Through Customer-Supplier Alliances.* New York: The Free Press, 1995.

Deal, Terrence E., and Allan A. Kennedy. *Corporate Cultures: The Rites and Rituals of Corporate Life.* Reading, Mass.: Addison-Wesley, 1982.

Chapter 15

Peters, Tom. *The Pursuit of Wow! Every Person's Guide to Topsy-Turvy Times.* New York: Vintage Books, 1994.

Schultz, Ron. *Unconventional Wisdom: Twelve Remarkable Innovations Tell How Intuition Can Revolutionize Decision Making.* New York: HarperBusiness, 1994.

Hyde, Douglas. *Dedication and Leadership.* Notre Dame, Ind.: University of Notre Dame Press, 1966.

Chapter 16

Townsend, Robert. *Further Up the Organization.* New York: Harper & Row, 1984.

Tuchman, Barbara W. *The March of Folly: From Troy to Vietnam.* New York: Ballantine Books, 1984.

Bolman, Lee G., and Terrence E. Deal. *Reframing Organizations: Artistry, Choice, and Leadership.* San Francisco: Jossey-Bass, 1991.

Harrington, H. J. *Business Process Improvement: The Breakthrough Strategy for Total Quality, Productivity, and Competitiveness.* New York: McGraw-Hill, 1991.

Nadler, Gerald, and Shozo Hibino. *Breakthrough Thinking: Why We Must Change the Way We Solve Problems, and the Seven Principles to Achieve This.* Rocklin, Calif.: Prima, 1990.

Drucker, Peter F. *The Frontiers of Management.* New York: Truman Talley Books, 1986.

Chapter 17

Peck, M. Scott. *The Road Less Traveled.* New York: Simon & Schuster, 1978.

Hedges, Charlie. *Getting the Right Things Right.* Sisters, Ore.: Multnomah Books, 1996.

Oakley, Ed, and Doug Krug. *Enlightened Leadership: Getting to the Heart of Change.* New York: Fireside, 1994.
Benfari, Robert. *Changing Your Management Style: How to Evaluate and Improve Your Own Performance.* New York: Lexington Books, 1995.

Chapter 18

Manfred F. R. Kets De Vries. *Leaders, Fools, and Imposters.* San Francisco: Jossey-Bass, 1993.
Doyle, Averil Marie. *Delusional Relationships: How They Are Formed, How They Falter and Fail.* Westport, Conn.: Praeger, 1995.
Contino, Richard M. *Trust Your Gut! Practical Ways to Develop and Use Your Intuition for Business Success.* New York: AMACOM, 1996.

Index

committing to, 188–190
difficulty of acknowledging, 21
facing, *see* soul sweating
ugliness of, 16
Tuchman, Barbara, on unity and consensus, 155
Twain, Mark, on lies, 13, 158

uncertainty traps, 186–187
uniqueness, focusing on, 111
unmet needs, 196–197

values, analyzing your, 196
victim mentality, 24, 199
virtual organization, 129
vision, 39–48
in benchmarking, 112–113
getting input on, 47–48
as illusion, 41–42
and leadership, 46
as motivator, 148
organizational perspective on, 44–46

people's responses to, 46–47
recognizing, as illusion, 42–43
shared, 148
"visionless," 40–41
vision statements, 40–48
components of, 44–45
as illusions, 41–42
one-sentence, 44
rating, 47–48
recognizing, as illusion, 42–43
vision vs., 40

Weaver, Earl, on learning, 189
Weaver, Robert A., on vision, 47
"what ifs," 187
Whitehead, Alfred North, on progress, 83
wishful thinking
and consequences, 98
and expectations, 74
worthiness, sense of, 44
writing, 201–202

Yamada, Kobi, on past, 89